VIETNAM AND THE UNITED STATES

Origins and Legacy of War
Revised Edition

TWAYNE'S INTERNATIONAL HISTORY SERIES

Akira Iriye, Editor
Harvard University

VIETNAM AND THE UNITED STATES

Origins and Legacy of War
Revised Edition

Gary R. Hess
Bowling Green State University

TWAYNE PUBLISHERS
AN IMPRINT OF SIMON & SCHUSTER MACMILLAN
NEW YORK

PRENTICE HALL INTERNATIONAL
LONDON • MEXICO CITY • NEW DELHI •SINGAPORE • SYDNEY • TORONTO

Twayne Publishers
An Imprint of Simon & Schuster Macmillan
1633 Broadway
New York, NY 10019

Library of Congress Cataloging-in-Publication Data
Hess, Gary R.
    Vietnam and the United States : origins and legacy of war / Gary
R. Hess. — Rev. ed.
        p.   cm. — (Twayne's international history series)
    Includes bibliographical references (p.   ) and index.
    ISBN 0-8057-1676-9 (alk. paper)
    1. United States—Foreign relations—Vietnam.   2. Vietnam—Foreign
relations—United States.   3. Vietnamese Conflict, 1961–1975.
I. Title   II. Series.
E183.8.V45H44   1998
959.704'31—dc21   98-35869
                                                                           CIP

This paper meets the requirements of ANSI/NISO Z3948-1992 (Permanence of Paper).

10 9 8 7 6 5 4 3 2 1

Printed in the United States of America

To the memory of
friend and colleague
Chuck DeBenedetti,
whose life and scholarship
were devoted to advancing
the cause of peace

CONTENTS

LIST OF MAPS

FOREWORD

Twayne's International History Series seeks to publish reliable and readable accounts of post–World War II international affairs. Today, nearly 50 years after the end of the war, the time seems opportune for a critical assessment of world affairs in the second half of the twentieth century. What themes and trends have characterized international relations since 1945? How have they evolved and changed? What connections have developed between international and domestic affairs? How have states and peoples defined and pursued their objectives, and what have they contributed to the world at large? How have conceptions of warfare and visions of peace changed?

These questions must be addressed if one is to arrive at an understanding of the contemporary world that is international—with an awareness of the linkages among different parts of the world—as well as historical—with a keen sense of what the immediate past has brought to civilization. Hence Twayne's *International History* Series. It is hoped that the volumes in this series will help the reader to explore important events and decisions since 1945 and to develop the global awareness and historical sensitivity required for confronting today's problems.

The first volumes in the series examine the United States' relations with other countries, groups of countries, or regions. The focus on the United States is justified in part because of the nation's predominant position in postwar international relations, and also because far more extensive documentation is available on American foreign affairs than is the case with other countries. The series addresses not only those interested in international relations but also those studying America's and other countries' histories, who will find here useful guides and fresh insights into the recent past. Now more than ever, it is imperative to understand the linkages between national history and international history.

This volume offers an up-to-date and comprehensive history of U.S.-Vietnamese relations. The long and tragic war, of course, occupies center stage, but it is preceded by a discussion of the historical circumstances leading to the conflict and followed by a careful discussion of events since the withdrawal of American forces from Vietnam in 1975. Such a comprehensive account helps us understand how the war affected both American and Vietnamese history. Gary R. Hess is a specialist on the history of American foreign relations who has written extensively on America's involvement in South and Southeast Asia. He brings to the volume years of archival research, a personal knowledge of the region, and a sense of balance that has distinguished his other works. This book offers insights into the ways in which the destinies of two peoples in seemingly distant parts of the world become intertwined. And this story is not limited to the United States and Vietnam: it is a main theme of contemporary history.

AKIRA IRIYE
Series Editor

PREFACE

While completing the first edition of *Vietnam and the United States*, I kept hoping for a breakthrough in the slow movement toward normalization of relations between the United States and the Socialist Republic of Vietnam. That hope reflected both a matter of conviction—that the long impasse between the two governments made no sense politically or economically—and a practical consideration: the establishment of formal diplomatic relations would provide an appropriate conclusion to my book. In the absence of progress on the issue, I had to conclude my narrative with a question; chapter 7 was titled "Toward Reconciliation?" As the Clinton administration moved toward normalization, I suggested a revised edition that would bring the story of U.S.-Vietnamese relations more up-to-date with the extension of diplomatic recognition in July 1995 the concluding point. With the enthusiastic support of Akira Iriye, the the International Series editor, and Margaret Dornfeld, the former editor at large at Twayne Publishers, the Twayne editorial board concurred. I acknowledge the assistance of three Bowling Green State University graduate students—Matt Young, Jeff Grim, and Jack Benge—for their contributions to the revisions of chapter 7, the bibliography, and final editing/indexing respectively.

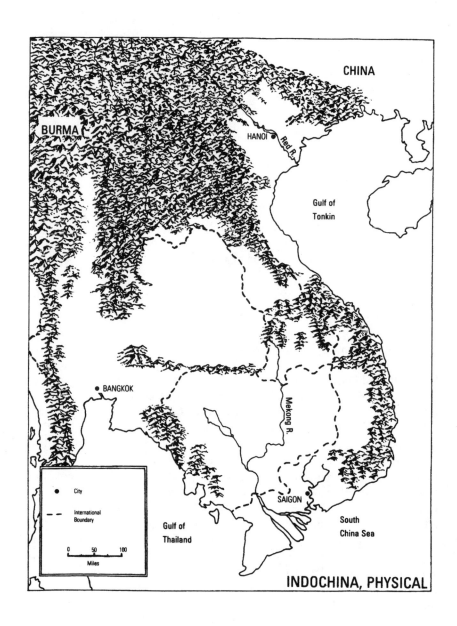

CHINA

BURMA

HANOI

Red R.

Gulf of
Tonkin

BANGKOK

Mekong R.

SAIGON

Gulf of
Thailand

South
China Sea

City

International
Boundary

0   50   100

Miles

INDOCHINA, PHYSICAL

chapter 1

TO THE AUGUST REVOLUTION: THE VIETNAMESE NATIONAL TRADITION

The dominant characteristic of the Vietnamese is, in the words of one historian, a "spirit of resistance." The Vietnamese, another scholar writes, have a tradition of "highly-charged, historically self-conscious resistance to oppressive, degrading foreign rule."[1] That resistance has combined a capacity to assimilate the ideas and institutions of others with a profound sense of national distinctiveness. The Vietnamese trace their cultural origins to the centuries-long period of Chinese rule, which at the same time inspired their determination to assert independence. Vietnamese history is largely the story of a struggle for national identity. The greater part of that history is of a people, not a distinct geographical area, for it was not until the last three centuries that the Vietnamese people came to control the area known today as Vietnam.

It is through China that ancient Vietnam passes from legend to recorded history. Chinese annals of 208 B.C. tell of warfare against peoples to the south of China, the earliest recorded reference to the area that eventually became known as Vietnam. A century later, in 111 B.C., China conquered the peoples living in the Red River Delta, an act that marked the beginning of one thousand years of Chinese rule. That long era of Chinese control was critical to Vietnamese cultural development, for as they adopted the institutions brought by the Chinese, the peoples of China's southernmost province (known as Giao Chi) gradually took on their own distinctive characteristics. That process took generations but eventually led to a Vietnamese national identity.

The Chinese brought numerous innovations and techniques that improved agricultural production in the fertile lands of the Red River Delta. They built dams, roads, and canals. Although at first the Chinese showed little interest in the peoples of Giao Chi, they eventually sent many officials to the province

1

and sought—as they did throughout their empire—to impose Chinese customs, using force when necessary. Clothing and hairstyles were dictated, the Chinese language replaced the native language in official transactions, and Chinese characters became the basis of the written language. The Chinese also instilled among their subjects the great religious and philosophical teachings of Chinese tradition: Confucianism, Buddhism, and Taoism.

On many occasions the Vietnamese rebelled against Chinese dominance, but without success. The most famous of these abortive revolts—one revered among Vietnamese to this day—was that led by the Trung sisters in A.D. 39. So long as China was ruled by strong dynasties, however, such efforts were doomed. After the fall of the powerful T'ang dynasty in A.D. 907, the Vietnamese renewed their struggle. Finally in 939 they won a decisive victory over a Chinese army, forcing its retreat, an event that ended the millennium of Chinese rule.

THE VIETNAMESE STATE: SURVIVAL AND EXPANSION

By the time the Chinese left, the Vietnamese culture had taken on its distinctive characteristics. The system of government, social structure, and ways of thought reflected the Chinese influence and strengthened the Vietnamese as they struggled over ensuing centuries to retain their independence.

The Vietnamese state was a miniature of the Chinese. The emperor—the "son of heaven"—was seen as the deputy on earth of the natural forces of the universe. As in other Asian societies, the Vietnamese conceived of a close parallel between the natural world and the affairs of state. The emperor's success was determined by whether his rule brought bountiful crops. To the peasants, natural disasters like floods or droughts were evidence of cosmic displeasure with the emperor. As a result, much of the time of the emperor and his court was devoted to enhancing agricultural production.

The emperor's power was limited by the dictates of Confucian tradition. The emperor, above all, had to set a moral example. As a scholar trained in the Confucian classics, the emperor was expected to bring to his court other men of similar training, who in turn expected him as the "son of heaven" to rule wisely. Maintaining prestige was the indispensable quality for effective leadership from the imperial court through the bureaucracy and down to the village chief. An individual emperor could not break significantly from the policies of his predecessor, for that would be considered disrespectful in a society that valued filial loyalty. As a result of these influences, leadership was passive, not bold or innovative.

The effectiveness of the Vietnamese state relied on an extensive bureaucratic system. Government positions carried high status, and bureaucrats enjoyed many privileges, including exemption from taxes; their sons were assured entry into the national college, which prepared them for the govern-

[handwritten annotation: They established a good community and a good government abteor giving China the best]

ment examinations. Those rigorous examinations, which were based on a thorough knowledge of Confucian writings, produced officials who embodied the Chinese emphasis on the importance of moral example and looking to the past for enlightenment. The Vietnamese built an effective governmental system that, in the words of a leading authority, "was well in advance of any other native administration in Southeast Asia."[2]

At the center of Vietnamese society was the village, which despite frequent wars retained its self-sufficiency and autonomy. With its huts enclosed for protection from the outside world, the village instilled in its families a strong sense of community. When the government demanded taxes, undertook public works, or needed men for the army, its assessed the entire village, which in turn was responsible for determining how to meet its obligations. These were decisions of the village chief and a council of notables, which governed local affairs. The chief and council reflected the same values as the emperor and his court, a characteristic underlined in the Vietnamese saying, "The village association is a small imperial court."

The landholding system and custom discouraged social distinctions. Most families held modestly sized parcels of land, and those who acquired larger holdings were obligated to fulfill various social functions for the benefit of the entire village. Prestige was expensive, as parties, banquets, subscriptions, and other devices enabled the community to share in the wealth of the larger landholders. This leveling effect of customs is reflected in a proverb borrowed from China: "No family stays rich for three generations, and no family stays poor for three generations."

While the overwhelming majority of villages engaged in cultivating rice, some villages specialized in single crafts to the exclusion of agriculture. In such villages, autonomy was jealously guarded. Determined to retain their expertise, such villages refused to divulge their skills and prohibited their young women from marrying outsiders.

Social structure followed the Confucian teachings. The "three principles" guiding life were loyalty to the emperor, a son's loyalty to his father, and a wife's loyalty to her husband. Although the emperor theoretically demanded the highest loyalty, in practice familial loyalty transcended that to the state. The government typically yielded its authority to permit individuals to fulfill personal obligations; for instance, officials were permitted prolonged absences from their positions in order to return to their villages on occasions such as the death of parents.

This Vietnamese society developed in a context of political uncertainty and frequent warfare, for the independence gained in 939 was precarious. The country faced the persistent threat of renewed Chinese invasion as well as the challenge of other powerful neighbors: the Champa kingdom to the south and the Cambodian (Khmer) empire to the west. Internally, the state suffered often from ineffective leaders and the fragmentation of political power. Ngo Quyen, the general who had defeated the Chinese, founded the first Vietnamese dynasty but died without having established firm control, and his successors failed to maintain control over the country. Subsequent dynasties, each founded by a strong emperor but undermined by weak successors, led to a century of chronic instability with power often in the hands of feudal lords. Finally, under the leadership of two dynasties—the Ly, which ruled from 1009 to 1224, and the Tran, which followed it and ruled until 1400—Vietnam gained four centuries of generally effective leadership, which brought improvements in transportation, communication, agriculture, and civil administration.

These accomplishments were continually threatened by hostile neighbors. To appease the Chinese, the Vietnamese court paid tribute, but that did not prevent Chinese invasions in 981 and 1057, which the Vietnamese repelled. In addition, the Cambodians and Champa frequently attacked the Vietnamese. The greatest danger, however, was always from the north. When the Mongolian armies of Kublai Khan overran China in the thirteenth century, they continued to the south. A large army of some 500,000 men attacked the Vietnamese in 1284. That Vietnamese rallied to defend their homeland and forced the Mongolians to retreat. Another large Mongolian assault in 1287 met similar resistance and prompted the triumphant Vietnamese general to proclaim that "this ancient land shall live forever." The hero of the battles against the Mongols, Tran Hung Dao, remains a revered figure.

The victory over the Mongols, however, came at great cost. The country was left devastated and suffered from widespread famine. Renewed and persistent warfare with Champa and numerous internal revolts eventually led to the overthrow of the Tran dynasty. Shortly thereafter, in 1407, a reinvigorated Chinese empire, under the Ming dynasty, invaded and imposed a period of harsh rule. Once more the Vietnamese had to fight, and after a decade of bitter warfare, they forced the Chinese to leave in 1428.

Having again expelled the Chinese, the Vietnamese now turned against their other enemies. Under the Le dynasty, which was established by Le Loi in 1428, the Vietnamese began their March to the South. Over the course of 250 years they advanced slowly down the coast, a distance approximately the length of the state of Florida. It was more a militant migration than a march. The Vietnamese eliminated the Champa empire. The Chams and other ethnic groups were bypassed and left isolated mostly in mountainous areas while the Vietnamese took the rich agricultural lands. Entire villages were established in the conquered areas and became links in a chain that took the Vietnamese as far as the Mekong Delta by the early eighteenth century. The March to the South thus ultimately defined the general territorial confines of the modern Vietnamese nation.

This cultural expansion, however, was not accompanied by political unity, as the power of the Le dynasty fragmented. Governing the expanded territory from Hanoi proved difficult, so the Le rulers delegated administrative responsibilities for the southern territories to the Nguyen family in the city of Hué.

Eventually the Le dynasty lost authority not only in the South but in the North as well, where the Trinh family asserted control.

Then in the late eighteenth century a movement leading to national unity developed out of political and social discontent and a renewed invasion by China. For three decades—from 1771 to 1802—Vietnam went through a peasant rebellion initiated by the three Tay-son brothers. The Tay-son revolt ended the moribund Le dynasty, but soon the Tay-son rulers faced massive Chinese invasions in 1788 and 1789. Once again, the Vietnamese resisted the Chinese in a series of battles, the most decisive being that waged at Dong-da, near Hanoi, in 1789. With their resources drained by the warfare with China, the Tay-sons lost their power to the resurgent Nguyen family. At length, the Nguyen dynasty was established in 1802.

That was a moment of historic importance, for it marked the first time that a single ruler governed the region from the Chinese border to the Gulf of Siam—the essential boundaries of the modern Vietnamese nation. Never before had a dynasty controlled both the Red River and Mekong deltas. With the founding of the Nguyen dynasty under Emperor Gia Long, political unification at last paralleled the cultural unification achieved by the March to the South.

This marked the culmination of a process that reflected the extent to which the prolonged pursuit of national identity had given the Vietnamese a sense of patriotism unique among the peoples of Southeast Asia. "Two millennia of struggle for survival against the political and cultural domination of China," the historian William Duiker notes, "had created in Vietnam a distinctly 'national' ethnic spirit, more self-conscious, and more passionate than that found virtually anywhere in Southeast Asia." Another historian, Huynh Kim Khanh, concurs: "unlike most other European colonies, by the time of the French invasion, Vietnam had developed the social and cultural attributes of a nation—a unified tradition, culture, and language and an effective political and economic system."[3]

THE INFLUENCE OF FRENCH RULE

The hope that Vietnam was about to enter a "golden age" under the Nguyen dynasty was threatened by the pressures of European expansion. In the late nineteenth century France established control over Vietnam and its neighbors; in the process, French imperialism challenged traditional society in many ways, but it failed to destroy Vietnamese patriotism.

The French conquest was one phase of the vast expansion of Europe that carried Western ideas and institutions throughout the world. The Western movement into Vietnam was typical of European expansion in Asia. The process was gradual, beginning with traders and missionaries, and eventually leading to political control. Warfare, of course, inevitably accompanied Western penetration, which came to be rationalized as a "civilizing" influence—a reflection of the unquestioned assumption of the West's racial superiority.

The Portuguese explored the coast of Vietnam and established a trading center at Hoi An in the early sixteenth century, but the trade never became substantial. Vietnam's limited economic value to Europe was underscored further when, during the late seventeenth century, the British, French, and Dutch each failed to establish profitable trading posts and abandoned their efforts within a few years.

In the meantime, Roman Catholic missionaries went to Vietnam, and those from France played a prominent role in the early French expansion. Indeed, a French Jesuit scholar, Alexander of Rhodes, became the first Westerner to study Vietnamese history and language. The principal objective of the missionaries was proselytizing, and their teachings and conversions threatened the authority of the mandarins, who began to persecute the missionaries and native Catholics. The French became involved in Vietnamese politics; missionaries recruited mercenaries and supplies on behalf of Gia Long's military campaigns, which resulted in the establishment of the Nguyen dynasty. If their objective was to make the Nguyens dependent upon them, the missionaries were disappointed, for the anti-Catholic campaigns reached a peak during the reigns of Gia Long's successors. Those campaigns were brutal, resulting in the executions of several missionaries and a large number of their converts.

By the mid–nineteenth century tensions between the French and Vietnamese reached a crossroads. The Vietnamese rulers, who saw in Christianity and Western institutions a threat to their values, persecuted the missionaries. The missionaries, supported by economic interests in France, pressed their government to undertake a military campaign against the Vietnamese. Naval commanders twice took the initiative, bombarding Da Nang in 1847 and again in 1856. The proponents of a military campaign held out the vision of Vietnam as a valuable colony that would serve France's economic needs. Coming at a time when other European powers were consolidating their position in Asia (the British in India and Malaya, and the Dutch in the East Indies), these pressures on the government of Napoleon III became irresistible.

It took 40 years for the French to complete their conquest of Vietnam. Beginning with an assault on Da Nang in 1858, which was followed by the extension of control in the South, and ending with an offensive that consolidated power in the central and northern regions in 1883, the French established their Asian empire. The imperial movement had to overcome not only the Vietnamese army but also critics in France who argued that the nation's resources were being drained by warfare on behalf of a prize of dubious value and that priority ought to be given to enhancing France's position in Europe. Indeed, the Vietnamese resistance continued: widespread opposition to the French led to several insurrections, with the result that it took the French military another 14 years before completing the "pacification" of Vietnam. It was not until 1897 that French control was firmly established.

By that time Vietnam had become part of French Indochina, along with its smaller and less populous neighbors, Cambodia and Laos, which the French annexed in 1863 and 1893 respectively. Following the historic imperial tactic of "divide and rule," France divided Vietnam into three political units: Cochin China in the south, Annam in the center, and Tonkin in the north. The tactics of colonial administration varied. The French governed Cochin China directly, but in Tonkin and Annam they retained a facade of native rule. In Cochin China the French established their own governmental structure, and Vietnamese who worked within that system adhered strictly to French rules and practices. A different system prevailed in Annam and Tonkin, where the Nguyen dynasty, with its capital at Hué, remained nominally in power. The emperor was a figurehead, though; real political power was held by French officials. The governments of Annam and Tonkin were cumbersome and inefficient: a French administration, responsible for the interests and affairs of French and other foreigners, was paralleled by a Vietnamese administration, which dealt with the natives. The Vietnamese bureaucracy retained its traditional practices, and the Confucian-based civil service system remained the basis of entry into government service. Indirect rule through native rulers and bureaucracies also prevailed in Cambodia and Laos. The distinction between direct and indirect rule, however, was meaningless, for everywhere French power was absolute. The native rulers and their courts had no real authority while the native bureaucrats carried out the policies of the French.

The French changed Vietnamese politics, society, and economy in far-reaching ways. The authority of the French, headed by the governor-general of Indochina, permeated all levels of government. The mandarins lost influence and were forced into secondary positions. As their status eroded, so too did the morality of the Confucian tradition, with the result that much of the mandarinate not only collaborated with the French but also were corrupted in the process. An ancient Vietnamese saying held that the power of the emperor stopped at the gates of the village, but the French shattered even the traditional autonomy of the villages. Local authorities lost power to French or French-trained Vietnamese officials. The communal land, which had formed a kind of social insurance for the entire village, was lost as it passed into the hands of wealthy landowners.

Paul Doumer, who served as governor-general from 1897 to 1902, established policies that exploited the Vietnamese for the benefit of French interests. Under his leadership the colonial administration undertook an extensive program of building railroads, roads, harbors, canals, and other public works that facilitated the extension of French economic influence. Financial power was centered in the hands of French investors and the Bank of Indochina, which became a symbol of imperialism. French capital was invested principally in products that would be profitable exports. This led to the development of large rice and rubber plantations in the South and mines in the North

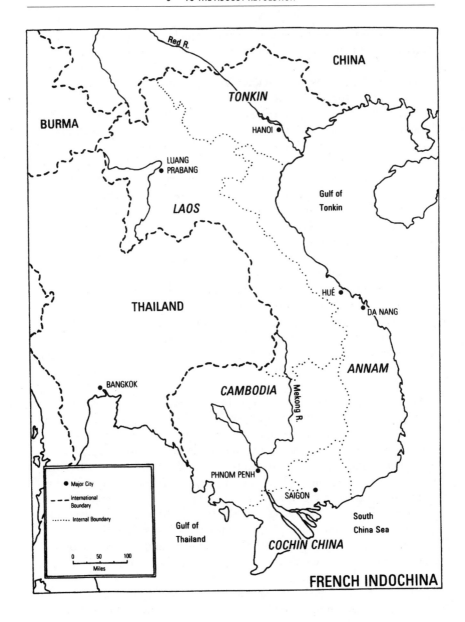

CHINA

Red R.

TONKIN

BURMA

HANOI

LUANG
PRABANG

Gulf of
Tonkin

LAOS

THAILAND

HUÉ

DA NANG

ANNAM

BANGKOK

CAMBODIA

Mekong R.

Major City

International
Boundary

Internal Boundary

PHNOM PENH

SAIGON

South
China Sea

0   50   100

Miles

Gulf of
Thailand

COCHIN CHINA

FRENCH INDOCHINA

that extracted coal and other minerals. By the 1930s Indochina had become the world's third largest exporter of rice and a major source of rubber. French investors exercised virtually complete control over these highly profitable enterprises. The long-term development of Vietnam was of no concern, so earnings were not reinvested in the country. The enormous profits benefited a small group of French private businesses, typically controlled, if not owned, by the Bank of Indochina. The French government and public did not gain from their Asian empire, which was one reason why colonial policy was frequently the subject of intense debate in Paris.

The French exploited the Vietnamese in many ways. The growth of the rubber industry created a demand for labor, and thousands of workers migrated from the North only to be forced into living and working in conditions that amounted to a peonage system. The new lands that were developed in the South through irrigation and other public works did not go to the peasants but were sold to the highest bidder or given away to powerful French or Vietnamese landholders. The French established government monopolies on salt, alcohol, and opium, thus forcing higher prices for those commodities while depriving villagers of traditional secondary means of income. As a result of the government monopoly, the price of salt increased 10 times. The colonial administration imposed a head tax—a classic example of regressive taxation—requiring that all men pay the same annual tax; in other words, the landless peasant owed exactly the same as the wealthy landowner.

French rule brought much hardship to the peasantry, which constituted about 85 percent of the population. In the northern and central areas of the country, peasants typically continued to own their land, but as population increased, pressures on the land intensified and the size of holdings declined. The result was that in Tonkin and Annam over 60 percent of the peasants had holdings of less than one acre, with about one-third farming less than half an acre. Besides the iniquitous head tax, peasants were obliged to pay other taxes. In addition, high interest rates were charged on loans, leaving the peasantry in a cycle of perpetual indebtedness. On the large southern plantations workers typically rented their lands, often paying 60 percent of their crops.

The French rationalized empire initially through the belief in their *mission civilisatrice*. The objective was to assimilate native peoples into French culture and, in the process, turn Vietnamese into *français de couleur*. The ideal of assimilation was challenged by advocates of *association*, who argued that the imperial objective should be the preservation of certain Vietnamese institutions to help legitimize French rule. Although this approach was more tolerant of Vietnamese culture and suggested a willingness to cooperate with the Vietnamese, *association* in no way implied acceptance of Vietnamese equality. *Association* became official policy in 1908, but the French never fully reconciled these conflicting approaches to dealing with the Vietnamese. Their policies fostered considerable resentment, for aside from the small elite who became *français de couleur*, few Vietnamese benefited from, much less identified with, French rule.

The French attitudes toward Vietnamese culture were strikingly evident in the "reform" of the educational system. In the precolonial period the Vietnamese had an extensive educational system. About 20,000 one-teacher village schools were spread throughout the country; in addition, district and provisional classes provided more advanced training. At the top of the system was a national college for royal princes and mandarins. About 80 percent of the population had some degree of literacy.

The colonial administration thoroughly changed the educational system, establishing French schools and altering the instruction in the traditional schools. The French language was introduced and written Vietnamese was changed to romanized script (*quoc ngu*) in place of Chinese characters. Whatever the value of the new educational programs, they were limited to a small group of Vietnamese. By 1939 only 15 percent of school-age children were being educated. The contrast with precolonial society was striking; 80 percent of the population was illiterate. Only one university, with an enrollment of 700 students, served the entire country. There were only 14 secondary schools throughout the country. The best education was available through the *lycées*, which were primarily intended for French children and to which few Vietnamese were admitted.

The system thus produced a small number of educated Vietnamese, including the pro-French elite, largely centered in Cochin China. The majority of French-educated Vietnamese, however, became disillusioned by the lack of opportunities. Invariably they were denied higher administrative positions in the government, which were reserved for French officials, many of whom were less qualified. The Vietnamese thus spent their careers in second-level government positions. The French thus inadvertently created a disgruntled educated class, which would eventually express its discontent.

The vast majority of Vietnamese suffered from the exploitation of their country. Most were demonstrably in worse condition than before the establishment of French rule. For instance, while rice production quadrupled between 1880 and 1930, the individual peasant's consumption decreased. The peasantry did not share in the profits made from the development of the rice export market. In those areas where they still owned their land, peasants typically received only 15 percent of the export price; a variety of Vietnamese and French middlemen took most of the remainder. Moreover, French policies created a growing landless peasantry. This occurred not only in Cochin China, where peasants were forced to rent lands on the large plantations, but in Tonkin and Annam as well, where peasants were forced from the land. Caught in a cycle of indebtedness that was aggravated by inequitable taxes and high prices for necessities like salt, more and more farmers lost their lands to the large landholders. They were reduced to renters or left the land entirely. Those who sought jobs on the rubber plantations, mines, or public work projects found not only low wages but also no protection from often dangerous working conditions.

Paralleling their economic policies was a French determination to prevent Vietnamese political expression. Civil liberties were not recognized, and political parties were virtually prohibited. When combined with the economic policies that prevented the rise of a substantial Vietnamese middle class, the effect of French policy was to preclude the development of a liberal, Western-oriented political movement. By contrast, the more enlightened colonial policies of other Western powers—such as the British in India and the United States in the Philippines—facilitated the rise of broadly based nationalist groups that were sympathetic with Western political and economic institutions.

RESURGENCE OF VIETNAMESE NATIONALISM

Opposition to the French accompanied the establishment of the colonial order and continued, in various forms, as long as the French remained in power. The earliest resistance, which was ultimately suppressed through the French "pacification" campaigns, was led by mandarins, scholars, and officials who sought to restore the traditional imperial system. After being defeated militarily, these movements quietly died, as they seemed to be outdated in the midst of the political, economic, and social changes brought by the French.

The first expression of national consciousness that broke from the past was led by Phan Boi Chau during the first two decades of the twentieth century. This movement reflected an effort to relate Vietnamese discontent to the modern world that was being forced upon their country; as he wrote in his memoirs, Chau and his followers knew that a new era was dawning, but they were uncertain what it all meant. They found an answer in the example of Japan, which had embraced Western ways in its dramatic modernization that began with the Meiji restoration in 1868. Many Asians living under Western domination found inspiration in Japan's transition to a modern state and its victory over Russia in their 1904–1905 war. With Japan as his model, Chau organized the Modernization Society, which sought to use Western ideas, technology, and science to establish a modernized Vietnamese state. It was to be led by a progressive emperor. Chau gained much sympathy for his movement in Japan, and hundreds of Vietnamese youth went there to study. The Modernization Society engaged in ceaseless propaganda and organized mass demonstrations.

The French reacted swiftly, condemning some protestors to death and sending others to the island of Poulo Condore, which became a concentration camp for Vietnamese patriots. Forced into exile, Chau went back to Japan seeking help, only to be expelled. The Japanese had higher international priorities than encouraging revolts in a small Asian country, and the French exerted sufficient influence—including a timely loan in 1910—to dissuade the Japanese from backing Vietnamese aspirations. Chau fled to China and, while exiled in that country, encouraged his followers to continue the struggle against the French. Though some agitation continued, the Modernization Society had lost its momentum. In 1925 French agents kidnapped Chau and brought him back to Vietnam for trial. He was sentenced to house arrest for the remainder of his life; he died in 1940.

Phan Boi Chau's failure rested partly in his naive expectation of Japanese support, but the more important reason was the narrowness of his own program. While he consistently called upon Vietnamese of all classes to resist the French, he never built the kind of mass organization that was essential for the realization of his objectives. His ideas had their greatest appeal for the elite, but they never became part of the outlook of the peasantry. The Modernization Society squandered its resources on ill-considered and poorly prepared attacks, which the French easily suppressed. In sum, this early expression of Vietnamese nationalism lacked widespread support, a disciplined organization, and a careful program. Despite his failure, Phan Boi Chau remains a respected figure in the history of Vietnamese nationalism, revered for his patriotism and sacrifice.

As the Modernization Society was declining, a conservative expression of Vietnamese nationalism was beginning. Led by Vietnamese who benefited from French rule, especially the landed aristocracy and the urban upper class of Cochin China, this movement was based on the assumption that collaboration with the French would benefit the country politically and economically. This elite constituted the first generation of Vietnamese to reflect the effects of French efforts at assimilation. In their outlook and orientation these Vietnamese were essentially Francophiles. The writings of Pham Quynh gave expression to the thinking of this small but influential group. Critical of traditional Vietnamese culture for its narrow-mindedness and Confucian-based veneration of the past ("taking the four books and five classics as sacred books synthesizing all knowledge in the world for mankind"), Pham Quynh found in France's arrival a "breath of fresh air" bringing Western ideas and institutions.[4] The key to his country's future development, he believed, rested in a synthesis of the best of Western and Vietnamese values, a careful mixture of progress with tradition.

Pham Quynh's vision of an ideal society found political expression in the Constitutionalist party, which voiced the Vietnamese elite's interest in altering French colonial policy to its advantage without alienating the French. The party's principal leader was Bui Quang Chieu, an agricultural engineer and large landowner, and one of the first Vietnamese to become a French citizen. In the 1920s the Constitutionalist party pressed the French for political and economic reforms. It achieved only minor concessions, however, as the French largely ignored its entreaties. By the 1930s the Constitutionalist party had become an anachronism within the nationalist movement.

At the heart of the failure of the Francophiles was the paradox in their outlook. They admired French civilization to such an extent that they wanted to preserve its presence. They were distrustful, even disdainful, of the Vietnamese peasants. This mentality thus precluded the building of a mass movement. The Francophiles were too thoroughly addicted to French culture—living in French-styled homes, sending their children to French schools, drinking French wine, and dining on French cuisine—to express meaningful nationalist aspirations.

The failure of the conservative approach gave impetus to renewed revolutionary activity, especially in Annam and Tonkin. The Vietnam Nationalist party—typically called the VNQDD, the abbreviation for its formal designation, the Viet Nam Quoc Dan Dang—was the most important of several groups that were led principally by urban intellectuals. Nguyen Thai Hoc, a 23-year-old teacher, led the VNQDD's establishment in 1927. Because the French refused to recognize the legitimacy of nationalist parties, the VNQDD had to function clandestinely. (Only the Constitutionalist party was sanctioned by the French, and its activities were restricted to Cochin China.) The VNQDD recruited students, lower-level government employees, small businessmen, soldiers, and women. By 1929 it had some 1,500 members, organized in small groups, mostly in the Red River Delta area. Convinced that armed revolution was the only means to gain Vietnamese freedom, the VNQDD concentrated on penetrating the ranks of Vietnamese serving in the French army and stockpiled arms and supplies to support an insurrection.

The turning point in the VNQDD's history came on the night of 9 February 1930. The leadership had plotted a general uprising by native troops throughout the country, but only the garrison at Yen Bay in northern Vietnam mutinied. There 20 French officers headed units totalling some 600 native troops. Even that single uprising disappointed VNQDD expectations in that not all of the native troops participated in the mutiny and many actually supported the French. A few French officers were killed, but the mutiny quickly failed. The French sent reinforcements the next day, and the mutineers were summarily executed.

The abortive uprising spelled the end of the VNQDD as an important nationalist group. The French reaction was, in the words of one scholar, "swift and brutal."[5] The army and police suppressed VNQDD activities and arrested its leaders and thousands of suspected followers and sympathizers. Hundreds of Vietnamese were killed, and hundreds more were given life sentences of hard labor in concentration camps. Eighty leaders were condemned to death. These included Nguyen Thai Hoc, who was beheaded in June 1930. The remnants of the VNQDD were forced into exile in China, where they retained the party's identity with support from Chinese authorities. By the time the VNQDD would return to Vietnam, however, the nationalist leadership had passed into the hands of the Communist-led Viet Minh.

The failure of the VNQDD can be traced partly to the dangerous impetuosity of its leadership, reflected especially in the unrealistic expectations for a general mutiny and in the poor planning for its execution. Nguyen Thai Hoc and other VNQDD consistently exaggerated the strength of their movement and often acted impulsively. In that sense, the VNQDD's shortcomings paralleled those of the Modernization Society headed by Pham Boi Chau. Like that movement, the VNQDD failed to enlist mass support. The VNQDD had no plan to incorporate peasants and workers and thus remained an urban-centered movement with limited appeal.

The demise of the VNQDD left revolutionary nationalism in the hands of the Vietnamese Communist movement. In the aftermath of the Russian Revolution and the establishment of a Communist state in that country, Marxist ideas began attracting the interest of urban intellectuals in the early 1920s. The Revolutionary League of Vietnam, established in 1925, and other leftist groups were active in the late 1920s, but it was not until the founding of the Communist party of Indochina in 1930 that the Communist movement achieved coherence and was positioned to exert significant political influence.

The major figure in this development was Ho Chi Minh, whose leadership gave decisive direction to the course of the Vietnamese struggle against the French. Born Nguyen Sinh Cuong in 1890, he used several aliases after becoming active in politics. He was known for many years as Nguyen Ai Quoc ("Nguyen the Patriot"); during World War II he took the Chinese name Ho Chi Minh ("He Who Enlightens"). Since that is the name that has endured, it is appropriately used in describing his career.

Ho Chi Minh was born into a family of high social status. During his youth Ho was strongly influenced by his father's alienation from traditional Vietnamese culture. After completing a master's degree, Ho's father passed the civil service examination and took a government position in Hué. But he quickly became disillusioned with government work and returned to his home village, where he taught school. Coming to detest the system of education and the Confucian literature at its core, which he vowed his children would never be taught, he eventually became a wandering scholar. Implicit in his father's alienation was the message that the Vietnamese needed to understand Western civilization, a message reflected in Ho's attitude toward the nationalist program of Phan Boi Chau. Ho declined an invitation to study in Japan as part of Chau's movement, presumably because he distrusted the reliance on Japanese help, which he allegedly described as "driving the tiger out the front door while welcoming the wolf in through the back."[6] At the age of 20 Ho spent a year studying in a French academy at Hué and then went to southern Vietnam, where he briefly taught school. By that time he was determined to visit France and observe Western civilization. Ho was not certain what he was looking for, but it seemed clear that the key to understanding how Vietnam could regain its independence lay in the West.

Ho Chi Minh left Vietnam, marking the beginning of an extended exile from his country. His experiences in France, Russia, and China not only shaped his political philosophy but also made him into a preeminent Vietnamese nationalist. The journey began humbly, with Ho working on board a transport liner. After spending several years working on ships and visiting a number of countries, including England, where he held menial jobs, Ho went to Paris after World War I. He quickly became politically active and organized, among the small Vietnamese community, the Association of Vietnamese patriots. To Ho and other leaders in this group the peace program of the victorious Allies offered an opportunity for Vietnamese freedom. Stirred especially by President Woodrow Wilson's call for the "self-determination of peoples," Ho presented a petition calling for recognition of his country's independence to the Allied leaders who assembled in Paris in 1919 to draft the postwar peace treaties. The United States, Britain, France, Japan, and the other Allied governments ignored this entreaty from an unknown figure representing a cause that was of no concern to them. Ho's audacious actions on behalf of his country, however, earned him renown as a Vietnamese patriot. Disillusioned by the lack of Allied support, Ho turned to the French Socialist party and became one of its more prominent spokesmen. Again, however, he was disappointed, for the Socialists showed little interest in the colonial issue.

Ho then turned toward communism, for he found in the ideology of Lenin and the Communist International (Comintern) the "path to our liberation." Unlike earlier Marxist writings, which had been directed to the problems of industrialized countries, Lenin's *Thesis on the National and Colonial Questions* spoke directly to the problems facing preindustrial, colonial societies. Lenin argued that to end Western capitalist imperialism in Asia Communists had to work with all nationalist groups in their countries and had to organize the peasantry as a basic force in the struggle. Ho, who was among the founding members of the French Communist party in 1920, seized upon the ideas of Lenin to build an anti-imperialist movement that was both rooted in the country's strong nationalist tradition and part of the Communist international proletarian struggle.

Ho Chi Minh became well known in French radical circles for numerous anti-French articles and pamphlets he wrote before going in 1923 to Moscow, which he saw as "the home of the revolution." A year later Ho went as a Comintern agent to Canton, in China, where his energies were devoted to organizing Vietnamese opposition to French rule. Ho worked with young Vietnamese radicals who had fled to China; he established the Revolutionary Youth League of Vietnam, edited the journal *Thanh Nien* (Youth), and wrote a book, *Road to Revolution*, which became the bible of the revolutionary movement. Mindful of the failures of earlier nationalists and of Lenin's teachings, Ho wrote that revolution "is not the work of a few people, but must come from the union of thousands and thousands of individuals. . . . Workers and peasants are the principal forces of the revolution." [7] This became a central part of the indoctrination of hundreds of young radicals who were trained in Canton. Upon returning to Vietnam, they worked with the peasantry and working class and began organizing militant labor unions and peasant associations. The

Communists sought to appeal simultaneously to anti-French nationalism and to the need for social and economic justice.

The first efforts to translate this ideology into political power met with French repression, but not before the Communist movement demonstrated an impressive capacity to mobilize mass support. In 1930 (shortly after the abortive VNQDD uprising) Communist leaders exploited rising peasant discontent with harsh economic conditions to organize protests and to seize power in some areas; local "soviets" replaced the French-controlled administration in large parts of Annam and Tonkin. By 1931 the French, however, massed their military strength and reasserted political control. It was done brutally: some 10,000 Vietnamese were killed and perhaps 50,000 were deported. "There is no darker year in the history of French rule in Vietnam than 1931," the historian Joseph Buttinger writes. "People were killed not in the heat of battle—there were no battles—but rather they were chased, hunted down, and murdered by a soldiery drunk on blood."[8] It seemed that the Communist movement was stillborn. The governor-general of Indochina proclaimed that "as a force capable of acting against the public order, communism has disappeared."[9]

In fact, the Communists survived and within a decade organized a broadly based nationalist movement. After the suppression of 1931 the Communist party smuggled many of its cadres into China. Those remaining behind cooperated with moderate patriotic groups and recruited new members to their cause. This meant that the Communists were the only nationalist group that was able to take advantage of opportunities presented by dramatic international changes.

WORLD WAR II: RISE OF THE VIET MINH

World War II altered French-Vietnamese relations in far-reaching ways. French authority eroded and nationalism gained the ascendancy. The transition began with the outbreak of war in Europe in September 1939, when France and Great Britain declared war on Germany following Hitler's invasion of Poland. The following spring, Germany launched an offensive that overran France within a few weeks, forcing France into a humiliating armistice in June 1940. France's crippled position was exploited by Germany's ally Japan, which, as a first step in its drive to dominate Southeast Asia, demanded special privileges in northern Indochina. To Ho Chi Minh and other Communist leaders France's inability to defend Vietnam offered the promise of an eventual opportunity to assert independence. Thus in May 1941 Ho met with other leaders in a small village near the Chinese border and established a nationalist front organization, the Viet Minh (the abbreviation for *Viet Nam Doc Lap Dong Minh Hoi*, "League for the Independence of Vietnam"). The Viet Minh represented moderate as well as radical nationalists, but from its inception the Communists dominated its program and operations. The Viet Minh appealed to nationalist instincts; in Ho's widely circulated "Letter from Abroad" of June 1941 he wrote:

> National salvation is the common cause of our entire people. Every Vietnamese must take part in it. . . . The hour has struck. Raise aloft the banner of insurrection and lead the people throughout the country to overthrow the Japanese and the French. The sacred call of the fatherland is resounding in our ears, the ardent blood of our heroic predecessors is seething in our hearts. . . . Let us unite and unify our action to overthrow the Japanese and the French. The Vietnamese revolution will certainly triumph. The world revolution will certainly triumph.[10]

The Viet Minh leadership saw their movement as part of the world struggle against fascism. Hitler's attack on the Soviet Union on 22 June 1941 transformed Communist movements everywhere into enemies of the Axis powers. The Vietnamese identity with the Allied cause was enhanced when Japan, in July 1941, forced the French into further concessions in Indochina, allowing Japan to extend its control throughout the colony. The French administration became an instrument of Japanese imperialism. Japanese troops were stationed throughout Indochina, and the colony became a principal supplier of rice for the Japanese. Hence, the Viet Minh saw both the Japanese as well as the French, now functioning as collaborators, as the enemy. Then when Japan attacked Pearl Harbor on 7 December 1941, the Viet Minh associated its cause with that of the United States.

By the time the Viet Minh was established, Ho Chi Minh's nationalist ideology had taken its distinctive characteristics. It drew upon Vietnamese tradition by emphasizing the persistent struggle for national identity and moral precepts akin to the Confucian teachings. Ho would often narrate for his followers the history of the world in ways that carefully linked international events to those in Vietnam. He composed a 236-line poem, "The History of Our Country from 2879 B.C. to 1942," which stressed resistance to foreign aggression, recalling in particular the peasant-based Tay-son revolt of the late eighteenth century. Ho also insisted that revolutionaries had to set the highest moral example, especially "industriousness, frugality, incorruptibility, and correctness." If revolution was to succeed, militants had to behave in upright, exemplary fashion. Ho's reputation for embodying the principles that he urged upon his followers enabled him to build the image of the selfless revolutionary. (Later in his life Ho advised young Vietnamese not to emulate two of his practices: smoking cigarettes and never marrying, but among Vietnamese only the former was a vice, for the latter enhanced Ho's status as the patriot who looked upon all of his countrymen as his family.) This blending of tradition with a vision of national destiny was fully embodied in Ho Chi Minh's personality.

He was at once a typical Vietnamese as well as the personification of the nation's new independent identity. The popular reference to him as "Uncle Ho" was an indication of both familiarity and respect.

As the leadership of the Viet Minh recognized, the political changes resulting from World War II promised to be a turning point in their nation's history. Indeed, for Vietnamese and other Asian peoples the war had a liberating influence, paving the way for the end of foreign domination. Following its attack on the United States, Japan quickly expanded across much of the Pacific and Southeast Asia. Japan's dominance of the region destroyed the last vestiges of notions of white superiority. Having already forced the French into accepting its occupation of Indochina, Japan, in the early weeks of 1942, conquered the Netherlands East Indies, the Philippines, Malaya, and Burma. With the exception of the Philippines, where American and Filipino troops fought gallantly but futilely against the invaders, the Japanese experienced little resistance from either the colonial armies or the native peoples. The most telling moment of this rapid transformation of power in Southeast Asia was the Japanese seizure, with little opposition, of the supposedly impregnable British naval base and commercial center at Singapore. In a few days in early 1942 that symbol of the British imperial system fell.

The Japanese promised the peoples of Southeast Asia a "New Order" based on economic interdependence. The Japanese, however, proved to be ruthless rulers, and in one sense the war marked a transformation of one type of imperial domination into another. Yet while the Japanese never allowed any challenge to their domination of the region, they did, in various ways, encourage nationalism. This meant that by the end of the war, nationalist movements had gained strength in all the colonial areas of Southeast Asia, thus challenging the resumption of Western domination.

Planning to exploit the opportunities presented by the war, the Viet Minh built a strong revolutionary base in Cao Bang province in northern Vietnam, close to the Chinese border. The movement was in a position to capitalize upon three momentous events of 1945—the Japanese coup of 9 March, widespread famine, and the Japanese surrender of 14 August.

The Japanese abruptly seized control of the Indochina government on 9 March, thus ending five years of collaboration with French authorities. This step was undertaken to protect Japan's position in the country, for the Japanese feared that the French officials were plotting against them. Indeed, as the war had turned in favor of the Allies, the defeat of Germany and Japan became a matter of time. The liberation of France in the summer of 1944 brought to power Charles de Gaulle, whose Free French movement denounced collaboration with the enemy. Realizing that the French authorities in Indochina could no longer be counted upon, the Japanese disarmed the French and took power directly.

For the Viet Minh, the Japanese coup created a political opportunity: the passing of the French administration meant that when the war ended there would be a political vacuum. Accordingly, the Viet Minh extended its operations, with the result that by the summer it controlled six northern provinces with a total population of one million. The Viet Minh's political structure was based at the village level, where owing to the breakdown in government structure, it was able to establish "liberation committees"; from the villages, the Viet Minh spread its control over larger towns and cities. Taking advantage of the indifference of the Japanese authorities, the Viet Minh became very active in Hanoi; its propaganda flooded the city, and its flag appeared atop buildings. Terrorism, while not widespread, was sufficient to intimidate opponents. The Viet Minh singled out for reprisal Vietnamese traitors, that is, those who had collaborated with the French or were known to be pro-Japanese. The Viet Minh presence in the Hanoi area thus became ubiquitous—a portent of political change stirring in the country.

The appeal of the Viet Minh was based not only on its promise of national liberation but also on its capacity to deal with the serious economic and social problems caused by a devastating famine. Throughout the war, Japan demanded that Indochina export much of its rice production and divert some lands from rice cultivation for other commodities needed by the Japanese military. As a result, Vietnam suffered from a serious food shortage that resulted in widespread starvation. The suffering was especially acute in the northern provinces, which traditionally relied upon shipments of rice from the South. The French authorities, when they were in power, and later the Japanese responded with an indifference that bordered on contempt for the plight of the Vietnamese. The Viet Minh, however, took measures on behalf of the peasantry. It organized peasants to "borrow" rice from landlords. It led attacks on granaries where rice was being stored for export and on the convoys carrying food from the country.

Besides its effort to work with the peasantry, the Viet Minh also sought international support for its political aspirations. Ho Chi Minh and other leaders looked in particular to the United States. Viet Minh representatives had contact with American military and intelligence personnel in southern China. The Viet Minh became important to the Allies, for after the elimination of the French administration it was the only reliable source of information on Japanese movements and activities in Indochina. As a result of contacts between Ho Chi Minh and the Office of Strategic Services (OSS), the American wartime intelligence organization, Americans parachuted into Viet Minh–controlled parts of northern Vietnam. The Viet Minh hoped that this collaboration would lead to U.S. endorsement of their political objectives. (This episode in U.S.-Vietnam relations is discussed fully in chapter 2.)

The Viet Minh was thus in a position to seize power when Japan abruptly surrendered. Events moved quickly in early August 1945: on 6 August, the United States dropped an atomic bomb on Hiroshima; on 8 August, the Soviet Union declared war on Japan; on 9 August, the United States dropped an atomic bomb on Nagasaki; on 10 August, Japan offered to surrender. When news reached Vietnam on 13 August that Japan was preparing to surrender, the Viet Minh called for a national insurrection, and its political cadres and army moved southward. The August Revolution swept the Viet Minh to power. In almost every town and city, political demonstrations and rallies erupted, and Viet Minh flags, songs, and propaganda were everywhere. Hanoi was taken on 19 August with three revolver shots—to salute the Viet Minh flag. A mass demonstration in Hué, the capital of the Nguyen dynasty, brought the Viet Minh to power there on 23 August. The same day Da Nang—with two persons with rifles leading a mass demonstration—came under the Viet Minh. The irresistible momentum carried the movement to the Mekong Delta, and on 25 August an enormous demonstration brought the Viet Minh to power in Saigon. In sum, between 18 and 28 August the Viet Minh's power spread through virtually the entire country, including some 60 cities and provincial capitals.

The August Revolution reached its conclusion with two dramatic events. On 30 August, Emperor Bao Dai, the last of the Nguyen dynasty, which had ruled since 1802, abdicated in favor of the new government. Bao Dai, who had come to power in 1932 at the age of 18 only to be used for political purposes by both the French and the Japanese, had no power, but he was important symbolically, representing the continuity of the Vietnamese state dating back to the pre-French period. In handing over the imperial seals and sword to the Viet Minh, Bao Dai thus added to the legitimacy of the new government. Then on 2 September Ho Chi Minh addressed a mass meeting of half a million people in Hanoi and proclaimed independence in the name of the Democratic Republic of Vietnam. The Vietnamese Declaration of Independence read in part:

> The French have fled, the Japanese have capitulated, Emperor Bao Dai has abdicated. Our people have broken the chains of colonialism which have fettered us for nearly a century in order to create an independent Vietnam. . . . We—the Provisional Government of the Democratic Republic of Vietnam—solemnly declare to the world that: Vietnam has the right to enjoy freedom and independence and has in reality become a free and independent country. The entire people of Vietnam are determined to mobilize all their physical and mental strength, to sacrifice their loves and property to preserve their right to freedom and independence.[11]

This assertion of Vietnamese independence marked the culmination of the August Revolution. To the Vietnamese it represented the reclaiming of a national identity that had survived six decades of French rule and five years of Japanese domination.

Notes

1. John T. McAlister Jr. and Paul Mus, *The Vietnamese and Their Revolution* (New York: Harper & Row, 1970), 49; David G. Marr, *Vietnamese Anticolonialism,*

1885–1925 (Berkeley and Los Angeles: University of California Press, 1971), 4.

2.   D. G. E. Hall, *A History of South-East Asia*, 3d ed. (London: Macmillan, 1968), 419.

3.   William Duiker, *The Rise of Nationalism in Vietnam, 1900–1941* (Ithaca, N.Y.: Cornell University Press, 1976), 16; Huynh Kim Khanh, *Vietnamese Communism, 1925–1945* (Ithaca, N.Y.: Cornell University Press, 1982), 32.

4.   Pham Quynh cited in Duiker, *Rise of Nationalism*, 120.

5.   Paul Isoart, *Le phénomène national vietnamien: De l'indépendance unitaire a l'indépendance fractionée* (Paris: Librairie Général de Droit et de Jurisprudence, 1961), 287.

6.   Quotation attributed to Ho cited in Duiker, *Rise of Nationalism*, 195.

7.   *Thanh Nien* and *Road to Revolution* cited in James P. Harrison, *The Endless War: Fifty Years of Struggle in Vietnam* (New York: Free Press, 1982), 45–46.

8.   Joseph Buttinger, *Vietnam: A Political History* (New York: Praeger, 1968), 180.

9.   Pierre Pasquier cited in Buttinger, *Vietnam*, 180.

10.   Ho Chi Minh, *Selected Writings, 1920–1969* (Hanoi: People's Publishing House, 1973), 46.

11.   Declaration of Independence of the Democratic Republic of Vietnam, 2 September 1945, in Gareth Porter and Gloria Emerson, eds., *Vietnam: A History in Documents* (New York: New American Library, 1981), 28–30.

chapter 2

TO THE JUNGLES OF TONKIN: AMERICANS IN SOUTHEAST ASIA

World War II marked an expansion of the power of the United States, and nowhere were the ramifications of that development more significant than in Southeast Asia. The United States became an important political force there; its position on regional issues often determined their outcome. Indochina, in particular, was destined to present a particularly difficult set of problems for the United States.

The United States' emergence as a power in Southeast Asia during the 1940s reflected an extension of interests and ideology that accompanied American expansion across the Pacific. For decades Americans had thought of Asian problems in ways that reflected a combination of national interest and democratic ideology. In dealing with the politics and peoples of Japan, China, the Philippines, and, later, Vietnam, the United States assumed that its power and influence could not only serve its economic and political interests but also extend its institutions and ideology. American leaders held to a vision of national greatness that suggested the need to promote liberty overseas. This vision was reinforced by a sense of racial superiority that assumed that the Anglo-Saxon peoples were obliged to tutor the "backward" races. Eventually, critics of U.S. foreign policy would see in such policies an "illusion of omnipotence" or an "arrogance of power." Whatever the label, the American approach to Asian problems—which was destined to reach its most critical challenge during the conflict in Vietnam—has deep roots.

From its inception the United States has been an expansionist nation. During the first century after independence, as political expansion concentrated on the North American continent, Americans crossed the Pacific in search of markets. Trade with China and India began within a decade of achieving independence, while in 1853 Americans forced the reopening of

Japanese trade. The United States shared in the Western exploitation of China, enjoying commercial privileges and extraterritorial rights that infringed upon Chinese integrity. The modest but steadily increasing trade with China, Japan, and other Asian countries encouraged many American business and political leaders to envision vastly expanded commercial opportunities.

Those dreams were enhanced by an ideology of expansion that found wide acceptance in the late nineteenth century. If the United States were to resolve internal problems and to achieve national greatness, proponents of the so-called New Manifest Destiny argued, expansion would be necessary. The spectacular growth of American industry had been accompanied by recurrent economic crises, which were blamed on excess productivity; increased exports would end the glut and sustain profits and employment. In his widely read book *Our Country*, Josiah Strong, a well-known Congregationalist minister, built upon concerns about industrial overproduction and warned that urbanization and immigration threatened the very character of American life. The moment was opportune, Strong contended, for Americans to civilize and Christianize the world. Strong's argument for cultural expansion was reinforced by Captain Alfred Thayer Mahan's case for strategic expansion. In his epochal work *The Influence of Sea Power on History*, Mahan maintained that to survive commercially and strategically in a highly competitive world the United States needed a large navy, overseas bases, and an interoceanic canal. Adding to the imperatives for expansion was the force of example, for in the late nineteenth century the principal European powers were building their empires in Asia and Africa. Between 1870 and 1900 European nations acquired control of one-fifth of the world's land area and one-tenth of its population. This imperial movement was celebrated in popular and scholarly writings of the era as an indication of the superiority of the West over "backward" peoples; an empire became a measure of a nation's greatness. If the United States was to take its rightful place "as one of the great nations of the world," Senator Henry Cabot Lodge of Massachusetts said, it needed to join in the race for "the waste places of the earth."[1]

Between 1898 and 1900 the United States thrust its way into Asian prominence, as it annexed Hawaii, seized the Philippine Islands, and proclaimed an open-door policy for China. The Spanish-American War of 1898 enabled expansionists to fulfill their Pacific dreams. Although the United States went to war with Spain for the avowedly anti-imperial objective of freeing Cuba, it took advantage of the conflict to become an Asian imperial power itself by annexing the Philippine Islands, which had been Spain's major Asian possession. In the first week of the war the American navy attacked and destroyed the Spanish Pacific fleet at Manila Bay, a mission undertaken in large part at the initiative of expansionists in the Navy Department. When the war ended following the defeat of Spanish forces in Cuba and Puerto Rico, the United States demanded that Spain cede control of the Philippine Islands.

That momentous step, which gave Americans responsibility for governing and defending an archipelago about which they knew precious little, reflected the prevalent ideology of the era. To advocates of commercial expansion, the possession of the Philippines offered a base for protecting growing interests throughout Asia and for enhancing trade, principally with China. Shortly after the annexation of the Philippines, the United States boldly asserted its open-door policy, which was intended to assure freedom of economic expansion into China. At the same time, Americans saw in the Philippines an opportunity to achieve greatness through fulfilling its duty to "enlighten" a supposedly "backward" people. The British writer Rudyard Kipling championed imperialism in the name of the "white man's burden"— an embodiment of the prevalent racial thinking of the late nineteenth century, which established a hierarchy of races with Anglo-Saxon peoples destined to control "lesser peoples," including Asians. President William McKinley, who was ultimately responsible for the decision to annex the Philippines, spoke of the "great obligations which we cannot disregard." The United States had to fulfill its "great trust . . . under the providence of God and in the name of human progress and civilization." Republican Senator Albert J. Beveridge, an outspoken expansionist, described Americans as "a people imperial by virtue of their power, by right of their institutions, by authority of their Heaven-directed purposes" who now were called upon "to lead in the regeneration of the world."[2]

With its annexation of the Philippines the United States became part of the Western imperial system that dominated Asia. Japan, which had become thoroughly modernized, resisted Western domination, but China's internal divisions were intensified and exploited by the foreign powers. In Southeast Asia only Thailand, which excelled at accommodating the imperialist powers, retained its independence. The British empire was at its apogee, with its political and economic power stretching across Asia. From their control over India, which was heart and symbol of their empire, the British extended their power to Ceylon, Burma, and Malaya, including the naval-commercial center of Singapore; from their colony at Hong Kong the British dominated the foreign commercial and financial structure that turned trade with China to the West's advantage. Besides the British, the Netherlands and France had important possessions. The Netherlands East Indies gave the Dutch control over an area rich in mineral resources. And just a few years before the United States took the Philippines, France completed its conquest of Vietnam, thus establishing Indochina as the center of its Asian power.

The American and French empires in Southeast Asia were connected not only in temporal terms but in other ways as well. The rhetoric of the American creed of national greatness bore similarities to the thinking of European imperialists. The New Manifest Destiny was not far removed from the French sense of a *mission civilisatrice*. Moreover, both the French and Americans encountered native peoples who resisted their control. Just as the

French had spent years "pacifying" the peoples of Indochina, the Americans soon found themselves suppressing Filipinos.

The Philippine resistance movement had begun in 1896 against Spanish domination. When the United States waged war against Spain in 1898, Filipinos took the initiative and seized control of most of the archipelago outside Manila. Emilio Aguinaldo and other leaders anticipated that the United States would support their independence. Thus when the United States decided to annex the Philippines, it faced immediate and widespread opposition that led to three years of war between the U.S. Army and an ill-equipped but determined Philippine army. The United States persisted in labeling the conflict of 1899–1902 the "Philippine insurrection," while to Philippine nationalists it has always been seen as a war for national liberation.

Regardless of how it is labeled, the American-Filipino struggle of 1899–1902 was savage, filled with atrocities on both sides. It was, in some ways, a harbinger of the experience of the American army in Vietnam six decades later. The Filipinos, facing the more numerous and better-equipped Americans, engaged in guerrilla tactics. The United States sent 125,000 troops to the Philippines in a war that cost over $160 million. To combat an enemy that was both everywhere and nowhere, American forces engaged in large-scale attacks on enemy positions. The American army destroyed villages, forced peasants into concentration camps, and tortured prisoners. Racial superiority was used to rationalize the brutal warfare. "It is not civilized warfare, but we are not dealing with a civilized people," one correspondent wrote. "The only thing they know and fear is force, violence, and brutality; and we give it to them."[3] To the mosquito-bitten, exhausted, and ill-fed American soldiers, the campaign lacked any lofty purpose. The Americans quickly came to despise the Filipinos, whom they called the "goo goo." Soldiers, laden with heavy packs, searched the jungles for an elusive enemy that lived off the land and found themselves constantly at the mercy of a sudden and hidden death. They often sang a bitter song:

> Damn, damn, damn the Filipino . . .
> Underneath the starry flag,
> Civilize him with a Krag
> And return us to our own beloved home!

And as would happen during the war in Vietnam six decades later, the prolonged and nasty war in the Philippines led many Americans to question national purpose. The romance of imperialism eroded, and one cynic wrote:

> We've taken up the white man's burden
>   of ebony and brown;
> Now will you tell us, Rudyard,
>   how we may put it down?[4]

After three years of fighting, in which 4,000 American and 18,000 Filipino soldiers were killed, the United States suppressed the revolution. In addition, nearly 200,000 civilians died either in torched villages or of starvation and disease in concentration camps. The U.S. victory resulted not only from its military superiority but also from the weaknesses of the fledgling Philippine Republic. It had only the most rudimentary administrative structure, and its president, Aguinaldo, became increasingly dictatorial. More basically, the sense of Philippine nationhood was not well-developed, and the republic's assertion of national unity foundered in regional, linguistic, religious, and class differences.

Once the "insurrection" ended, the United States solidified its rule by coopting important segments of Philippine society. The economic elite of the islands, which had pressed the Spanish for moderate reforms and had been alienated from Aguinaldo's movement, shared the American objective of order, reform, and modernization. A structure of accommodation linking the interests of the American government and business interests with those of the Filipino elite became the basis of four decades of U.S. rule of the islands. This economic relationship led to a seriously imbalanced trade between the United States and the Philippines and to Philippine dependence upon the American market.

Aside from its economic aspects, the American imperial record, when compared with that of other powers, was relatively enlightened. Never comfortable governing "subjects," the United States began a gradual transition of political power. Within five years of the end of the "insurrection," the United States established an elected legislative assembly; in 1916 the U.S. Congress passed the Jones Act, which promised eventual independence. The Tydings-McDuffie Act of 1934 provided for an autonomous Philippine commonwealth, with a commitment to grant complete independence by 1946. These political reforms were accompanied by programs that improved and expanded communications and transportation, the educational system, and public health services. Thus, at a time when the French in Indochina were refusing to grant even a modicum of self-rule and to deal with social problems, the Americans were planning to end control of the Philippines. At a time when the suppression of political movements in Indochina was forcing nationalists underground and toward leftist ideologies, Filipino nationalists had few complaints with the Americans; one leader lamented, "Damn the Americans, why don't they tyrannize us more?"[5]

Besides its control over the Philippines, the United States had steadily increasing economic interests elsewhere in Southeast Asia. British Malaya (rubber and tin), the Netherlands East Indies (rubber and oil), and, to a lesser extent, French Indochina (rubber) were important sources of raw materials.

The tumultuous events of World War II forced the United States into a far more prominent role in the region. Japan's promise of a New Order for Asia, which was to be based on Japanese political and economic hegemony, threatened the position of the United States and the other Western powers. Having established control over large parts of China, Japan envisioned expanding into Southeast Asia, thus gaining the area's mineral resources, especially oil, tin, and rubber. With its ally Germany conquering France and the Netherlands in the spring of 1940 and poised to strike Britain, Japan realized that only the United States could prevent its advance into Southeast Asia. The Japanese thus threatened important interests of the United States, which benefited not only from its own strong commercial ties with the Philippines but from the European predominance of Southeast Asia as well. Forced into defending the Western position in Southeast Asia, the United States sought to negotiate with Japan, but the differences defied compromise. In the end, Japan's leaders believed that national survival necessitated war.

The Japanese attack on Pearl Harbor on 7 December 1941 was quickly followed by the conquest of Southeast Asia. With one exception, the Japanese encountered little resistance, as native troops had no incentive to fight to preserve Western empires. In the Philippines, however, American and Filipino troops fought a determined campaign. Lacking reinforcements, the outnumbered, inadequately equipped, and ill-fed defenders eventually surrendered in May 1942. Despite its ultimate futility, the American-Filipino resistance underscored the fundamental solidarity of the relationship between the United States and its colony. Americans interpreted this bond as evidence of the beneficial aspects of their colonial administration.

As the United States waged war in Europe and Asia from 1941 to 1945, its leaders envisioned a postwar system of peace that would be based on continued cooperation among the wartime allies, the establishment of the United Nations to adjudicate problems among nations, and the end of the colonial system that had dominated prewar Asia. The strong commitment to anticolonialism reflected several widely held assumptions: first, if the Allies were waging a war on behalf of freedom from fascist domination, they could hardly justify the preservation of the white man's imperialism; second, the colonial system had increased the West's vulnerability in confronting Japan, which had skillfully used the concept of pan-Asianism to appeal as a liberator from Western domination; and third, economic barriers among nations intensified rivalries, and colonies, by definition, restricted the economic development of native peoples and commercial-investment opportunities for other countries. In sum, the end of imperialism would liberate subject peoples, would open markets, and would facilitate political and economic stability.

"The western nations," the prominent columnist Walter Lippmann wrote in 1942, "must identify their cause with the freedom and security of the peoples of the East, putting away the 'white man's burden' and purging themselves of the taint of an obsolete and obviously unworkable white man's imperialism. In this drastic reorientation of war policy, the leadership of the western nations must be taken by the United States."[6] In a speech three months later Under Secretary of State Sumner Welles stated unequivocally that the "age of imperialism is ended."[7] President Franklin D. Roosevelt championed anti-colonialism. He privately lamented to his son, "Don't think for a moment that Americans would be dying in the Pacific tonight, if it hadn't been for the shortsighted greed of the French and the British and the Dutch." The president then promised that he would "work with all might and main to see that the United States is not wheedled into the position of accepting any plan that will further France's imperialistic ambitions, or that will aid or abet the British Empire in its imperial ambitions."[8]

The American sense of destiny in Asia was reinforced by the intense hatred of Japan that grew out of the Pearl Harbor attack. The peoples of Asia, Americans believed, had to be liberated from the "Japs," who were depicted in wartime propaganda as a cunning, ruthless, barbaric people. Pearl Buck, the popular novelist renowned for her works on China, stated in 1942: "If the American way of life is to prevail in the world, it must prevail in Asia. . . . In Europe our influence has been of little importance. In Asia it has long been the chief influence. We have so far the ideological leadership in Asia."[9]

Those sentiments led the State Department to plan for the transition of Southeast Asian countries from colonialism to independence. Americans believed that their administration of the Philippines served as a model of enlightened imperialism, and thus the United States sought commitments from European powers that their return to power in Asia would be accompanied by measures of progressive self-government and promises of eventual independence.

In addition to those general plans President Roosevelt took a special interest in the future of Indochina and sought to prevent any restoration of French rule. Roosevelt envisioned the establishment of an international trusteeship for Indochina, whereby several nations would be responsible for postwar administration and for implementing measures leading to eventual independence. While his ideas for Indochina were vague, Roosevelt firmly believed that the French should not be permitted to resume their colonial administration. His opposition to French rule was summarized during a meeting in 1943 with various Allied officials:

> Roosevelt said that he felt Indo-China should not be given back to the French Empire after the war. The French had been there for nearly one hundred years and had done absolutely nothing with the place to improve the lot of the people. . . . The President said that he felt 35,000,000 people should not be exploited; that the French had taken a great deal from them. . . . The President said that after the war we ought to help these 35,000,000 people. Naturally they could not be given independence immediately but should be taken care of until they could govern themselves. . . . In the meantime we would treat Indo-China as a trustee.[10]

Roosevelt, armed with his limited but not inaccurate knowledge of French rule, pursued his trusteeship plan in meetings with other Allied leaders, espe-

cially Premier Joseph Stalin of the Soviet Union and President Chiang Kai-
shek of China. While he found them sympathetic, Roosevelt encountered the
implacable hostility of Britain's Prime Minister Winston Churchill, who feared
the implications of American anticolonialism for the British Empire.

Why did Roosevelt, confronting countless problems in the midst of a global
war, concern himself with the future of a small country in which the United
States historically had scant interests? In part, the answer lies in Roosevelt's
conviction that France had relinquished its claim to be a major world power.
At a time when others had been resisting the Axis powers, France's abrupt collapse after the German invasion of 1940 and the capitulation of French colonial authorities in Indochina in the face of Japanese pressures in 1940–1941
had been instrumental in the German-Japanese military ascendancy. Besides
punishing France by taking away part of its empire, Roosevelt believed that
the postwar status of Indochina was directly related to American long-term
objectives. Recognizing that the days of Western domination of Asia were
ending and seeing colonies as one of the causes of the war, the president
wanted to give impetus to the liquidation of imperialism. He knew that the
British and Dutch would resist U.S. pressures to liberalize their colonial
administrations. An international trusteeship for Indochina, when combined
with the fulfillment of the American promise to grant Philippine independence in 1946, would not only affirm the Allied commitment to anticolonialism but also make it more difficult for the other Western powers to ignore
the nationalist aspirations of peoples in their own colonies. Roosevelt was
sensitive to the forces that were changing Asia; in early 1945 he discussed the
need for the United States to identify with nationalism: "The President said
he was concerned about the brown people in the East. He said there are
1,100,000,000 brown people. In many Eastern countries, they are ruled by a
handful of whites and they resent it. Our goal must be to help them achieve
independence—1,100,000,000 potential enemies are dangerous."[11]

Roosevelt's trusteeship plan was undermined, however, by considerations
largely beyond his control. First, the division of military administration in the
Pacific gave the British responsibility for Allied occupation of Indochina,
which would be instrumental in determining the postwar political status of the
country. Second, once France was liberated from Germany in 1944, its new
government under the leadership of General Charles de Gaulle reasserted
France's stature as a major power, which included retaining its empire. Third,
Britain and the Netherlands, in collaboration with a resurgent France, ignored
Roosevelt's ideas and worked for colonial restoration in Southeast Asia.
Finally, many State Department officials believed that the United States
could not treat Indochina differently from other colonial areas and could not
afford to alienate France, whose cooperation was considered necessary in
meeting postwar problems in Europe. As a result of these developments, the
Indochina trusteeship plan, which had already become increasingly fragile,
ended with Roosevelt's death on 12 April 1945. One can only speculate how

the transfer of authority in Indochina to an international trusteeship might have changed the course of history, but at the very least, it would have precluded the return of the French, which touched off 30 years of warfare. On the other hand, pursuit of the trusteeship in the face of France's opposition would have led to a crisis in Franco-American relations.

Meanwhile, far removed from State Department and White House deliberations about postwar Southeast Asia, a number of Americans came into contact with the Viet Minh. In the jungles of Tonkin in early 1945 a small group of Americans collaborated with the Vietnamese. Ho Chi Minh and his movement had been known for some time to American intelligence officers in southern China, but they paid little attention to the Vietnamese until the Japanese coup of March 1945. Because the end of the French administration had deprived the Allies of their source of information about developments in Indochina, the OSS entered into an agreement with Ho whereby the Americans provided radio equipment, arms, and ammunition in return for Viet Minh assistance in gaining intelligence, sabotaging Japanese installations, and rescuing U.S. pilots shot down over Indochina. OSS personnel joined the Viet Minh at Ho's headquarters in northern Vietnam.

The Viet Minh–American collaboration quickly took on important political overtones. Anticipating that U.S. support could be critical in his bid for national independence, Ho cultivated the Americans. Like other Asian nationalists, Ho expected that the United States would champion the aspirations of colonial peoples. Thus the Americans were enthusiastically welcomed to the Viet Minh headquarters. Nearly all of the Americans who had contact with the Viet Minh were impressed by its popular support and determination to achieve independence. Like their countrymen, those Americans held strong anticolonial convictions and thus identified with Vietnamese aspirations. They were not ignorant of Ho's Communist background, but they considered it irrelevant. "The Viet Minh League," one officer cabled Washington, "is not Communist. Stands for freedom and reforms from French harshness." Another American observed that the Viet Minh was "not Communist or Communist controlled or Communist led."[12]

Americans not only witnessed the August Revolution but in fact became part of the Viet Minh's bid for independence. The Viet Minh appealed for U.S. support of its political objectives and Vietnam's economic development. As it prepared to seize power, the Viet Minh, in a message of 15 August, expressed the hope that "the United States, as a champion of democracy, will assist [Vietnam] in securing this independence [by] . . . prohibiting or not assisting the French to enter Indo-China . . . sending technical advisors to assist the Indo-Chinese to exploit the resources of the land . . . [and] developing those industries that Indo-China is capable of supporting. In conclusion, the Indo-Chinese would like to be placed on the same status as the Philippines for an undetermined period."[13] In a conversation with an American, Ho expressed his admiration for the Russian Revolution but was skeptical whether the Soviet Union could contribute to the building of a modernized Vietnam; American investment capital and technology, however, could clearly benefit his country. The affinity with the Americans was underscored when Ho, while drafting a declaration of independence for his country, asked an American for a copy of the U.S. declaration. When Ho proclaimed national independence on 2 September, the influence of Thomas Jefferson was evident; the Vietnamese declaration referred to the precedents of the American and French (but not Russian) revolutions and spoke of the expectation of Allied support: "We are convinced that the Allied nations which . . . have acknowledged the principles of self-determination and equality of nations, will not refuse to acknowledge the independence of Viet Nam. A people who have courageously opposed French domination for more than eighty years, a people who have fought side by side with the Allies against the fascists during these last years, such a people must be free and independent."[14]

By the time Ho proclaimed his country's independence, additional Americans had come to Vietnam, and by October a Vietnam-America Friendship Association was established with great fanfare in Hanoi. The strength of the Viet Minh continued to impress the Americans. "My personal opinion," one OSS officer wrote, "is that Mr. Ho Chi Minh is a brilliant and capable man, completely sincere in his opinions. I believe that when he speaks, he speaks for his people, for I have . . . found that people of all classes are imbued with the same spirit and determination as their leader."[15] Another American official observed, "The enthusiasm with which liberated peoples greeted the American troops in various parts of the world is by now an old story. But nowhere did the coming of the Americans, in this case a mere handful of them, mean so much as they did to the population of northern Indo-China. To [the Vietnamese], our coming was the symbol of liberation not from Japanese occupation but from decades of French colonial rule. For the [Vietnamese] government considered the United States as the principal champion of the rights of small peoples."[16]

Repeatedly Ho appealed to the U.S. government for recognition of the Democratic Republic of Vietnam. Despite the numerous reports from Americans who expressed respect for the Viet Minh, Ho's leadership, and the widespread popular support for independence, Ho's efforts to elicit U.S. support failed.

In Washington the State Department dutifully filed Ho's messages, but no official suggested that the United States take any steps on behalf of the Vietnamese. The momentous political, economic, and social dislocations caused by World War II were of overriding concern to the administration of Harry S. Truman, who had succeeded to the presidency upon Roosevelt's death. In the American global perspective of late 1945, Vietnam was a diplomatic backwater. Moreover, developments there were seen as the problems of the French; shortly after Roosevelt's passing, U.S. officials had assured their French counterparts that the United States would not interfere in their control over Indochina.

And by late 1945 the Americans were leaving Vietnam. The missions that had brought them into contact with the Viet Minh were completed. Their departure ended a unique moment in the Vietnamese-American encounter.

Notes

1. Henry Cabot Lodge, "Our Blundering Foreign Policy," *Forum* 19 (1895): 16–17.

2. McKinley and Beveridge speeches cited in Michael H. Hunt, *Ideology and U.S. Foreign Policy* (New Haven: Yale University Press, 1987), 38.

3. Cited in Stuart C. Miller, "Our Mylai of 1900: Americans in the Philippine Insurrection," *Transaction* 7 (1970): 24.

4. Song and poem cited in H. Wayne Morgan, *America's Road to Empire: The War with Spain and Overseas Expansion* (New York: Wiley, 1965), 111–12.

5. Manuel Quezon cited in James C. Thomson Jr., Peter W. Stanley, and John Curtis Perry, *Sentimental Imperialists: The American Experience in East Asia* (New York: Harper & Row, 1981), 120.

6. *Washington Post*, 21 February 1942.

7. *Department of State Bulletin* 6, 30 May 1942, 488.

8. Elliot Roosevelt, *As He Saw It* (New York: Duell, Sloan, Pearce, 1946), 115–16.

9. Cited in Christopher Thorne, *Allies of a Kind: The United States, Britain, and the War against Japan, 1941–1945* (New York: Oxford University Press, 1978), 156.

10. Pacific War Council Minutes, 21 July 1943, Map Room Files, Franklin D. Roosevelt Library, Hyde Park, N.Y.

11. Memorandum of Conversation with Roosevelt, 15 March 1945, FDR Papers, Roosevelt Library.

12. Report No. 1, Deer Mission, 17 July 1945, in U.S. Senate Committee on Foreign Relations, *Causes, Origins, and Lessons of the Vietnam War* (92d Cong., 2d sess.; Washington, D.C.: U.S. Government Printing Office, 1973), 244–48.

13. OSS to Truman, 22 August 1945, Truman Papers, Harry S. Truman Library, Independence, Mo.

14. DRV Declaration of Independence, 2 September 1945, in Allen W. Cameron, ed., *Vietnam Crisis: A Documentary History* (Ithaca, N.Y.: Cornell University Press, 1971), 1:52–54.

15. OSS China Theater, SI Branch, 19 September 1945, in Senate, *Causes*, 306–7.

16. Report by Hale, 2 October 1945, in ibid., 23–31.

chapter 3

TO DIEN BIEN PHU: THE UNITED STATES AND THE FRENCH–VIET MINH WAR, 1946–1954

The end of World War II brought immense political changes throughout Asia. In the colonial areas of Southeast Asia, nationalists seized upon the suddenness of the Japanese surrender and the weakness of the European powers to demand an end to Western imperialism. The August Revolution, which brought the Viet Minh to power in Vietnam, was paralleled by a nationalist revolution in Indonesia, where leaders proclaimed their independence from the Netherlands. Meanwhile, the Burmese demanded an end to British rule, and Filipinos, in less strident terms, called for fulfillment of the prewar American promise to grant independence to their country. The forces of change swept across the rest of Asia. In India, the long and largely nonviolent struggle against the British gained irresistible momentum as Mohandas K. Gandhi, Jawaharlal Nehru, and thousands of other leaders, who had spent much of the war in prison for demanding independence in 1942, now pressed for immediate freedom. In China, the end of the war against Japan also ended the pretext of collaboration between the Nationalist government (Kuomintang) of Chiang Kai-shek and the Communist movement led by Mao Tse-tung; renewed fighting between the Kuomintang and Communist armies in 1945 marked the beginning of four years of civil war.

These changes in Asian politics concerned the United States, which emerged from World War II as the world's preeminent power. As the only major nation whose homeland had not been scarred by war, the United States was spared the enormous problems of postwar reconstruction faced by all the other belligerents, victors and vanquished alike. Despite its enormous military power, which was heightened by development of the atomic bomb, the United States approached the postwar world with much uncertainty. The deterioration of the wartime coalition with the Soviet Union soon led to the tensions of the cold war. To Americans it seemed that the Soviets, by using their military presence in Eastern Europe to establish political dominance, were following a path of aggression similar to that of Nazi Germany, Imperial Japan, and Fascist Italy in the 1930s. From the failure of the Western democracies to halt that aggression prior to World War II, it seemed clear to American leaders that any appeasement of aggressive powers was mistaken. Hence, much of U.S. foreign policy after 1945 was driven by a historical "lesson": aggression had to be resisted, for if not, the insatiable aggressors would keep expanding. World War III, in other words, could be avoided only by halting aggression in its early stages.

The United States' response to developments in Europe shaped its approach to postwar Asia. With Europe retaining its high priority in calculations of global interests, American leaders avoided actions in Asia that would weaken the nation's position in Europe. Since the United States sought close relations with Great Britain, France, and the Netherlands as part of the effort to contain the Soviet Union's power, it was reluctant to challenge their colonial policies. The British, recognizing their diminished economic and military resources, took the initiative and ended their control over India and Burma. The Dutch, however, fought to hold their empire against the forces of the Indonesian Republic. And when the French refused to compromise with the Vietnamese, the resulting conflict drew the United States into its initial political commitments in Indochina. Indeed, the roots of the subsequent large-scale U.S. involvement can be traced to the American response to the French–Viet Minh War of 1946–1954.

ORIGINS OF THE FRENCH–VIET MINH CONFLICT

The resort to arms in Vietnam was almost inevitable. It resulted from the inability of the French and the Democratic Republic of Vietnam (DRV) to reconcile their differences over the fundamental issue of sovereignty. The August Revolution had concluded with Ho Chi Minh's bold assertion of independence, but the french ignored such claims and planned to reestablish their Indochina colony. They considered the DRV and its ill-equipped army as more of a nuisance than a serious challenge.

After proclaiming independence on 2 September 1945, the Viet Minh leadership saw the DRV's position as "quite fragile," for despite the extent of popular support, it faced a continuing food crisis and a lack of financial resources. More important, the arrival of Chinese and British occupation forces to receive the Japanese surrender undermined the position of the Viet Minh. A Kuomintang army of 150,000 troops crossed into northern Indochina, while British forces took key areas in the South. Neither the British nor the Chinese governments acknowledged the DRV's claim to independence, although initially the Chinese forces helped the Viet Minh by providing arms and supplies captured from the Japanese. Shortly afterward, however, the

Chinese government recognized French sovereignty in Indochina in return for a promise of special economic concessions. In the South the British sought a brief occupation. Assuming that the early restoration of French authority would assure political stability, the British facilitated the return of French forces and the reestablishment of a degree of French political control. The strong French position in the South reflected not only the support of the British but also the fact that French power had historically been concentrated in that area and that the Viet Minh had been unable to build the kind of support there that it enjoyed in the North.

The French endeavored to exploit the weaknesses of the Viet Minh. The resumption of French authority in much of the South left the DRV in control of only the northern areas. In the face of French plans to send troops to the cities of the North, the Viet Minh leaders feared that their ill-trained forces would have to fight alone against the much better equipped French army. Ho Chi Minh recognized his government's isolation: the Americans, who had embraced the August Revolution, had departed; his several appeals to President Truman for support had gone unanswered; the Chinese, about to depart, had agreed to permit French forces in the North; the French had an invasion force off the coast near Haiphong; and even the leading Communist state, the Soviet Union, took no evident interest in the DRV's plight.

Ho desperately sought an agreement that would acknowledge the legitimacy of the DRV and would buy time to complete the nationalist revolution. Accordingly, on 6 March 1946 he entered into an agreement with Jean Sainteny, who as head of the French mission in northern Vietnam was one of the few French leaders to recognize that the popularity of the Viet Minh necessitated a liberal colonial policy. But even between two men who shared a determination to avoid conflict, compromise was difficult, and their agreement amounted to an "armistice that provided a transient illusion of agreement when actually no agreement existed."[1] Ho accepted the stationing of 15,000 French troops in northern Vietnam; in return France agreed to recognize the DRV as a "free state" within the Indochina Federation and promised to conduct a referendum on Vietnam's national unity and to withdraw their army from the north gradually over the next five years. Many of his followers criticized Ho since in agreeing to a French military presence, he seemingly compromised the independence that he had proclaimed just six months earlier. However, Ho justified that concession on the grounds that the Ho-Sainteny Agreement gave a partial recognition to the DRV's legitimacy and that the referendum, if held, would almost certainly lead to national unity under the DRV. Yet even Ho was disappointed, for he told Sainteny, "You know I wanted more than has been granted. . . . Nevertheless, I realize that one cannot achieve everything in one day."[2]

French actions over the next several months revealed that Ho's confidence in their good faith had been ill-placed. France refused to carry out the plebiscite and instead established its own government, the Republic of Cochin China, with a few compliant Vietnamese acting as figureheads; in sum, France simply continued its historic colonial policy of dividing Vietnam and using Frenchified Vietnamese as puppets. (Even the puppets, however, often resented the French; the head of the Republic of Cochin China committed suicide a few months later when he realized that his government had no real power and was only a facade for French rule.) France also reestablished control over Laos and Cambodia, meaning that in the Indochina Federation the DRV would face three French-controlled governments. When Ho Chi Minh traveled to France in the summer of 1946 for negotiations that were to implement the Ho-Sainteny Agreement, he found the French uncompromising; he left Paris in September with only an innocuous joint statement endorsing the earlier agreement.

While in Paris Ho once again sought American support. In meetings with U.S. embassy officials, he urged pressure on the French to negotiate in good faith and spoke of his government's interest in foreign investment capital. The Vietnamese leader promised an end to France's special economic privileges and talked of the possibility of a U.S. naval base at Cam Ranh Bay. A few State Department officials believed that the United States should use its influence to moderate French policy. Most notably, Abbott Low Moffatt called for "express[ing] to the French, in view of our interest in peace and orderly development of dependent peoples, our hope that they will abide by the spirit of the [Ho-Sainteny] agreement."[3] Yet at the time the overriding concern of high-level policymakers was with events far distant from Indochina, which seemed a minor problem and one that the French could handle.

Indeed, the French were preparing to deal with the situation by military means. The presence of French military forces in DRV-controlled areas in the North created a tenuous situation in which clashes were inevitable. In November, following two days of fighting between French and Viet Minh forces at Haiphong, which had been virtually blockaded by the French navy, the French decided to deal forcefully with the DRV. A French cruiser opened fire and destroyed the Vietnamese section of the city, killing 6,000 Vietnamese. Buoyed by that show of strength, the French commander demanded that the Viet Minh yield military control of Haiphong, Hanoi, and the roads connecting those cities. By December French units had occupied Hanoi, taking control of DRV government buildings. On 19 December, General Vo Nguyen Giap, commander of Viet Minh forces, ordered a war of national resistance.

As French-Vietnamese relations deteriorated, the United States belatedly tried to prevent war. The State Department sent Moffat on a special mission to Vietnam. Meeting with Ho and Giap in Hanoi, Moffat assured the Vietnamese leaders of American interest in a peaceful settlement. The Vietnamese reiterated their overriding commitment to independence, while stressing the willingness of their people to pay whatever price was necessary to achieve that objective. The Vietnamese still trusted the United States, but Moffat's mission could not alter the drift to war. To the DRV a resumption of negotiations with the French, as Moffat implicitly suggested, however attractive as a means of avoiding or at least delaying war, seemed too risky. Ho's pursuit of negotiations in 1946 had been criticized by many of his followers, including Giap, who pointed to the French record since the Ho-Sainteny agreement as proof that they could not be trusted. Moffat's role as an intermediary was also limited by the American government's distrust of the Viet Minh; his instructions admonished Moffat not to forget "Ho's clear record as an agent of international communism" and that "the least desired eventuality would be the establishment of a Communist-dominated, Moscow-oriented state in Vietnam."[4] That preoccupation with the Viet Minh's Communist leadership projected the worst-case scenario—a Soviet-dominated Communist state in Vietnam—and left the United States a hostage of French policy.

A striking aspect of the American preoccupation with Ho Chi Minh's Communist background is that the Soviet Union took virtually no interest in the Viet Minh's problems. It did not extend diplomatic recognition to the DRV and continued to regard France as the legitimate ruler of Indochina. Stalin's response to the Vietnamese revolution reflected his country's international priorities, which gave little importance to the aspirations of relatively obscure Communist comrades in a small country that had never been of strategic, economic, or political significance to the Soviet Union. Moreover, Moscow may have distrusted Ho's independence, which had been evident in his looking to the West, specifically the United States, for diplomatic and material support. Such national communism made Ho a maverick who could not be controlled. Most important, the Soviet Union, like the United States, was preoccupied with European developments. Stalin sought to enhance the French Communist party, which showed considerable strength in postwar elections, anticipating that if it came to power it would lead toward French-Soviet collaboration at the expense of American interests. Since holding the empire in Indochina was popular among the French public, the Communist party supported the get-tough policy in Vietnam. If the Soviet Union had supported the DRV, it would thus have weakened the association of the French Communist party with French colonialism. In sum, Soviet stragetic interests pointed toward acquiescing in French suppression of the Vietnamese Communists.

It was thus an isolated Vietnamese people who followed the Viet Minh's call for a war of national resistance. The French, with a well-equipped and well-trained force of some 100,000 troops, looked with disdain upon the Viet Minh army. Among the 150,000 soldiers in the Viet Minh force, only one-third were equipped with even small arms. The Viet Minh had neither air force nor navy. Accordingly, the French easily secured control of the cities and major towns, and with their superior firepower were able to defeat the Viet Minh in open battles.

Yet the French could not achieve a military victory, for the Viet Min controlled most of the countryside, where they retained the loyalty of the vast majority of the population. This strength in the rural areas provided the base for an effective campaign of guerrilla warfare. The French minister of war recognized the no-win situation: "It is evident that the greater part of the country remains in the hands of the Viet Minh. I do not think that we should undertake the conquest of French Indochina. It would necessitate an expeditionary corps of at least 500,000 men."[5]

The challenge facing the French was more political than military. General Jacques Philippe Leclerc warned his superiors in 1947 that "anti-Communism will be a useless tool as long as the problem of nationalism remains unsolved," and advised that the "capital problem from now on is political. It is a question of coming to terms with an awakening xenophobic nationalism."[6]

THE U.S. COMMITMENT: THE "BAO DAI SOLUTION"

Facing the prospects of a prolonged war, the French government eventually heeded Leclerc's advice and fostered an anticommunist, nationalist alternative to the Viet Minh. The central problem was finding a leader around whom the Vietnamese would rally. In their search for a noncommunist leader who could challenge Ho Chi Minh's nationalist stature, the French eventually settled upon the former emperor, Bao Dai. With much fanfare, the French, through the Elysée Agreement of March 1949, granted "independence" to the "State of Vietnam," Laos, and Cambodia, which became "associated states" within the French Union. In fact, the "independence" was a sham, for the French retained control over foreign affairs and defense and held various special privileges. Bao Dai thus returned to Vietnam in July 1949 as "head of state" of the nominally independent State of Vietnam.

The Bao Dai solution—as the French referred to this alleged liberalization of their colonial policy—reflected the weakness of France's position, for Bao Dai stood little chance of building a viable political base that could challenge the credibility of the Viet Minh. Bao Dai's capacity, as a representative of the Nguyen dynasty that had united Vietnam 150 years earlier, to appeal to national tradition was tarnished by the Nguyens' long record of subservience to the French. Bao Dai had made a career of offering his services to whomever had power in his country: before World War II, he worked with the French, as a nominal ruler from the throne at Hué; when the Japanese seized control of his country, he collaborated with them; during the August Revolution, he abdicated in favor of the Viet Minh; when it became evident that the Viet Minh would give him no special favors, he left Vietnam and spent the greater part of three years living on the French Riviera, where he earned a reputation as the "playboy emperor." In a completion of the cycle, Bao Dai in 1949 was again doing the bidding of the French. Not only did Bao Dai lack credentials as a nationalist, he lacked any real power as "head of state"; to his credit, Bao

Dai sought concessions from the French, but none of any significance were forthcoming. For the French, the Bao Dai solution was intended principally to provide a facade for a continuation of French military rule. It enabled the French to respond to critics of their war against the Viet Minh, for they could now claim that the struggle in Indochina was not a colonial war but a civil war in which the French were supporting one of two Vietnamese contestants. That rationale, of course, completely ignored the vast differences between the Viet Minh and the State of Vietnam in terms of nationalist stature and popular support.

The French nonetheless accomplished a major objective—gaining U.S. support for their Indochina policy. Indeed, the United States, in response to the Bao Dai solution, made the first commitment of American political and economic resources to Vietnam. American officials, however, recognized Bao Dai's limited chances for success; one observed, "the majority of natives stoutly maintain that Ho Chi Minh is the man, and the only one, who represents them and they will oppose the putting forward of any other candidate as the creating of but another puppet and the erecting of a smoke screen of France's real intentions."[7] Supporting Bao Dai risked "in view of his very dubious chances of succeeding . . . follow[ing] blindly down a dead-end alley, expending our limited resources—in money and most particularly in prestige—in a fight which would be hopeless."[8]

If the prospects for the Bao Dai solution appeared so bleak, why did the United States support it? Within the framework of American global strategy in 1949–1950, the commitment to the French seemed imperative. In view of the importance of France to the containment policy in Europe, the United States refused to alienate its ally over the war in Vietnam. "We have an immediate interest in maintaining in power a friendly French government to assist in the furtherance of our aims in Europe," a State Department policy statement maintained, and that "vital interest has in consequence taken precedence over active steps toward the realization of our objectives in Indochina."[9] Moreover, in the French-American exchange over the war with the Viet Minh, the French always held a high card—the threat of withdrawal. This meant that the United States had virtually no leverage with the French and had to accept the Elysée Agreement as the best that the French were prepared to offer. French officials recognized that the Americans preferred their presence in Indochina to the alternative of allowing the Viet Minh to come to power. The Bao Dai government, French as well as U.S. officials recognized, would not survive without the French army. While the Americans argued that more liberal concessions to noncommunist nationalists were necessary to enhance France's credibility, the French were able to ignore such advice and gave Bao Dai minimal responsibilities.

Finally, the victory of the Communist movement in the Chinese civil war provided irresistible momentum to support of Bao Dai. For the momentous events that culminated in the proclamation of the People's Republic of China in October 1949 made it seem that Southeast Asia would be the next target of Communist expansion. Alarmed U.S. policymakers looked in 1949–1950 upon a world that was far different from what they had anticipated at the end of World War II, for everywhere, it seemed, the forces of communism were gaining. The establishment of Soviet control over Eastern Europe had now been followed by the success of the Communist movement in the world's most populous country, an event made all the more disconcerting by the traditional assumption of a special Chinese-American friendship. Southeast Asia appeared to be vulnerable to the agenda of Soviet-Chinese expansion. Events seemed to support that interpretation: the Chinese Communists provided material support for the Viet Minh and in January 1950 extended diplomatic recognition to the Democratic Republic of Vietnam; shortly afterward, the Soviet Union, at last, also recognized the DRV as the legitimate government of Vietnam. The prospects appeared ominous; in the words of a National Security Council policy statement: "The extension of communist authority in China represents a grievous political defeat for us. . . . If Southeast Asia is also swept by communism, we shall have suffered a major political rout, the repercussions of which will be felt throughout the rest of the world. . . . It is now clear that Southeast Asia is the target for a coordinated offensive directed by the Kremlin."[10]

To U.S. policymakers Vietnam stood as the key to the entire region, for if the Viet Minh—now drawing support from the Soviets and Chinese—succeeded, that would enhance the prospects for Communist success in Thailand and the newly independent Philippines, Indonesia, and Burma. Economic problems and political instability in these countries seemingly facilitated the appeal of communism and weakened resistance to external pressures.

To stabilize the region, American policy drew upon recent U.S. experience in Europe, where a strategy of containment had been directed against the Soviet Union. The use of American political, economic, and military resources was strengthening the Western democracies and reducing the region's vulnerability to the influence of the Soviet Union. Thus, in response to the Chinese civil war, American leaders redefined Asian policy with the objective of again "drawing the line," which resulted in an extension of U.S. economic assistance to friendly governments (notably the Philippines, Indonesia, and Thailand), the rebuilding of the Japanese economy (for which Southeast Asia would be important as a source of raw materials and as a market for manufactured goods), and support of the French in Indochina. As part of this general redefinition of its Asian policy, the United States in February 1950 formally took sides in the Indochina war as it extended diplomatic recognition to the State of Vietnam. The success of the Bao Dai solution had thus become critical to U.S., as well as French, objectives.

Shortly after the commitment to the Bao Dai solution, the American association with the French became even more imperative. The unanticipated outbreak of the Korean War in June 1950 brought American forces to the defense of South Korea. By the end of that year, they were fighting not only the North Koreans but the Chinese as well; China intervened to prevent North Korea's defeat and the unification of Korea under a pro-Western government. Thus the French fight against the Vietnamese Communists and the American war against the North Korean–Chinese Communists came to be seen as two fronts of a struggle to prevent the Communist conquest of Asia. Such an outlook ignored numerous differences in the origins of the two wars. Yet to the American government and people, who were suddenly caught in a nasty war on a small peninsula just five years after their armies had won the greatest war in history, such nuances were meaningless; it seemed vital to hold the line in both Indochina and Korea. Writing in *Foreign Affairs* in 1950, Jacques Soustelle linked the wars:

> The glow from the Korean battlefields lights up the whole Asiatic front from Manchuria to Malaya. . . . Along two portions of this immense arc, the cold or tepid war has given place to, simply, war. There two Western powers have engaged their armies. The United States has been in Korea since June 26, 1950 and France has been in Indo-China since December 19, 1946.
>
> The two conflicts differ from each other in many ways. However, each clearly has a place in the same strategic and political complex. They share a basic common factor. Each results from the expansion of Soviet power toward the area, pushing its satellites ahead, and exploiting against the West the nationalism, even xenophobia, of the Asiatic masses.[11]

U.S. support became critical to the continuation of the French war effort. Assistance began on a modest scale in the spring of 1950, but pressures for more aid quickly mounted. Indeed, as Soustelle was writing in the fall of 1950, Viet Minh forces were about to overrun French outposts near the Vietnamese-Chinese border, an attack that would result in heavy casualties and an erosion of French morale. To sustain the French, the United States supplied aircraft, tanks, naval vessels, combat vehicles, automatic weapons, small arms, machine guns, bombers, transportation planes, artillery, and ammunition. By the end of 1952 the total value of American military support amounted to $775 million.

Despite this assistance, the French remained caught in an impossible political-military situation. To defeat a guerilla army requires overwhelming numerical military superiority and popular support. The French lacked both. By 1953 the forces under France's Indochina Command had grown to 517,000 troops, including an influx of Vietnamese who had been recruited into Bao Dai's "national army"; the Viet Minh forces, however, had grown proportionately, to nearly 300,000 soldiers. While the French continued to control the major towns and cities in the Mekong Delta, along the coast, and in the Red River Delta, the Viet Minh dominated the countryside, where their identification with the peasantry gave them enormous advantages. In a war waged in the villages, jungles, and mountains, French operations were principally directed toward three objectives: pacification (securing rural areas against the Viet Minh and establishing political control), offensive probes against Viet Minh strongholds, and protection of convoys carrying supplies through enemy-infested areas. Yet all three objectives were elusive: pacification absorbed large numbers of troops, took much time, and frequently failed to secure areas for extended periods; offensive operations rarely resulted in engaging regular Viet Minh units, but nonetheless cost the French heavy casualties; and the convoys also required substantial units for what proved to be a precarious protection at best.

By the summer of 1953—after six and a half years of indecisive campaigns—the frustrated French were prepared to negotiate an end to the war. The French public had grown weary of a seemingly endless conflict. Total French casualties reached nearly 150,000, and even with U.S. support the war was costing nearly one-half of the country's defense expenditures. Moreover, this drain on human and material resources left the French army in a weakened position in Europe. This became an especially sensitive matter because the United States was proposing the creation of a European Defense Community (EDC), which included the rearming of West Germany. With vivid memories of two German invasions within the previous 40 years, France refused to endorse EDC, especially so long as the Indochina War continued. A leading critic of the war, Pierre Mendes-France, warned that pursuing the war meant "rising prices and further social unrest" and "never succeed[ing] in organizing our defenses in Europe if [we] continue to send all [our] cadres to Asia, to sacrifice them every year without any result."[12] Finally, the French were influenced by the armistice signed in July 1953 ending the Korean War. It increased the possibilities that China, now that it was no longer at war with the Americans in Korea, might send troops to Indochina; at the very least, the Chinese could be expected to increase their levels of supplies to the Viet Minh. Moreover, many French asked, If the Americans, unable to achieve military victory in Korea, had negotiated a settlement, why should France not do the same in Indochina? Ending the unpopular war in Korea had fulfilled a campaign promise of the new U.S. president, Dwight D. Eisenhower. A leading supporter of the French war stated that his country would be in an "untenable position . . . [if] peace were re-established in Korea while the war continued in Indochina."[13]

Reflecting these pressures for a settlement, the French Parliament in late 1953 endorsed resolutions calling upon Premier Joseph Laniel to pursue negotiations. Shortly afterward Laniel announced that "if an honorable end were in view . . . France, like the United States in Korea, would be happy to welcome a diplomatic solution of the conflict."[14] The DRV quickly responded, as Ho Chi Minh indicated his willingness to discuss a cease-fire. Major power initiatives added to the pressure for a negotiated settlement. Following the death of Stalin in March 1953, the new leadership of the Soviet Union called, in the name of "peaceful coexistence," for a reduction of cold war tensions and negotiation of outstanding issues. Negotiation of the Indochina situation gained the support of Britain, France, China, and, reluctantly, the United States. In early 1954 it was agreed that the Indochina issue would be included on the agenda of a conference to be held that spring at Geneva.

THE DIEN BIEN PHU CRISIS

In anticipation of a negotiated settlement, both sides in Vietnam sought to enhance their bargaining positions by military means. In the summer of 1953 the French had gained U.S. support for an ambitious military effort advanced by General Henri Navarre, who had recently been named commander of French forces in Indochina. The Navarre Plan called for sending another 10 French batallions to Indochina, a sizable increase in the native segment of their Indochina forces, and a major offensive to drive the Viet Minh from their stronghold in the Red River Delta. While American officials were skeptical that the Navarre Plan would achieve its objectives, they had little choice but to support it (in the amount of $400 million in additional assistance), for the French threatened to withdraw entirely, thus forcing the Americans to deal on their own with the intractable Indochina problem. By the end of 1953 the maintenance of the French presence was becoming more important to the United States than it was to France.

The initiatives of the Viet Minh, however, lured the French into operations not anticipated in the Navarre Plan. In the spring of 1953 General Vo Nguyen Giap had decided to send Viet Minh units into Laos, assuming that the French would be determined to protect that part of their Indochina colony; defense of that small landlocked country, however, would force France to stretch long supply lines across Viet Minh–dominated territory. The foray into Laos was launched from the remote village of Dien Bien Phu, located in mountainous northwestern Vietnam just a few miles from the Laotian border. Having demonstrated his army's capacity to invade Laos, Giap withdrew his forces; but the French expected that the Viet Minh would attack again in 1954.

Thus, to the French command, the taking of Dien Bien Phu became a critical objective in order to prevent another attack on Laos and to establish a "mooring point" from which an offensive could be launched to destroy a major part of the Viet Minh army. Accordingly, in the fall of 1953 General Navarre ordered the air force to drop paratroopers into the valley, about 11 miles long and 5 miles wide, in which Dien Bien Phu was located. Navarre was convinced that the Viet Minh could not match French strength, but Giap calculated that by controlling the mountains surrounding the valley, the Viet Minh would have a decisive advantage. Accordingly, the Viet Minh moved some 33 infantry battalions, 6 artillery regiments, and a regiment of engineers toward Dien Bien Phu. Many units traveled long distances, marching by night and

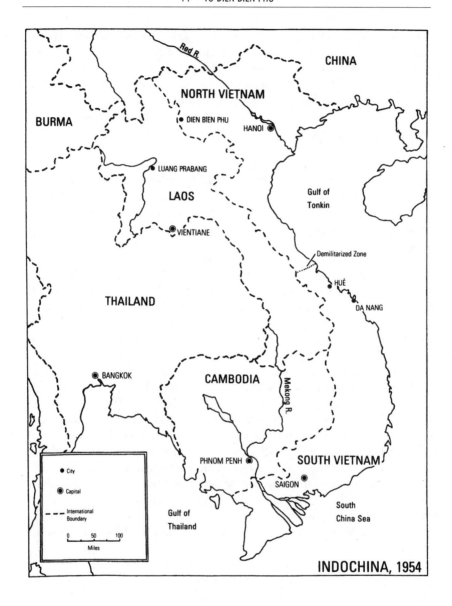

CHINA

NORTH VIETNAM

Red R

DIEN BIEN PHU

HANOI

BURMA

LUANG PRABANG

LAOS

Gulf of
Tonkin

VIENTIANE

Demilitarized Zone

HUÉ

THAILAND

DA NANG

BANGKOK

CAMBODIA

Mekong R.

PHNOM PENH

SOUTH VIETNAM

SAIGON

● City

◉ Capital

--- International
Boundary

0   50   100

Miles

Gulf of
Thailand

South
China Sea

INDOCHINA, 1954

sleeping by day in order to avoid French bombing and surveillance. The Viet Minh transported heavy equipment up mountainous paths. By early 1954 some 35,000 Viet Minh troops held the high ground around Dien Bien Phu.

The Viet Minh's capacity to move men and equipment to the hills surrounding the French position was but the first instance of Giap's confounding Navarre's calculations. "The French did not lose at Dien Bien Phu itself," the journalist Stanley Karnow has written, "but in General Navarre's airconditioned headquarters at Saigon, where he had woefully miscalculated Giap's intentions and capabilities even before the fighting started."[15] The French commander made other mistakes: he refused to consider that wellcamouflaged Viet Minh artillery would cut off flights into the valley; he assumed that the area would be suitable for armored vehicles, only to discover that tanks could not function in the thick bush and the soggy terrain. In his most serious error, Navarre calculated that the Viet Minh would launch a massive assault against the French garrison at the center of the valley; accordingly, Col. Christian de Castries, the French commander at Dien Bien Phu, built three outlying artillery bases named Gabrielle, Beatrice, and Isabelle (so named, according to legend, for de Castries' mistresses) to protect the center. But when the Viet Minh attacked on 13 March, they assaulted those three artillery bases. After overruning them in four days of intense fighting, the Viet Minh then laid siege to the garrison.

The Eisenhower administration now faced the prospects of a humiliating French defeat that might lead to their withdrawal from Indochina. When France appealed to the United States for support, specifically a large air strike against Viet Minh positions at Dien Bien Phu, the American dilemma quickly became clear: only U.S. intervention could avert such an outcome. Indochina's strategic importance remained a given; no one questioned that Communist domination of Vietnam would weaken noncommunist governments throughout Southeast Asia, with widespread ramifications. Because of the "interrelationship of the countries in the area," a National Security Council study in early 1954 observed, Communist ascendancy in any country would lead others to submit to or align themselves with the Sino-Soviet bloc; "Communist control of all of Southeast Asia . . . would seriously jeopardize fundamental U.S. security interests in the Far East."[16]

At a press conference on 5 April President Eisenhower gave public expression to such thinking in what was to become the most frequently cited justification for U.S. involvement in Vietnam over the next several years—the "domino theory." Answering a question about Indochina's importance at a press conference, the president, in a characteristically rambling statement, warned:

> Finally, you have broader considerations that might follow what you would
> call the "falling domino" principle. You have a row of dominoes set up, you
> knock over the first one, and what will happen to the last one is the cer-

tainty that it will go over very quickly. . . . But when we come to the possible sequence of events, the loss of Indochina, of Thailand, of the [Malay] Peninsula, and Indonesia following, now you begin to talk about areas that not only multiply the disadvantage that you would begin to suffer through loss of materials, sources of materials, but now you are talking really about millions and millions and millions of people. . . . Finally, the geographical position achieved thereby does many things. It turns the so-called island defensive chain of Japan, Formosa, of the Philippines, and to the southward, it moves in to threaten Australia and New Zealand. . . . So the possible consequences of the loss are just incalculable to the free world.[17]

Yet despite Indochina's strategic importance, the United States decided against intervention on behalf of the French. Careful consideration of the political-military situation led Eisenhower to conclude that the option of intervention lacked five essential ingredients.

1. *Lack of reasonable prospects for success*. U.S. military leaders questioned whether an air strike would be sufficient to hold Dien Bien Phu. If it were not, the United States might find itself drawn into sending ground troops—a process that once started would be difficult to limit. Like the French, the Americans would find themselves fighting in jungles against an elusive enemy.

2. *Lack of compatibility with overall strategic priorities*. The Eisenhower administration was committed to a containment strategy that emphasized nuclear deterrence and a reduction of conventional forces. The diversion of military power to Indochina risked undermining that global strategy and U.S. capacity to meet its obligations in Europe and elsewhere.

3. *Lack of congressional support*. Eisenhower was unwilling to commit U.S. military forces without the support of Congress. Accordingly, he instructed Secretary of State John Foster Dulles and Admiral Arthur Radford, chairman of the Joint Chiefs of Staff, to meet confidentially with congressional leaders on 3 April to determine whether they would give the president discretionary authority to intervene. The congressional leaders adamantly opposed unilateral and unconditional intervention; they warned that once committed more would be required and that the United States would appear to be supporting French colonialism. Recalling the Korean War, where the United States had provided virtually all of the support for what was presumably a United Nations effort, they insisted that any intervention be multilateral and include prior commitments from Allies, especially Great Britain. They also insisted that France be obliged to grant genuine independence as a condition of any intervention.

4. *Lack of international support*. The congressional position effectively left the decision for intervention in the hands of America's allies. The Eisenhower administration had assumed that intervention would need to be on a multilateral basis. Indeed, prior to the meeting with congressional leaders Secretary Dulles, in a speech on 29 March, addressed the necessity for "United Action" whereby the United States together with France, Britain, Australia, New Zealand, the

Philippines, and Thailand would guarantee the security of Southeast Asia. While "United Action" was vague, it was intended to warn the Soviet Union, China and the Viet Minh of the possibility of some form of multilateral action in Indochina. Any such initiative, however, depended principally upon the willingness of the British to participate, and their support was not forthcoming. Prime Minister Winston Churchill and Foreign Secretary Anthony Eden did not share the U.S. assumption that the loss of Indochina would have serious international ramifications and considered their interests in Malaya, where they were supporting anticommunist forces, to be an overriding priority. They were, in any event, opposed to sending British troops into what seemed to be a situation that was both hopeless (given the French weakness) and unpredictable (given the uncertainty of Chinese and Soviet reaction to Allied intervention). The British accordingly looked favorably upon the prospects for a negotiated settlement, and they refused to discuss any alliance for Southeast Asia until after the Geneva Conference participants had an opportunity to reach agreement.

5. *Lack of agreement with the French.* Discussions with the French on the terms of U.S. intervention underscored a continuance of fundamental differences between the two countries. The Americans insisted that direct military support should be accompanied by French commitments to accelerating the movement to independence of Vietnam and to giving the United States a prominent role in the training of native troops and in determining strategy. The French refused to make such concessions, since to do so would have undermined the very sovereignty that they had been fighting to preserve. Thus, to the end of the war, the French fought principally to hold an empire, while the Americans wanted them to liquidate that empire in order to build an anticommunist nationalist base.

THE GENEVA AGREEMENTS AND SEATO: THE U.S. "HOLDING ACTION"

Although these factors effectively precluded intervention, the United States used the threat of intervention as diplomatic leverage during the Geneva Conference. The United States approached that conference with great misgivings, for the Western allies were clearly bargaining from a position of weakness—a point made all the more dramatic by the fall of Dien Bien Phu on 7 May, the day before the conferees began discussion of the Indochina issues. The Viet Minh had achieved a major victory, making their victory appear inevitable if the war continued. With the disheartened French and the British both anxious to negotiate an end to the war, the Viet Minh seemed to be in a strong position to achieve their objective of national unification.

Yet after 10 weeks of negotiation, a settlement was reached at Geneva that gave the Viet Minh significantly less than it had seemingly earned on the battlefields. The DRV was forced to compromise, as the fate of Indochina was determined by the major powers and their interests. The United States played a shrewd diplomatic game. It engaged in what Dulles called "holding action" diplomacy intended to prevent a settlement that would turn Indochina over to the Viet Minh. Accordingly, the United States used its influence in ways calculated to keep the Communist powers uncertain about its plans. It assumed a limited role at the conference, more that of an observer than a participant. It continued to speak of the necessity for "United Action," thus retaining the option of intervention should it not be satisfied with the settlement. France sought to retain some influence in Indochina and used the issue of its participation in the European Defense Community for bargaining purposes. The Soviet Union, which was anxious to prevent the creation of EDC, accommodated some of France's interests in Indochina as a way of lessening France's commitment to the Western alliance. More generally, the new Soviet leadership was willing to compromise with the West on Indochina, which remained an area of marginal interest, to demonstrate its commitment to "peaceful coexistence." To China, of course, Southeast Asia was a major concern, but its overriding priority was keeping a U.S. military presence from its southern frontier. The Chinese sought a settlement that would be satisfactory to the United States, thus avoiding any reason for U.S. intervention. Moreover, the Chinese were desperate for a period of peace to facilitate their economic development; having been involved in civil and international wars almost constantly for two decades, China needed a respite and toward that end was prepared to force the DRV to compromise. In addition to the pressures from the major Communist powers, the DRV itself inclined to compromise; it too feared the possibility of U.S. intervention and believed that so long as provisions were made for eventual unification, the objectives of the August Revolution would be achieved. (The State of Vietnam, Laos, and Cambodia were also represented at Geneva.)

After 10 weeks of negotiation, the settlement reached at Geneva was, in the words of one U.S. official, "the best that could be expected in the circumstances. Diplomacy is rarely able to gain at the conference table that which cannot be gained or held on the battlefield."[18] Two interrelated agreements ended the French–Viet Minh conflict. A bilateral armistice signed between the French and the DRV was supplemented by a multinational 13-point Final Declaration; together, they provided for (1) the temporary partitioning of Vietnam at about the 17th parallel to permit regrouping of French and Viet Minh forces to the south and north, respectively; (2) reunification elections to be conducted in 1956 under the supervision of an international commission composed of India, Poland, and Canada; (3) a prohibition on the introduction of new forces or equipment, the establishment of foreign military bases, and membership of either part of Vietnam in any military alliances. Participants were asked to give their "oral assent" to the Final Declaration; Britain, France, the Soviet Union, China, and the DRV did so, but the State of Vietnam and the United States refused. The U.S. declaration was a "calculated ambiguity," giving conditional assent while maintaining freedom of action. After promising to "refrain from the threat of the use of force to disturb" the agreement, the United States affirmed a commitment to supporting unification of countries "divided against their will" through "free elections, supervised by the United Nations to ensure they are conducted fairly." Referring to the State of Vietnam, the U.S. declaration added "that peoples are entitled to determine their own future and . . . [the U.S.] will not join in an arrangement which would hinder this."[19] Immediately American officials disassociated the United States from the settlement; Eisenhower stated that the nation "had not itself been party to or bound by the decisions taken by the conference."[20]

If the Geneva Agreements had fallen significantly short of the DRV's expectations, why were they unacceptable to the United States? American officials realized that the agreements, if fulfilled, worked to the advantage of the Viet Minh. True, the Viet Minh had been obliged to accept not only the division of Vietnam but also a demarcation line far to the north of its original demands. True, the Viet Minh had been obliged to withdraw its troops from southern Vietnam, Laos, and Cambodia. True, the Viet Minh had been obliged to allow others to determine the political future of Laos and Cambodia. Yet on balance the DRV gained more than it lost. Its legitimacy in northern Vietnam now had international sanction. Assuming that the provisions for French withdrawal and nonintroduction of other outside military forces were fulfilled, the Viet Minh would be in a position to achieve its objectives through the political process established in the agreements. Its only rival was the weak State of Vietnam, which had administrative responsibilities in the South; but the lack of popular support for the Bao Dai government virtually assured Viet Minh success in the unification elections.

To prevent that eventuality, the United States moved quickly after the Geneva Conference to implement a regional multilateral defense system. "The important thing," Dulles publicly asserted on 23 July, "was not to mourn the past but to seize the future opportunity to prevent the loss in northern Vietnam from leading to the extension of Communism throughout Southeast Asia and the Southwest Pacific." It was vital "to bring about the collective arrangements to promote the security of the free peoples of Southeast Asia."[21] Accordingly, the United States provided the leadership in the establishment of the Southeast Asia Treaty Organization (SEATO). At a conference held in Manila in early September, three Asian countries—Thailand, the Philippines, and Pakistan—joined with the United States, Britain, France, Australia, and New Zealand in organizing a mutual defense system that was intended to deter aggression in the region. The SEATO treaty circumvented the provisions in the Geneva Agreements that prohibited the Indochina governments from being part of a military alliance. SEATO's "protective area" was simply extended to include the "free territory of Vietnam under the jurisdiction of the State of Vietnam" as well as Laos and Cambodia.[22] While SEATO had serious limitations, including the lack of substantial Asian membership and its incapacity to deal with Communist subversion, it clearly signaled the U.S. intention to hold the line against the further extension of Communist influence in the region. That line was now at the 17th parallel in Vietnam.

Notes

1.   Ellen Hammer, *The Struggle for Indochina, 1940–1955* (Stanford, Calif.: Stanford University Press, 1966), 159.

2.   Jean Sainteny, *Histoire d'une Paix Manguée: Indochina, 1945–1947* (Paris: Amoit, Dumont, 1953), 167.

3.   Moffat to Vincent, 6 August 1946, in *Foreign Relations of the United States 1946*, vol. 8, *The Far East* (Washington, D.C.: U.S. Government Printing Office, 1971), 52–54.

4.   Acheson to Reed, 5 December 1946, in ibid., 67–69.

5.   Paul Coste-Floret cited in Hammer, *Struggle for Indochina*, 207.

6.   Leclerc Report cited in George McT. Kahin, *Intervention: How America Became Involved in Vietnam* (New York: Knopf, 1986), 24.

7.   Reed to Marshall, 14 June 1947, in *Foreign Relations of the United States 1947*, vol. 6, *The Far East* (Washington, D.C.: U.S. Government Printing Office, 1972), 103–5.

8.   Reed to Butterworth, 14 April 1949, Department of State files, 851 G.00/4-1449.

9.   Policy Statement on Indochina, 27 September 1948, in *Foreign Relations of the United States, 1948*, vol. 6, *The Far East and Australia* (Washington, D.C.: U.S. Government Printing Office, 1974), 43–49.

10.   NSC 48-1, 23 December 1949, in U.S. House Armed Services Committee, *United States–Vietnam Relations 1945–1967*, book 1, 2:A–45.

11.   Jacques Soustelle, "Indo-China and Korea: One Front," *Foreign Affairs* 29 (October 1950): 56–66.

12.   Mendes-France cited in Stanley Karnow, *Vietnam: A History* (New York: Viking, 1983), 188.

13.   Georges Bidault cited in ibid., 191.

14.   Laniel cited in ibid.

15.   Ibid., 194.

16.   Report to NSC (NSC 5405), 16 January 1954, in *Foreign Relations of the United States, 1952–54*, vol. 12, *East Asia and the Pacific* (Washington, D.C.: U.S. Government Printing Office, 1984), 366–81.

17.   Eisenhower press conference, 7 April 1954, in *Foreign Relations of the United States, 1952–54*, vol. 13, *Indochina* (Washington, D.C.: U.S. Government Printing Office, 1982), 1280–81.

18.   *New York Times*, 24 July 1954.

19.   Declaration by Smith, 21 July 1954, in Porter and Emerson, eds., *Vietnam*, 161–62.

20.   *New York Times*, 22 July 1954.

21.   *Department of State Bulletin*, 51, 2 August 1954, 163–64.

22.   *Southeast Asia Treaty Organization*, Department of State Publication 6305 (Washington, D.C.: U.S. Government Printing Office, 1956).

chapter 4

TO THE GULF OF TONKIN: THE UNITED STATES AND THE TWO VIETNAMS, 1954–1964

Having seen the "loss" of the northern half of Vietnam, the United States was determined to limit further Communist expansion. As the Geneva Conference ended, Secretary of State John Foster Dulles told a congressional committee, "Whether [communism] can be stopped at this point, and whether Laos and Cambodia and the southern part of Vietnam, Thailand, Malaya, and Indonesia can be kept out of Communist control depends very much on whether we can build a dike around this present loss. The only thing we have to build that dike is this [economic assistance] money.... There are some good people there who are well disposed, but they are weak and they are feeble, and they cannot stand alone.... It will be a domino business, unless we can bolster this thing alone."[1]

Over the next decade the central objective of American policy in Southeast Asia was to "build that dike" through extensive assistance to the "well disposed but . . . weak and . . . feeble." Bolstering the "dominoes" would prove to necessitate considerably greater levels of involvement than anticipated in 1954, but U.S. leaders, driven by the unquestioned assumption of the region's overriding importance to American security, nevertheless committed national resources and prestige to Indochina.

INDOCHINA, 1954

The end of nearly eight years of warfare brought independence to the peoples of Indochina but under foreboding conditions. In Vietnam, French and Viet Minh troops regrouped, as dictated by the Geneva Agreements. Over 130,000 French Union forces moved from the North to the South, while nearly 150,000 Viet Minh left the South and headed north. Two governments functioned but in significantly different ways. The Democratic Republic of Vietnam emerged from the jungles to reestablish its capital at Hanoi, from which Ho Chi Minh and other leaders had been forced to flee seven years earlier. Having controlled much of the countryside during the struggle against the French, the DRV quickly moved from that base to control the region north of the 17th parallel. Having led the fight against the French and having been a principal participant in the Geneva negotiations, the DRV had earned a national following and international status. On the other side, the State of Vietnam, still headed by Bao Dai, had limited influence in the area south of the 17th parallel; even in Saigon it faced strong opposition. If reunification elections were held, as scheduled by the Geneva Agreements, no one questioned that the Vietnamese people would choose Ho Chi Minh as their leader. (Since the Democratic Republic of Vietnam and the State of Vietnam [renamed the Republic of Vietnam in 1955] were typically called North Vietnam and South Vietnam respectively and not by their formal titles, they will be referred to as North Vietnam and South Vietnam in discussing the period from 1954 to 1975, when the country was reunified.)

The United States assumed a dominant role in Vietnam. Determined to prevent unification under Communist leadership, the American objective was to perpetuate the division of the country. Balancing the Communist North with a noncommunist South was considered essential to preventing the advance of communism throughout the region.

If Vietnamese nationhood was undermined by the division of the country, in Laos it was limited by even more fundamental factors. Laos lacked the essential characteristics of a nation; a leading scholar wrote that "Laos is neither a geographical, nor an ethnic, nor social entity, but merely a political convenience."[2] Laos comprised four major ethnic groups and numerous tribes representing various languages and cultures. Living in a mountainous, landlocked country with a poor system of roads and communications, these remote peoples had little sense of nationhood. The Royal Laotian Government had few direct links to the people outside the few cities. The isolation of the peoples of Laos was underscored in a 1956 opinion survey in which fewer than half the people knew the name of their own country. Only 10 percent knew the name of the prime minister or where the king lived. Indeed, the name of the king, who had been on the throne for 50 years, was known to barely one-fourth of the people.

The struggle for political power generally followed ethnic and ideological lines. Conservative leaders, who had been closely identified with the French administration, represented the Lao, the largest ethnic group, and dominated the newly independent Royal Laotian Government. The Viet Minh had controlled much of Laos during the French–Viet Minh War and had fostered the establishment of the Pathet Lao. After the withdrawal of the Viet Minh as provided in the Geneva Agreements, the Pathet Lao, drawing its support from various smaller ethnic groups, stood as the principal leftist challenge to the right. In the political center was a neutral faction, headed by Prince Souvanna Phuoma, which sought a coalition government that would include conservatives and the Pathet Lao.

The overriding objective of the United States was to buttress the conservative control of the government. This led to military assistance, including the dispatch of an advisory group, to the Royal Laotian Army. Within a few years the American effort to uphold the rightist leadership would lead to substantially greater involvement in Laos.

In contrast with Vietnam and Laos, the political situation in Cambodia appeared relatively stable. Unlike Laos, a clear sense of nationhood developed from a strong cultural tradition, which grew out of the ancient glory of the Khmers and their struggle for national identity against the Thais and Vietnamese. Norodom Sihanouk, who had become king in 1941 at the age of 19 and had pressured the French to grant independence, was firmly in control of the Cambodian government as the French withdrew. A constitutional monarchy was established. Sihanouk abdicated the throne (retaining the title "prince") and became prime minister after his party (the Socialist People's Community party) won all the seats in the legislature.

Sihanouk's foreign policy was cleverly contradictory. To avoid antagonizing any of the major powers, he proclaimed Cambodia's neutrality in the cold war. He thus disavowed the protection afforded Cambodia under the SEATO Treaty. Yet at the same time, Sihanouk, recognizing his country's vulnerable position between its historic enemies Thailand and Vietnam, believed that foreign military assistance was essential to security. Hence he entered into a military aid agreement with the United States; under this program the Americans funded, equipped, and, through an advisory group, trained the Cambodian army. Sihanouk's prestige enabled him to ignore his critics who argued, quite reasonably, that assistance from the United States was inconsistent with the principles of nonalignment.

Thus, throughout the former French colony the United States quickly became the dominant external power. U.S. influence, principally reflected in economic and military assistance programs as well as various covert operations, essentially sought to underwrite governments that had been closely identified with French rule: the royal governments of Laos and Cambodia, through which the French had indirectly ruled those countries, and the South Vietnamese government, which was the remnant of the political structure through which the French had controlled the southern parts of that country.

SOUTH VIETNAM: ILLUSION AND REALITY, 1954–1960

One could scarcely imagine a more difficult assignment than that undertaken by the United States to build a strong anticommunist nation in the southern half of Vietnam. The fundamental problem was a lack of national identity of the peoples in the South with the government in Saigon.

American hopes centered on the ability of Ngo Dinh Diem to build a strong South Vietnamese government. From the American perspective, the greatest strengths of Diem, whom Bao Dai appointed premier in June 1954, came from what he stood against: he was anti-French and anticommunist. Diem was unquestionably a Vietnamese nationalist, but his patriotic credentials had been undermined by lack of participation in the struggle against the French. His capacity to lead the disparate peoples of the South was further weakened by his dominant personality traits: an inability to compromise, an unshakable family loyalty, and a paternalistic approach to leadership, reflected in his frequent statement "I know what is best for my country."

Diem's emergence as premier in 1954 has sometimes been seen as American manipulation of an obscure, apolitical, austere recluse to serve the U.S. interest in fostering an anticommunist government. The story, however, is a good deal more complex, for Diem's career before 1954 suggests a persistent pursuit of political power, provided it was granted on his terms. Diem was born in 1901 in a province that in 1954 became part of North Vietnam but spent most of his childhood and youth in the imperial capital of Hué. His family had long before converted to Catholicism, and his father worked for the imperial government only to be dismissed for anti-French sympathies. From his father Diem thus acquired an abiding antagonism toward the French. As a youth, he became immersed in both Catholic and Confucian traditions; at age 15, he spent several months in a monastery to prepare for the Catholic priesthood but abandoned that objective. Instead, Diem pursued a career in government service, which, he believed, would provide valuable experience even though it meant working with the hated French. Accordingly, he studied at the French-run School for Law and Administration at Hanoi, graduating first in his class in 1921. Diem entered government service and at the age of 28 became governor of a small province to the northwest of Saigon. Known for his integrity and fairness, Diem was recruited to the imperial court by the young emperor Bao Dai, who was determined to reform his government. Bao Dai appointed him minister of the interior in 1933, but Diem served only a few months, resigning in indignation over the failure of the French to grant any real power to the imperial government and accusing Bao Dai of being nothing but an instrument of French authorities. Diem's assessment may have been basically correct; the incident, though, underscored both his aversion to French colonialism and his uncompromising self-righteousness.

For the next 20 years Diem retreated from public life but did not put aside political ambitions. Living in Hué from 1933 to 1945, he corresponded with Vietnamese nationalists as well as with nationalists in other Asian countries. When the Japanese occupied Indochina during World War II, he correctly distrusted their promises to grant independence and turned down an offer to participate in their puppet government. As the war ended and Ho Chi Minh's movement swept to political power in the August Revolution, the Viet Minh arrested Diem. Although various political groups and leaders supported the nationalist revolution, Diem demurred. In a gesture that may have reflected respect for Diem as well as an interest in assuring a wide range of political support for the revolution, Ho allegedly offered him a position in his government, but Diem rejected it.

During the French–Viet Minh War, Diem was among the small group of Vietnamese nationalists who refused to support the Viet Minh and hoped for a liberal French colonial policy as the means to his country's independence. Diem supported the Bao Dai solution, but when the emperor invited him to become his premier in 1949, he refused on the grounds that the French had made no real concessions to Vietnamese nationalism. Shortly afterward Diem left Vietnam for the first time, spending nearly three years in the United States. He lived at Maryknoll seminaries, but his American mission was as much political as it was spiritual. He established contacts with Catholic leaders and several prominent politicians, and he spoke at universities and elsewhere about the problems facing his country. His message was simple: to prevent Communist control of Vietnam, it was necessary to foster the establishment of an anticommunist nationalism, but the French refusal to make concessions undermined the opponents of Ho Chi Minh. Diem's position thus approximated the official American view of the Vietnam situation. In 1953 Diem left the United States for Belgium, where he took up residence at another monastery. It was while Diem was in Europe that Bao Dai again offered him the position of premier, but characteristically Diem refused until he could define the terms of the appointment. Only when Bao Dai granted him virtual dictatorial powers did Diem accept. On 26 June 1954 Diem returned to Saigon as premier.

American officials were not enthusiastic about Diem's emergence, for they were aware of his arrogance and lack of popular support. "Diem is a messiah without a message," the U.S. chargé d'affaires in Saigon wrote. "His only formulated policy is to ask for American assistance in every form . . . [and] his only present emotion, other than a lively appreciation for himself, is a blind hatred for the French."[3] Yet the American interest in building an anticommunist bastion in South Vietnam necessitated finding an alternative to Ho Chi Minh, and Diem, for all his weaknesses, appeared to be the best of a bad lot of potential leaders. One official summarized the American dilemma: "We are prepared to accept the seemingly ridiculous prospect that this yogi-like mystic could assume the charge he is apparently about to undertake only because the standard set by his predecessors is so low."[4]

Diem faced enormous problems. As the new premier of a government that was associated with the lost French cause, he had a narrow base of support. Bao Dai's government had never been able to control the countryside, but in addition to the legacy of the alienated peasantry, Diem faced opposition from within his own government, especially the army, as well as from two prominent religious sects and the Saigon underworld. The army opposition centered in the political ambitions of its commander in chief, General Nyugen Van Hinh. Hinh's intrigues against Diem were encouraged by the French, who, although preparing to leave Vietnam, wanted to preserve their influence. France preferred to see South Vietnam under the leadership of Hinh, who was a French citizen with a French wife, rather than the virulently anti-French Diem. Unable to count on the loyalty of his government's army, Diem also confronted the opposition of the religious sects—the Hoa Hao and Cao Dai— and the Binh Xuyen, the Vietnamese equivalent of the Mafia. All three of these groups, which shared an aversion to communism, had enjoyed a symbiotic relationship with the French, having been supported by the French in return for their cooperation in the struggle against the Viet Minh.

These were powerful groups that enjoyed considerable popular support and had their own military forces. The Cao Dai, which had been established in the 1920s, was a mystical religious movement that synthesized the major world religions. With perhaps as many as 2,000,000 adherents concentrated to the northwest of Saigon along the Cambodian border, the Cao Dai's strength in the region was enforced by its own army, which numbered some 30,000 troops. The Hoa Hao sect, which emerged in 1939, claimed to have 1,500,000 adherents; it too was a mystical blend of religious thought, described as "Buddhist Protestantism." Centered in the rich farm areas of the Mekong Delta, the Hoa Hao had an army of 9,000 soldiers. As the French–Viet Minh War ended, both the Cao Dai and Hoa Hao sought to extend their political power beyond their areas of traditional strength; their leaders functioned very much as independent warlords, who had no loyalty to the new premier in Saigon. The final group to challenge Diem was in no sense religious: the Binh Xuyen constituted the underworld of gangsters who ran the Saigon opium trade, the gambling casino known as Le Grand Monde, and an enormous brothel, the Hall of Mirrors, which employed some 1,200 prostitutes. The Binh Xuyen also controlled the Saigon police force, having allegedly purchased it from Bao Dai for $1 million so that the emperor could pay his gambling debts.

To the astonishment of many Vietnamese and Americans, Ngo Dinh Diem appeared to overcome these obstacles. His success resulted from a combination of good fortune, a capacity to play off one group of opponents against others, and, above all, the support of the United States. Between 1954 and 1957 Diem's position was strengthened as a result of several initiatives and circumstances that created the impression of a "miracle" occurring in South Vietnam.

First, in the fall of 1954 Diem forestalled a coup plot led by General Hinh. With the support of the army and the religious sect leaders, Hinh was in an excellent position to overthrow Diem. The United States played a critical role in Diem's survival. Although many American policymakers doubted Diem's capacity to lead, they regarded him as preferable to Hinh, whose nationalist stature was tarnished by his association with the French. The leading U.S.

officials in Saigon—Ambassador Donald R. Heath and Lt. Gen. John W. O'Daniel, the head of the American military mission—warned Hinh and his co-conspirators that the United States would not continue its support of South Vietnam if Diem were overthrown. Hinh later recalled, "The Americans let me know if [the coup] happened, dollar help would be cut off . . . but the country could not survive without American help."[5] In the midst of the political tensions in Saigon, the United States affirmed its support of Diem. On 25 October it made public a letter from Eisenhower to Diem in which the American president offered an "intelligent program of aid . . . to assist Viet Nam in its present hour of trial."[6] The Hinh plot finally collapsed when, under pressure from the United States, he reluctantly left Vietnam and, shortly thereafter, was dismissed as chief of staff.

Second, having eliminated Hinh, Diem decided to assert control over the sects. In January 1955 he announced his intention to break the power of the Binh Xuyen. Although U.S. officials could only applaud this campaign against the Saigon underworld, they also feared that it would induce the Cao Dai and Hoa Hao to join the Binh Xuyen in a common front against Diem. To prevent that eventuality, the United States, through the Central Intelligence Agency, bribed the leadership of the religious sects. The leaders were not easily bought off; it cost the CIA about $12 million to win their support. The Americans thus took over the function of subsidizing the sects just as the French had done earlier. As a result, the majority of the sects' troops were integrated into the South Vietnamese army. At the same time, Diem guaranteed the support of the army by promoting several important officers. Diem then forced the showdown with the Binh Xuyen; in late April and early May 1955 the South Vietnamese army, in pitched battle on the streets of Saigon, defeated the Binh Xuyen troops and their police allies. Thus, in less than a year after his return to Saigon, Diem had gained a great deal of power. In the American press and the thinking of officials in Washington and Saigon, doubts about Diem's capacity to lead South Vietnam gave way to cautious optimism.

Third, the migration of hundreds of thousands of people from the North increased the Diem government's base of support and enhanced its stature in the United States. As the French relinquished power in the North to the Viet Minh, 900,000 persons, about two-thirds of whom were Catholics, moved to the South. These migrants included well-to-do landowners who had been associated with the French, many civil servants who had worked with the French governments, and the families of Vietnamese soldiers in the French army who had regrouped in the South. (In comparison, about 120,000 civilians migrated from South to North.)

The migration from the North was seized upon by the American government as proof that vast numbers of Vietnamese were fleeing from Communist dictatorship. The U.S. navy assisted in the movement, providing transportation for over 300,000 persons. Unquestionably, many migrants were strongly anticommunist and feared for their well-being under DRV control. Yet the migration was more complex than an instinctive anticommunism. The Catholic church organized a major campaign to encourage its followers to move south. Diem himself paid a brief visit to Hanoi (before the French relinquished control to the DRV) in June 1954 to encourage his fellow Catholics to take refuge in the South. Accompanying the departure of most of the clergy to the South were blunt propaganda slogans: "Christ has gone south" and "the Virgin Mary has left the North."

The idea that a "flight to freedom" had taken place in Vietnam quickly became engrained in the American popular consciousness. In a best-selling book, *Deliver Us from Evil*, Lt. Tom Dooley, a navy doctor who participated in the transportation of refugees, graphically described peoples fleeing from the "Goodless cruelties of Communism." No one reading Dooley's book or seeing the movie based on it could ignore his emotional appeal for U.S. support of South Vietnam: "We had come late to Vietnam, but we had come. And we brought not bombs and guns, but help and love."[7]

Fourth, having eliminated the principal challenges to his power and having an enlarged Catholic population as his most reliable base of support, Diem further consolidated his position by removing Emperor Bao Dai as chief of state. Bao Dai posed no threat, but Diem resented Bao Dai's monarchial pretensions and his flamboyant lifestyle. Taking advantage of Bao Dai's absence from Vietnam for his annual extended vacation on the French Riviera, the Diem government in 1955 launched a propaganda campaign against him and announced that the public would choose, in a national referendum, between Diem and Bao Dai. Rarely has an election been more cleverly rigged. The ballot gave the South Vietnamese electorate two choices: "I support the deposition of Bao Dai and recognize Ngo Dinh Diem as chief of state with the mission of installing a democratic regime" or "I do not support the deposition of Bao Dai and the recognition of Ngo Dinh Diem as chief of state with the mission of installing a democratic regime." To leave no doubt which candidate represented democracy, the first option was accompanied by a drawing of Diem among a group of smiling young people, while beside the second option was a portrait of Bao Dai in his imperial robes. In an election marked by extensive fraud (although Saigon had 450,000 registered voters, over 600,000 votes were cast there), Diem won 98.2 percent of the vote and proclaimed the establishment of the Republic of Vietnam with himself as president. The "democratic regime" for which the electorate voted in October 1955 took shape in 1956 with the election of a National Assembly, but it was both powerless and controlled by Diem.

Fifth, Diem subverted the national unification elections that had been scheduled for 1956. He contended that since his government had not signed the Geneva Agreements, it was not obliged to participate in elections. Moreover, Diem maintained that North Vietnam could not be trusted to conduct free elections. While such arguments provided a questionable rationale, Diem successfully undermined the Geneva Agreements' provisions for national unification in large part because the major powers supported, openly or tacitly, the division of Vietnam. The United States, of course, backed Diem. Neither the Soviet Union, to whom Vietnam remained a minor consideration, nor China, which was preoccupied with internal problems and was never anxious to see a strong Vietnam on its southern frontiers, considered it in their national interest to back North Vietnam's repeated efforts to assure fulfillment of the Geneva Agreements.

Above all, Diem's success depended upon the United States. It was American plotting, advice, and dollars that helped Diem overcome the various challenges to his position. It was with American personnel and dollars that the South Vietnamese government was built. Between 1954 and 1959, $1.2 billion in American assistance went to South Vietnam. About 80 percent of that government's military expenditures and nearly 50 percent of its nonmilitary expenditures were being paid in some way by the United States. The overriding priority was the security of South Vietnam, and about three-fourths of all American assistance was directed toward military objectives. The Army of the Republic of Vietnam (ARVN) was equipped through American assistance and trained by a U.S. military advisory program.

At the center of this large-scale assistance effort was the "commodity import program" through which the United States purchased with dollars various commodities for South Vietnamese importers, who paid for them in piasters. Those piasters, which were owned by the United States but remained in South Vietnam in so-called counterpart funds, underwrote the various American assistance programs in the country. The "commodity import program" served two distinctive functions: it prevented an inflationary cycle in South Vietnam, which would have resulted from the infusion of dollars, and it provided the United States with a large pool of piasters to support the South Vietnamese government.

Perhaps the high point of Diem's leadership was his invitation to visit the United States in 1957. By that time he was being extravagantly praised by American political leaders and in the press for having achieved the "miracle" of South Vietnam's survival and growth. Diem was accorded the honor of addressing Congress. It was fitting that Diem's presidency would reach a high point among his benefactors in the United States, where he enjoyed greater popularity than in his home country.

By the time of Diem's American visit, the underside of the "miracle" was eroding the South Vietnamese government. At the heart of Diem's problems was his very limited concept of political leadership. Diem lacked the capacity to compromise. The hard-line approach may have been essential in establishing the credibility of his government against the Binh Xuyen, but it could not be used against all opponents. Many anticommunists in the South, including much of the middle class and the intellectual community, distrusted Diem because of his Catholic background and his absence from Vietnam during the struggle against the French. Diem's major challenge came from the Communist strength in the countryside; it was estimated that during the French–Viet Minh War, the Viet Minh controlled most of the villages of what became South Vietnam. While the position of the Communists lessened as Viet Minh units regrouped to the North in 1954, they still enjoyed considerable strength and widespread sympathy among the peasantry in many areas. Rather than undertaking democratic and social reforms that might have rallied these disparate groups to support his government, Diem built a dictatorial state.

South Vietnam became a one-party country with an elaborate propaganda apparatus, concentration camps, secret police, rigged elections, and restricted liberties. Diem manipulated democratic processes to enhance his power. The tawdry election of 1955 that eliminated Bao Dai and made Diem president showed his contempt for democracy. That was further underscored in the elections in 1956 for a constituent assembly that was to draft a constitution; Diem controlled the election and the writing of the constitution. Presented as a victory for representative government, that document actually gave no real authority to the legislature and granted dictatorial powers to the president. The president could suspend legislation and civil rights and could rule by decree.

Diem used the Communist challenge as a rationale for widespread suppression. In 1955 his government began an anticommunist denunciation campaign in which villagers were forced to attend mass meetings for the purpose of identifying Viet Minh members and their sympathizers. In 1956 Diem promulgated an ordinance under which his government assumed unlimited powers in dealing with political opponents; anyone considered a threat "to the defense of the state and public order" could be imprisoned. Although this measure was justified as necessary to limit Communist activity, it was in fact used against all political opponents. Tens of thousands of opponents—Communist as well as noncommunist—were arrested and sent to concentration camps. Later, in 1959, the suppression went further, as another law gave military courts the power to sentence to death anyone who committed crimes infringing on the security of the state or who belonged to an organization that did so.

Diem's power depended upon the loyalty of the army and the government bureaucracy, both of which became notorious for widespread corruption. In essence, Diem, who was personally honest, tolerated dishonesty among the 138,000 government employees as the price for assuring his survival. To the people of South Vietnam, contacts with government typically entailed demands for bribes in return for services. Extortion, secret accounts, and bribery were part of the daily routine of South Vietnamese officials. "Careers in the civil service," an American journalist noted at the time, "too often are merely platforms for a lifetime of corruption."[8] He continued that of the thousands of South Vietnamese officials he had known, all more or less held the people in contempt. "The typical local political leader," another American observer has written, "was at best paternalistic and at worst a corrupt bully. But whichever he was, he considered himself vastly superior to the rest of the people."[9]

Power became concentrated in Diem and his family. Diem's innate distrust of others and sense of imperial authority led him to rely upon his brothers for advice and as the only trusted agents of political authority. The close tie between his government and the Catholic Church was symbolized by the fact that one of Diem's brothers, Thuc, was the archbishop of South Vietnam. Another brother, Can, enjoyed virtually dictatorial powers over several provinces in the central highlands. Other members of the family also held important positions. Perhaps the most powerful figure in the country was still another brother, Ngo Dinh Nhu, who under the title of "adviser" to Diem built the extensive political-military apparatus of the dictatorial regime. He controlled the Personalist Labor party, which embraced a vague ideology that blended a wide range of political and religious concepts with the objective of harmonizing material and spiritual needs of the individual and providing a middle path between capitalist individualism and Communist collectivism. Composed of trusted government officials who sought membership since it assured access to Nhu and to the regime's graft, the Personalist party's principal function was to provide Nhu with information about members of the government, army officials, and ordinary citizens. Nhu further controlled the government's notorious secret police as well as other organizations that were intended to assure loyalty of the bureaucracy and to eliminate critics of the government.

Nhu's wife, Tran Le Xuan ("Beautiful Spring"), exerted considerable influence as the official hostess for her bachelor brother-in-law. An energetic, determined, and outspoken woman, Madame Nhu engaged in various enterprises, including organizing her own feminist political party and a paramilitary women's corps. She prevailed upon the legislature to pass such measures as the "Law for the Protection of Morality," which declared illegal such activities as dancing, beauty contests, gambling, fortune-telling, cockfighting, prostitution, "and a hundred other things dear to hearts of Vietnamese men."[10] Along with her husband, the calculating and determined Madame Nhu reinforced Diem's authoritarian instincts.

The fundamental weaknesses of Diem's leadership were reflected above all in his government's approach to its most formidable task: building support in the countryside. Eighty-five percent of the population lived in villages. Every important action of the Diem government, however, alienated the peasantry. That process began with Diem's support of large landowners' claims to repossess land that they had lost during the French–Viet Minh War. While the Viet Minh had controlled much of the countryside during the war, most large landholders lived in the relative safety of the cities. The Viet Minh seized their estates and distributed the land to the peasantry, but when the war ended and much of the Viet Minh regrouped to the North, the landowners—with the backing of the South Vietnamese government—repossessed their lands. Under pressure from the United States, Diem finally undertook a program of land reform. This was desperately needed in a country where inequitable distribution of land forced millions of peasants to live in perpetual poverty. One-fourth of 1 percent of the rural population owned 40 percent of the rice land; 80 percent of the peasantry rented land for which they paid exorbitant rents, typically at least 50 percent of their crops.

The Diem government, which depended upon the support of the large landholders, undertook a limited program of reform. Some lands were confiscated for redistribution, but landlords were permitted to hold up to 284 acres; given the richness of the land, that was a substantial holding from which enormous profits could be made. Further, landlords had to be compensated in full for any lands that were lost as a result of redistribution; only a minority of the tenants could afford to pay the compensation or to repay government loans for land purchases. Much of the land went to government officials or to other large landowners. As a result, only about 10 percent of the more than one million tenant farmers actually obtained land. The economic status of the remainder did not improve. The Diem government established a rent limit of 25 percent of the crop, but that was not effectively enforced. Thus most peasants continued to pay exorbitant rents. The overall effect of land reform was simple: relatively little land went to peasants. The political implications were also simple: peasants found themselves losing land that the Viet Minh had given them, and when given the opportunity to regain that land as part of the Diem government's reform, they had to pay for it.

Besides the limited effectiveness of its land reform, the Diem government further alienated the peasantry through its assault on the traditional autonomy of the villages. Fearing Communist strength in the countryside, Diem ended the powers of the village councils and sent his own officials into the countryside to administer the villages. These officials owed their loyalty to Diem, not to the villagers, who resented their presence and power. The men sent by Diem indeed were "strangers" to the peasants, for many were Catholics of urban background who had migrated from the North. They lacked experience in dealing with rural problems, and many were corrupt and oppressive. In the countryside these officials thus stood as distinctly unpopular representatives of the Diem government.

NORTH VIETNAM: THE INCOMPLETE REVOLUTION

As the Communist leadership established a one-party government in North Vietnam, it faced serious problems. The completion of the revolution through national reunification remained an overriding objective, but circumstances forced Ho Chi Minh and his colleagues to acknowledge that national reunification would not be achieved as early as had been anticipated at the Geneva Conference. Not only could Hanoi not force reunification elections given Saigon's recalcitrance and lack of international support but also it had to give priority to meeting the North's economic crisis.

A food shortage and destruction from the war, which had been fought mostly in the North, necessitated outside support. Historically, the northern half of the country depended on the South for much of its food; about 60 per-cent of the country's rice was produced in the South. The Saigon government, however, ignored Hanoi's requests for discussion of economic integration. This hastened the North Vietnamese move toward the Soviet Union and China for assistance, including food, technicians, and equipment.

External aid was critical not only to meet immediate needs but also to the long-term objective of building a self-sufficient socialist state. The Commu-nist leadership moved gradually in modifying the economic system by devel-oping a mixed economy. The state took over utilities, banks, and some large businesses, but it permitted trade and manufacturing to remain in private hands. While the private sector was thus assured of the opportunity to earn profits, it was far from enjoying entrepreneurial freedom, for prices and wages were subject to government regulation. The key to economic development, however, depended upon a more efficient agricultural system. Per-capita rice production in North Vietnam was among the lowest in Asia, the result of a preponderance of small, inefficient landholdings and the related lack of mech-anization. The long-term Communist solution to agricultural reform was col-lectivization modeled on that of the Soviet Union and China. Recognizing that collectivization was not attractive to land-hungry peasants, the North Vietnamese government embarked on an intermediary measure of land reform. By taking land away from the wealthy owners and distributing it to the poor, the government's position would be enhanced, for not only would the peasantry come to support its policies but also the power of the conservative large landholders in the villages would be eliminated.

The ambitious program of land reform, carried out by cadres sent by the North Vietnamese government into the villages, produced substantial results. Some two million acres were distributed, and about two million families—about one-half of all of North Vietnam's families—received some land. The power of the traditional landed gentry was broken. Rice production increased significantly, from 2.6 million tons in 1954 to 4.21 million tons in 1956. Food supplies were adequate, albeit barely, for the North's needs.

Yet the land reform effort also threatened to undermine the very integrity of the government. Indeed, in 1956 Ho Chi Minh publicly acknowledged that errors had marred the program and ordered corrective measures. A fundamen-tal problem was the government's inability to control the cadres. The Hanoi leadership wanted to channel peasant resentment against the rich landlords—"local despots"—who did no work themselves and lived off the labor of others, but it wanted to avoid antagonizing other more or less well-to-do groups, those whom the government labeled as "middle peasants" and "rich peasants." The poorly trained cadres frequently classified many people as "local despots" whose economic status was not that of the wealthy landlord and who, in fact, supported the government. Cadres pressured peasants to demand punishment of the "despots"; after denunciations and trials, most "despots" were impris-oned, but a sizeable number were executed. Estimates on the number of executions vary widely. (In the most exaggerated claim, President Richard Nixon stated in 1972 that 500,000 North Vietnamese were executed and another 500,000 died in slave labor camps at this time.) The most reliable estimates set the total number of executions in the range of 2,500 to 15,000 victims.[11]

Despite Ho Chi Minh's promises to rectify the errors of the land reform program, peasant unrest mounted. The most notable instance occurred in late 1956 when thousands of peasants in Ho's home province marched in protest on the provincial capital. With its integrity at stake, the North Vietnamese government responded with force against the protesters (perhaps one thousand were killed) but also dismissed various officials who were held responsible for the land reform failures (including Truong Chinh, secretary-general of the Communist party). It also encouraged, albeit briefly, open criticism of the government.

Confronting these serious problems, Ho Chi Minh and other leaders in Hanoi had little choice but to concentrate resources on consolidating their position and advancing the socialist revolution in the North.

RENEWAL OF WARFARE: INSURGENCY IN THE SOUTH

Meanwhile in the South, the opposition to the Diem government led gradually to a large-scale Communist-led insurgency. During the first two years after the Geneva Conference, the former Viet Minh in the South anticipated that national unification would result from the 1956 elections. When those elections were not held, they looked to the Hanoi government for direction. In 1956 Le Duan, the senior Communist party leader in the South, issued a lengthy document, "The Path of Revolution in the South," which called upon the party's followers to prepare for a long-term political struggle while also implicitly pressuring the North to anticipate eventual militancy. Charting a long struggle—Duan's "path of revolution"—was necessary because the reunification elections had been sabotaged by the "American imperialist invaders and the feudalist dictator Ngo Dinh Diem" and because the Communist movement in the South had been weakened by the partition in 1954 and suppressed by the Diem government. Long-term success depended on "firmly consolidat[ing] the North," for "the North at present must be the firm and strong base to serve as rear area for the revolutionary movement to liberate the South."[12]

"The Path of Revolution in the South" thus left Communist cadres in the South with no promise of immediate support from the North at a time when they were facing Diem's determined campaign to eliminate them. During the next two years, they generally followed the party's dictates, concentrating on political activities. The Communist insurgents did undertake some limited military measures: self-protection demanded arming propaganda teams, and certain local political officials were targeted for assassination. Working with other opponents of Diem, the Communists also attacked some government outposts. True to the Communist practice of relying on united front tactics, they cooperated with others who were being suppressed by Diem's government. These included dissident elements within the Cao Dai, Hoa Hao, and Binh Xuyen—groups whose connections with the French had made them the Communists' archenemies a few years earlier, thus proving that politics in Vietnam, no less than anywhere else, can indeed make strange bedfellows.

Despite these activities, the former Viet Minh and their followers believed by 1959 that the struggle was becoming futile. This period constituted the "darkest days" of Southern insurgency. Communist party membership in the South had declined sharply, and many cadres left the party dispirited by the lack of Northern support and the strength of the American-backed South Vietnamese army. In the face of the Diem government's suppression, the Southern Communists reasoned, the movement's very survival depended upon armed insurgency. "It was then or never," one scholar has written; they "had no choice" but to change policy.[13] A militant policy, the Southern Communists believed, would enable them to take advantage of the wide-spread peasant discontent with the Diem government.

The North Vietnamese, while remaining cautious, gave their first implicit encouragement to a militant approach. In early 1959 a Vietnam Communist party directive reaffirmed that the political struggle had to remain "the principal form" of activity but permitted "to a certain extent . . . self-defense and armed propaganda forces."[14] Southern cadres quickly seized upon the new policy to lead a series of peasant uprisings. They were generally successful not only in gaining control over large areas in a few provinces but also in overrunning a few South Vietnamese army units. It was during this fighting in 1959 that the Communist-led insurgents were labeled by U.S. and South Vietnamese officials as the Viet Cong, a pejorative abbreviation for "Vietnamese Communist."

The insurgency gathered momentum beyond what the party leadership in Hanoi anticipated. Of special importance was the January 1960 uprising in Ben Tre province in the Mekong Delta, where Madame Nguyen Thi Dinh, a local Communist cadre, led a revolutionary movement. Beginning with 160 troops armed with a few old rifles and homemade mortars, the insurgents gathered widespread support, gaining control of a large part of the province and overrunning government outposts. When the Saigon government sent troops into the region, the revolutionaries easily forced them to retreat. Madame Dinh later claimed that the uprising resulted in the "liberation" of 70 percent of the province's villages; while that figure may be exaggerated, the revolt underscored the vulnerability of the South Vietnamese government. In the liberated areas, the insurgents immediately fulfilled their promise of giving land to the peasants, resulting in the transfer of some 60,000 acres of rice fields.

The remarkable growth of the Communist-led insurgency encouraged the Southern dissidents to press for a widespread offensive against Diem's government. In March 1960 a diverse group—including former Viet Minh and representatives of the various sects and of Buddhist and Catholic groups—met and issued the "Declaration of Former Resistance Fighters." Claiming to speak for "the vast majority of Vietnamese people," the document called for a "struggle to end the colonial regime and the fascist dictatorship of the Ngo family." It would be replaced by a coalition government that would work with North Vietnam "for the peaceful unification of the country."[15]

The "Former Resistance Fighters" statement was directed not only to the people of the South but also to the Communist leadership in the North. It anticipated "the active support of our northern compatriots," but that was not yet forthcoming. Ho Chi Minh and other leaders in the North were restrained by the fear that a "people's war" in the South would only invite further U.S. involvement and that large-scale warfare in the South would also involve the North, thus disrupting its economic development. Moreover, the Northern leaders assumed that the Diem government would sooner or later collapse of its own shortcomings, thus paving the way for a peaceful transition to Communist control. Le Duan, the Southern Communist leader, had returned to the North and in 1959 was appointed secretary-general of the Vietnam Communist party; he stated in 1960 that the "irretrievably doomed" Saigon regime would "rapidly decay" in the absence of any warfare. The Communists enjoyed "necessary conditions to develop strongly," but wide-spread insurgency, if it led to U.S. intervention, would alter the situation. "To maintain peace," he concluded, "is a revolutionary slogan."[16] Yet support of the Southern revolutionary movement could not be delayed without risking a loss of the Vietnam Communist party's influence and prestige. Pressed by Le Duan and others, the Vietnam Communist Party Congress, meeting in Hanoi in September 1960, agreed at last that the "two priorities" were "to carry out the socialist revolution in the North" and "to liberate the South from the rule of the American imperialists and their henchmen [and] achieve national reunification."[17] Communist in the South were urged to form a broadly based political alliance, uniting all the various political, religious, and ethnic groups that opposed the Diem government.

The Southern Communists moved quickly, and in December 1960 they announced the formation of the National Liberation Front, which called for the overthrow of the Diem regime, the end of military assistance from the United States, the establishment of a broadly based coalition government, and gradual reunification with the North. The NLF attracted a wide following, drawing the support not only of Communists but also of the dissatisfied elements within the Cao Dai and Hoa Hao sects, various small political groups, and numerous critics of the Diem government. They were joined by increasing numbers of former Viet Minh who had headed north after the Geneva partition but who now returned to their homes in the South to resume the struggle. Since the Diem government tried to prevent migration from the North, those returning had to infiltrate across the Demilitarized Zone or via Laos, along a footpath that later became known as the Ho Chi Minh Trail. (The Demilitarized Zone—or DMZ—was provided for in the Geneva Agreements;

it was intended to be a buffer, running along the 17th parallel demarcation line, between the two Vietnamese governments.) The NLF, operating alongside the Communist party, thus provided a broadly based direct challenge to the legitimacy of the Diem government. Its strategy called for political as well as military measures, depending upon the circumstances: in the mountainous and jungle areas, military means were given priority; in the cities, where the Diem government had its greatest strength, the stress would be on political means; and in the lowland agrarian region, equal emphasis was to be given to political and military approaches. While this program may not have been a full-fledged "people's war," the formation of the NLF was an important step in that direction. The number of armed resistance forces increased from some two thousand in 1959 to over ten thousand by 1961.

Thus the Communist movement in the South, which had appeared to be on the verge of extinction in 1958, had accomplished a remarkable resurgence. Having barely withstood Diem's suppression, it had finally forced support from North Vietnam and had capitalized on the fundamental weaknesses of the Diem government. The alienation of the peasantry and other groups from the Saigon regime constituted the basis for NLF's strength.

To those who launched this warfare, their struggle was seen as a continuation of the struggle that had begun earlier against the French and their puppet Bao Dai. The French and Bao Dai were gone, but in their place were the Americans and Diem. So evident was the South Vietnamese government's dependency upon the United States that the insurgents promised to liberate the country from the "My-diem"—an opprobrium meaning American-Diem. Throughout the countryside, "My-Diem" became a common way of referring to the South Vietnamese government.

THE "MESS": THE CRISIS IN LAOS, 1960–1961

As serious as the Vietnam situation appeared, the United States' overriding concern in Indochina by 1960 was the situation in Laos. When the outgoing Eisenhower briefed the incoming president John Kennedy on the day before the inauguration, he stated that the Laotian "mess" seemed the most intractable of the international problems facing the United States. Although Laos had not received the American official and popular attention that had been devoted to South Vietnam since 1954, that country's strategic importance had led to a steadily increasing level of involvement. As a small country between North Vietnam and Thailand, both of which sought a "friendly" neighbor, Laos faced immense difficulties in its pursuit of national independence.

The U.S. objectives were to prevent the Communist Pathet Lao from having influence on the Laotian government and to encourage the development of a pro-American leadership in the country. The terms of the Geneva Agreements—obliging the Pathet Lao to regroup in two provinces and pro-

viding for the Pathet Lao's integration into the Royal Laotian Government—
seemed to provide the means by which Communist influence could be limited. The United States provided considerable assistance to the Royal Laotian
Government, accounting for about 65 percent of the government's revenues
between 1956 and 1958.

The United States, however, distrusted the avowed determination of Premier
Souvanna Phouma to incorporate the Pathet Lao within his government and
to follow a neutralist foreign policy. The United States and Souvanna Phouma
shared an interest in limiting Communist influence, but they disagreed on tactics. Whereas the Americans wanted the royal government to use its army to
eliminate the Pathet Lao, Souvanna Phouma and other neutralists looked
upon military action as forcing the Pathet Lao into the arms of the North
Vietnamese; they believed that compromise with the Pathet Lao and participation in the government would assure its independence from North Vietnam.
Souvanna Phuoma's pursuit of a coalition government was always a perilous
course, for it faced the opposition of rightist leaders, who, like the Americans,
distrusted the Pathet Lao. The rightists' strongly anti–Pathet Lao position was
encouraged by the anticommunist government of neighboring Thailand and
supported privately by U.S. officials and agents. Undaunted, Souvanna Phuoma
negotiated with the Pathet Lao and eventually, in 1958, reached an agreement
whereby in return for representation in the government, the Pathet Lao agreed
to recognize government jurisdiction over the two provinces it occupied and to
merge its army with the Royal Laotian Army.

That effort to establish a broadly based coalition, however, quickly unraveled.
Rightists overthrew Souvanna Phuoma. The new premier, Phoui Sananikone,
repudiated the agreement with the Pathet Lao and excluded them from the government. As Phuoi embraced a stridently anticommunist policy, United States'
assistance to Laos increased significantly, reaching a total of $55 million in 1960,
including the dispatch of a small American military training mission.

The American aid program, however, had limited effect. Most notably, it
failed to build strong ties between the public and government, as nearly all of
the assistance was directed to the military and much of it went for private gain.
A Laotian official sympathetic to America stated: "the precious American aid
is very much appreciated—only the way in which it is applied is often the cause
of criticism. . . . The results are visible only to the government and the chiefs of
the various national services. They are seen with difficulty by the mass of people."[18] The assistance programs were often accompanied by graft, black marke-
teering, corruption, and inept administration. "Our greatest danger of communist subversion," one official stated, "arises from the bad use of foreign aid. . . .
It enriches a minority outrageously while the mass of the population remains as
poor as ever."[19] Finally, the aid was a principal cause of rampant inflation,
which further alienated the peasantry from the government.

Predictably, the American-encouraged rightist direction of Laotian leadership resulted in Pathet Lao warfare against the royal government. The Pathet

Lao propaganda exploited the weakness of Phuoi's leadership, criticizing his dependence upon the United States and charging widespread government corruption and indifference. Facing a challenge to its very existence, the Pathet Lao looked for increased support from North Vietnam and the Soviet Union. The North Vietnamese sent cadres to train and equip the Pathet Lao, which consolidated its control over the northeastern provinces and prepared for protracted warfare against the royal government.

When the Phuoi government was overthrown in August 1960, however, it was not by the Pathet Lao but by a group of army officers who wanted to eliminate the corruption associated with American aid. The king asked Souvanna Phuoma to return as premier, with the result that Laos resumed a neutralist foreign policy. Souvanna calculated that by establishing a coalition between rightist and neutralist groups, he could pressure the Pathet Lao into supporting the government.

The United States, however, remained distrustful of any effort to accommodate the Pathet Lao and supported rightist opposition to Souvanna Phuoma's leadership. It provided military assistance to the government as well as to Phuoi's forces, and the CIA recruited and supplied tribes that were prepared to support Phuoi. It encouraged Thailand to close its borders to Souvanna Phuoma's government, while allowing supplies to his opponents to cross the frontier.

The United States' unrelenting opposition to Laotian neutrality forced Souvanna Phuoma to turn to the Pathet Lao and Communist-bloc nations for support. He brought the Pathet Lao into his government and sent goodwill missions to China and North Vietnam. To Americans those maneuvers, of course, only confirmed their worst suspicions about Souvanna. The State Department and CIA thus became determined to force him from power. That did not take long, and in December 1960 the American-equipped army of Phuoi Sananikone overthrew the neutralist government.

That coup, however, brought only greater instability to the country and a widening of the international implications of the Laotian situation. Under pressure from North Vietnam, the Soviet Union, which had little interest in Laos, airlifted supplies to the Pathet Lao and to Souvanna Phuoma's forces. The vulnerability of the rightist government, which had alienated both the Pathet Lao and Souvanna Phuoma's neutralist followers, forced the Eisenhower administration in its last days to consider military intervention.

In his meeting with Kennedy, Eisenhower urged him to stand firm against any coalition government in Laos. The United States should be prepared to intervene militarily only "as a last desperate effort to save Laos." The secretary of defense even assured Kennedy that "we could handle the military situation successfully if we did intervene."[20]

The Laotian "mess" that Eisenhower passed along to Kennedy was largely of American making. The determined U.S. resistance to Laotian neutrality had contributed to the very conditions that it was intended to preclude: the resurgence of the Pathet Lao, a renewal of North Vietnamese activity, and the intervention of the Soviet Union. That Laos had become a major concern illustrated the difficulty of limiting American interests in Southeast Asia. That obscure, landlocked country had taken on critical importance because U.S. policymakers looked upon the region in zero-sum terms: any grain for communism was equated with a loss for the United States. That way of thinking not only ignored the internal sources of political divisions in a country like Laos but also assumed that any compromise with a Communist movement, even if favored by local noncommunist leaders as it was in Laos, would lead to that country's "loss." It assumed that with substantial levels of U.S. economic and military assistance, anticommunist movements could be fostered however weak their political base. That way of thinking led the United States to provide Laos with a higher per-capita level of economic aid that that given any other country.

Hence, by the time Kennedy took office in 1961 the United States faced two serious problems in Indochina. In South Vietnam and Laos the governments of Ngo Dinh Diem and Phuoi Sananikone, both dependent upon American support for their existence, were floundering.

KENNEDY: COMPROMISE IN LAOS AND COMMITMENT IN VIETNAM

John F. Kennedy and his principal foreign policy advisers shared the assumptions of their predecessors about the strategic importance of Southeast Asia. Their concern about the region was heightened when shortly before Kennedy's inauguration, Nikita Khrushchev, the premier of the Soviet Union, affirmed support for "wars of national liberation." In his inaugural address, Kennedy spoke of seemingly unlimited American commitments: "Let every nation know, whether it wishes us well or ill, that we shall pay any price, bear any burden, meet any hardship, support any friend, oppose any foe to assure the survival and the success of liberty."[21]

Vietnam and Laos were but two of several critical points in the global struggle. In Berlin, Cuba, and the Congo, the superpowers seemed on the verge of confrontation. If the challenges were many, the American response had to be diversified. Accordingly, the Kennedy administration broadened American strategic planning, embracing the concept of "flexible response." Nuclear deterrence, on which the Eisenhower administration had relied, would be augmented by a buildup of conventional forces and innovative programs. If the Communist powers were using "wars of national liberation" in the Third World, then the United States had to respond through counterguerilla warfare and encouraging anticommunist allies to undertake reforms that would blunt the appeal of communism. If the Communists were appealing to Third World peoples as being more sympathetic with their problems, the United States had to respond with greater economic assistance and through the people-to-people effort embodied in the Peace Corps.

This determined effort to seize the initiative in the cold war reflected the thinking not just of Kennedy but of a circle of action-oriented advisers. These included Secretary of State Dean Rusk, Secretary of Defense Robert McNamara, National Security Adviser McGeorge Bundy, and his deputy, Walt W. Rostow. In his book *The Best and the Brightest,* the journalist David Halberstam described the mood of the Kennedy era: "A remarkable hubris permeated this entire time. Nine years earlier Denis Brogan had written 'probably the only people who have the historical sense of inevitable victory are the Americans.' Never had that statement seemed more true."[22]

In Southeast Asia, Laos was the most immediate concern, and there Kennedy opted for a compromise. The United States accepted an initiative put forth by Cambodia, Britain, and the Soviet Union calling for a cease-fire and negotiations among the Communists, neutralists, and rightists. This reflected a departure from the Eisenhower approach, which had assumed that any compromise would lead to Communist domination. Why was Kennedy, who assumed that Laos was critical to U.S. interests, prepared to negotiate? First, the military commitment and risks seemed excessive. The Joint Chiefs of Staff warned that it would require 60,000 American troops to assure the victory of the rightist forces; moreover, such a step would likely result in Chinese intervention, which would risk a major confrontation. Second, Kennedy's experience in the ill-fated Bay of Pigs invasion left him cautious. That abortive effort in April 1961 to overthrow the government of Fidel Castro made the new president suspicious of those who argued that the United States could easily achieve political objectives through military intervention.

Beginning in May 1961, the three principal Laotian political groups entered into negotiations in Geneva. More than a year later, a compromise settlement provided for a coalition government in which the Pathet Lao shared power under neutralist leadership. Thus Laos, with Souvanna Phuoma again becoming premier, returned to the neutralist international position that it had followed from 1954 to 1958.

In meeting the challenge of the deteriorating situation in Vietnam, the Kennedy administration significantly increased the American commitment. Having appeared weak during the Bay of Pigs and having compromised in Laos, Kennedy needed to demonstrate his resolve somewhere if his cold war rhetoric was to be taken seriously. More importantly, the Kennedy team looked upon Vietnam as a place where the United States, through the calculated use of its power, could win a "war of national liberation." That relied on two major initiatives: a comprehensive "counterinsurgency" strategy and the "strategic hamlet" program.

Counterinsurgency marked a departure from the earlier U.S. military role. Military assistance to South Vietnam until almost the end of the Eisenhower administration had been directed toward preparing for its defense in the event of an invasion from the North. The Kennedy approach called for a buildup of the South Vietnamese army and shifting its emphasis to confronting the Communist insurgency in the countryside. This reorientation was accompanied by a dramatic increase in the U.S. military presence. While the Eisenhower administration had limited U.S. advisors to the 685 foreign advisers permitted in the Geneva Agreements, the Kennedy policymakers ignored such restrictions. By the end of Kennedy's first year in office, more than 2,000 American military personnel were in Vietnam. A year later, the number had increased to over 11,000.[23] The American advisers engaged in a wide range of activities: training the South Vietnamese army in counterinsurgency, accompanying their units into battle and their aircraft on strafing and bombing missions against Viet Cong positions, manning helicopters that provided the South Vietnamese with mobility in jungle warfare, and participating in propaganda and political activities.

These measures seemingly enabled the South Vietnamese to gain the initiative. The introduction of air power and the use of napalm, a jellied gasoline that burns deeply into the skin, caught the enemy by surprise. The helicopters, Americans reported, "were a terrifying sight to the superstitious Viet Cong peasants [who] turned and ran . . . [and] were easy targets."[24] Napalm, an enthusiastic General Paul D. Harkins, who headed the U.S. military command, noted, "really puts the fear of God into the Viet Cong . . . and that is what counts."[25]

The strategic hamlet program was intended to cut the Communist insurgents from their base of support. If they were denied access to villages on which they depended for food, intelligence, and recruits, the Viet Cong would be denied the capability of waging war. Modeled on a program that had been used successfully against Communist insurgency in Malaya, the strategic hamlet effort endeavored to move entire villages into secure areas where the South Vietnamese government would provide health, educational, and other social services. The peasant would thus come to see the Saigon government as supportive and protective. Since it provided a means of redressing his government's point of greatest vulnerability—the lack of rural report—Diem endorsed the strategic hamlet program, promising to build twelve thousand such communities, which would have been enough to protect all of the rural population. Diem's brother, Nhu, personally directed the program, which had another important objective as far as the ruling family was concerned: it offered a means of controlling the peasant population.

The Kennedy administration initiatives, however, failed to alter the political-military situation. The National Liberation Front more than compensated for the substantial increase in U.S. military assistance. The total number of Communist forces increased steadily from about 7,000 in 1960 to nearly 100,000 by 1963. The principal insurgent force was composed of guerilla militias, which through raids on military outposts, assassinations of local officials, propaganda work in the villages, recruitment of young men to their ranks, and other activities intensified the pressures on the Diem government.

The insurgency benefited from North Vietnam's assistance. According to U.S. estimates, the number of "infiltrators" from the North totaled 26,000 between 1961 and 1963 (as compared with 4,500 in 1959 and 1960). The vast majority of these "infiltrators" were "regroupees," that is, those who had gone to the North in 1954. Returning to familiar areas and often to home villages, these "infiltrators" were critical in rekindling patriotic sentiments and in building a strong resistance network. In sum, despite the infusion of American advisers and equipment, the South Vietnamese government and army remained on the defensive.

Likewise, the strategic hamlet program, despite repeated assurances of American and South Vietnamese officials of its success, proved unworkable. Like many U.S.–South Vietnamese efforts at enlisting peasant support, the strategic hamlet initiative was undermined by hasty and inadequate planning and by tensions between Saigon authorities and the rural population. Strategic hamlets were often located in remote areas, far from market towns. The compensation for lost and destroyed property ($21) was inadequate. Above all, peasants resented being moved from their ancestral villages and farmlands; in numerous cases villagers had to be forcibly relocated. Few young men of military age moved, an indication that many of them had gone over to the Viet Cong. "The strategic hamlet program," David Halberstam noted, "never separated the guerrillas from their source of greatest strength: young men."[26] A South Vietnamese official report on one district illustrated the problems: of the 38,000 inhabitants, 60 percent were "Communist-intoxicated," and after six weeks only 7 percent of the residents had been moved to the strategic hamlets. The social services in the hamlets were typically poor and understaffed. Moreover, the strategic hamlets were more akin to concentration camps than communities. An American reporter noted in 1962 that visiting a hamlet was like "blundering into some sort of prison camp."[27]

An incident in January 1963 underscored the vulnerability of the U.S.–South Vietnamese position. Near the village of Ap Bac, 50 miles southwest of Saigon, a South Vietnamese unit of 2,000 men surrounded a Viet Cong force of 400. The ARVN unit enjoyed not only numerical but also technological superiority, as it was equipped with armored personnel carriers and artillery and was supported by U.S. helicopters and air power. Yet it lost the engagement, sustaining heavy casualties (61, including 3 U.S. advisers, killed and 100 wounded; five helicopters shot down) and allowing the enemy battalion to escape. The Viet Cong unit lost only 12 men. "The implication was obvious to the U.S. and communist commands alike," one historian has written: the Viet Cong "could defeat the ARVN, despite the ARVN's U.S. arms, equipment, and advice."[28] As the Laos experience had indicated earlier, the battle of Ap Bac underlined the limits of U.S. power.

TURNING POINTS: THE U.S. AND THE VIETNAM CRISES, JUNE 1963–AUGUST 1964

Whatever lessons might have been learned from the Ap Bac episode were ignored when the United States confronted recurring crises in

Vietnam. Political instability and an eroding military position forced American policymakers to face the realization that still greater U.S. involvement would be necessary in order to assure the objective of preserving South Vietnamese independence. Beginning in the summer of 1963, the crises in Vietnam became a matter of considerable attention in the American media. At the time, however, few Americans questioned the decisions of their leaders to deepen the nation's commitment.

The United States became ensnarled in a morass in which Vietnamese culture and tradition—reflected in persistent resistance to external direction, the emergence of the Buddhists as a political force, and the strong appeal of North-South unification—undermined the American concept of South Vietnamese nationhood. Officials in Saigon and Washington were infuriated by Diem's indifference to their pleas for reform; Diem's continued obstinancy grew out of not only his own innate stubbornness but also his unwillingness as a Vietnamese nationalist to be seen as the puppet of a foreign power. Whatever his shortcomings, Diem correctly recognized that his dependence upon the United States was a major source of his unpopularity. The history of resisting foreign domination—whether it was Chinese, Japanese, French, or now American—left all Vietnamese leaders, Communist as well as the noncommunist, distrustful of outside powers.

The longstanding weakness of the Diem government, however, could not be remedied, and in the early months of 1963, opposition shifted from the countryside to the cities, with the leadership coming not from the Communists but from the large Buddhist community. Buddhists had long resented the dominance of the Catholic minority in the Diem government, a situation worsened by the arrogance of the Nhu family and its indifference to the religious sensitivities of the Buddhist majority. In a remarkably obtuse act, Diem in 1959 had formally dedicated his country to the Virgin Mary. In addition, the Buddhist leadership historically had played an important political role at times of crisis and through its moral influence had been instrumental in affecting change. Although there were divisions within the Buddhist community, generally it sought, beyond Diem's overthrow, an end to American influence and a neutral South Vietnam followed by reunification with the North under a coalition government.

The "Buddhist crisis" began in Hué on 8 May—the celebration of the birth of the Buddha—when provincial police enforced a hitherto largely ignored law prohibiting the display of religious flags. When the Buddhists protested, the troops opened fire and nine persons were killed. This incident led to a protest demonstration in Hué on 10 May in which Buddhists demanded an end to religious persecution, but Diem refused to compromise. The protest then took another traditional form, which had a devastating impact in the United States. At a busy intersection in Saigon on 11 June, Thich Quang Duc, an elderly monk, sat down and crossed his legs in the middle of a circle of other monks and nuns. One of them poured gasoline over his body, and then another ignited him. The victim left a plea to the Diem government to show "charity and compassion" to all religions. This self-immolation was widely covered in the U.S. news media (correspondents having been told about it in advance), and the photograph of the monk engulfed in flames led many Americans to question the character of the South Vietnamese government. In Vietnam much of the urban middle class, including large numbers of students, now rallied behind the Buddhist protest.

Despite American pressures to compromise, the Diem government forced a showdown. Protests mounted. Other monks engaged in acts of self-immolation. Madame Nhu added to the discrediting of the government when she described the self-immolations as "barbecues." "Let them burn," she said, "and we shall clap our hands."[29] Then, on 21 August, the Diem government sent its American-trained and -equipped special forces units to attack the Buddhist pagodas in Saigon, Hué, and other cities. The military units ransacked the pagodas, forcibly removed the monks, and arrested 1,420 of them.

The assault on the pagodas not only shocked U.S. officials but also galvanized opponents of Diem. Several military officers had been plotting a coup, but of critical importance to them was the position of the United States. They established secret contact with CIA personnel seeking assurances of support. Officials in the Kennedy administration were divided. The pro-Diem policymakers believed that the United States should stand behind Diem, albeit pressing him for some gesture (such as dismissing his widely despised brother Nhu) that would blunt the appeal of his opponents. They also warned about the disastrous implications of being associated with a coup attempt that failed. Anti-Diem officials, on the other hand, contended that Diem's policies were so bankrupt that his regime defied salvaging. Their criticism was reinforced by reports that Nhu had established secret contact with Hanoi presumably to strike a political deal; whether Nhu's overtures were genuine or were intended to pressure the Americans to support his brother, the effect was to cause doubt about the South Vietnamese government's anticommunist commitment.

In the end the Kennedy administration hesitantly embraced the coup. It tacitly encouraged the plotters and, through Ambassador Henry Cabot Lodge, assured them of U.S. assistance should the coup succeed. On 1 November the generals took control of key military positions and communications centers in Saigon. Diem and Nhu escaped from the palace, but army officers found and executed them.

For both North Vietnam and the United States, the overthrow of Diem and the coming to power of a 12-man military junta in Saigon resolved some problems and presented new difficulties. The Communist leadership in Hanoi welcomed the elimination of the dominant political figure in the South. Yet since Diem's policies had been so unpopular and had been a rallying point for the insurgency, his passing meant that it might be more difficult to sustain the opposition to the Saigon government. Indeed, in the weeks after Diem's fall, Viet Cong recruitment lagged, and some cadres deserted. If the Southern insurgency were to be sustained, it seemed necessary for the North to provide greater assistance, but that risked a response from the United States. Moreover, the North Vietnamese recognized that the military junta would be more receptive than Diem had been to an enlarged U.S. military presence. Thus from Hanoi's perspective this situation pointed toward the likelihood of increased warfare, which presented serious problems. The extent of U.S. involvement was difficult to project. North Vietnam's economic development, in any event, would be endangered by the costs of intensified warfare in the South and by the likely U.S. air attacks. In addition, conflict posed difficulties in relations with the major Communist powers, which by this time had sharp differences over relations with the West. The Soviet Union had muted its call for "wars of national liberation" and espoused the doctrine of "peaceful coexistence," while China, as the champion of wars of national liberation, seemingly supported conflict. Hence warfare meant that North Vietnam would appear to be aligning ideologically with its powerful neighbor while alienating the Soviet Union.

The Communist party leadership, at a major meeting in Hanoi in December 1963, decided to increase military commitment in the South. The dangers inherent in this approach were overcome by an appeal to patriotic sentiment, as advocates of greater involvement maintained that the Southern insurgents needed support. Whereas a few years earlier the Northern leadership accepted the proposition that liberation would be accomplished "by the Southern people themselves," they now embraced the argument that that objective was "not only a task of the Southern people, but also of the entire people, of the South as well as the North." Besides the influence of the patriotic appeal, Northern leaders' reservations were also mitigated by the prospects that they could quickly force the capitulation of the Saigon government before the United States would have time to react.

The United States also responded to postcoup developments in ways that pointed toward greater military involvement. American policymakers had tended to assume that once Diem was overthrown, the new leadership would enjoy greater popularity and would pursue the struggle against the Communists more forcefully. One American official later reflected: "Actually no one on our side knew what the new people were thinking at all. It was a fantastic vacuum of information. Our requirements were really very simple—we wanted any government which would continue to fight."[30] In fact, the junta, headed by General Duong Van Minh, quickly evidenced a determination to act independently. This reflected, in part, the continued influence of the Buddhists; Minh and many other new leaders had Buddhist backgrounds, and the junta immediately freed all of the Buddhists imprisoned by Diem. Convinced that the struggle with the NLF could be more effectively waged by political rather than military means, Minh and his colleagues believed (as did the leadership in Hanoi) that the NLF would be weakened by Diem's overthrow. Accordingly, the time was opportune to attract the noncommunist groups who had joined the NLF because of their opposition to Diem's policies. In particular, large numbers of the Cao Dai and Hoa Hao religious sects had been driven into the ranks of the NLF by Diem's repressive measures; they were seen as being responsive to conciliatory gestures from the new government in Saigon. Rather than relying on military measures and the discredited strategic hamlet program to confront the NLF in the rural areas, the Minh government embarked upon a rural welfare system that, it insisted, would be free of U.S. control and would be administered by local officials. The long-term objective was an eventual agreement with the NLF.

Besides distrusting Minh's conciliatory approach, American officials also feared that his government would be receptive to international pressures, current in late 1963, for the neutralization of Indochina. French president Charles de Gaulle offered to mediate differences between North and South Vietnam, and Prince Sihanouk of Cambodia called for a federation of neutral Indochina states. In Vietnam the NLF quickly endorsed Sihanouk's plan. To many Laotian, Cambodian, and Vietnamese leaders, neutralization had much appeal since it suggested an opportunity to be free of outside interference. Although Minh's government never endorsed neutralization, the idea was popular among much of the urban middle class and the Buddhist leadership in the South. To the United States, however, neutralization was anathema since it seemed to leave the Communists in a dominant position in Indochina, a situation that Americans believed would have adverse effects throughout Southeast Asia. Lyndon Johnson, who had succeeded to the presidency after Kennedy's assassination, warned Minh that neutralism would lead to Communist domination. "Nothing is further from [our] mind," an American official related, "than 'neutral solution for Vietnam.' We intend to win."[31]

Minh's government never had the opportunity to test its policies. It was troubled by dissension within its ranks, resentment from dismissed officials, and strained relations with the United States. Again, American officials, in this instance principally military personnel, conspired with opponents of a government in Saigon. In late January 1964 the Minh government was overthrown by a group of army officers led by General Nguyen Khanh. The "Pentagon's Coup" brought to power a pro-American leader who was committed to a military solution.

Having shifted support from Diem to Minh to Khanh within a few months, the United States was discovering the intractability of its Vietnam problem. American policy increasingly shifted from concern with the South's internal economic and political problems, which became critical again after Khanh's seizure of power, to reliance on military means. More American military advisers were sent (totaling over 23,000 by late 1964), increased assistance facilitated a substantial increase in ARVN's size, and General William Westmoreland was appointed commander of the American military mission. The United States also put sustained pressure on the North: sporadic raids, sabotage, and psychological warfare, which had been carried out secretly by the

CIA in cooperation with the South Vietnamese, were now upgraded into a program of continued harassment and surveillance, code-named Operation Plan 34A (OPLAN 34A). The North Vietnamese were warned through diplomatic channels that continued support of the war in the South would lead to direct attacks on its territory.

Thus, in the aftermath of Diem's overthrow, both North Vietnam and the United States interpreted events in the South in ways that pointed each toward greater reliance on military means. While war was not inevitable, a crisis in the Gulf of Tonkin in August 1964 brought the first direct use of American naval and air power against North Vietnam. The incident grew out of the OPLAN 34A operations, which were supplemented by the dispatch of U.S. naval missions, code-named DeSoto, into the Gulf of Tonkin to engage in electronic monitoring of North Vietnam coastal defenses. In July the destroyer *Maddox* sailed into the Gulf of Tonkin on a DeSoto mission, and the aircraft carrier *Ticonderoga* was stationed at the entrance to the gulf. On 30 July South Vietnamese commandos, as part of OPLAN 34A operations, raided two small islands off the North Vietnamese coast. The *Maddox* moved into the waters near the attack, and on the morning of 2 August it was pursued by North Vietnamese patrol boats, which assumed that the *Maddox* had been involved in the 30 July raids. The patrol boats fired three torpedos, but none hit the American vessel. In response, the *Maddox* opened fire, crippling two patrol boats and sinking a third. The *Maddox* commander summoned aircraft from the *Ticonderoga*, which attacked other patrol boats.

When word of the incident reached Washington, President Johnson sent a message to the North Vietnamese government warning of "grave consequences" in the event of "further unprovoked offensive military action."[32] He also ordered a second destroyer, the *C. Turner Joy,* to join the *Maddox* in the Gulf of Tonkin patrol.

On the night of 4 August a second "incident" took place when the commanders of the two American destroyers became confused in the pitch-darkness and believed that they were pursued by patrol boats. The American ships opened fire. In fact, there was no firm evidence of any North Vietnamese vessels or gunfire, and the commander of the *Maddox* urged that the event be completely reviewed.

The facts of the 4 August "confrontation," however, were ignored in Washington. Johnson and his advisers immediately accepted the proposition that the North Vietnamese, despite Johnson's warning, had engaged in "unprovoked" warfare. The United States now took two far-reaching steps. Johnson immediately ordered air attacks against North Vietnamese patrol boat bases and an oil depot; speaking on national television on the evening of 4 August, the president told the American public, "Repeated acts of violence against the armed forces of the United States must be met not only with alert defense, but with positive reply. That reply is being given as I speak to you tonight."[33] Described as "limited in scale," the air assault constituted 64 sorties, which "severely" hit all targets; they destroyed or damaged 25 patrol boats. (A few days later, Johnson privately acknowledged that he had not been honest with the public; of the second incident, he said, "Hell, those dumb stupid sailors were just shooting at flying fish."[34]

Taking advantage of the broad popular support for this defense of American national honor, Johnson secured congressional approval for a resolution that gave him virtually unlimited authority to pursue warfare in Southeast Asia. With only nominal debate, the House of Representatives approved the resolution unanimously, and the Senate followed suit with only two dissenting votes. The Gulf of Tonkin Resolution, as it became known, charged that the North Vietnamese attacks were "part of a deliberate and systematic campaign of aggression" and authorized the president to "take all necessary measures to repel any armed attack against the forces of the United States and to prevent further aggression."[35] (Again, Johnson's private characterization was apt; the resolution was "like grandma's nightshirt—it covered everything.")[36]

Considering that U.S. actions in the Gulf of Tonkin were reasonably perceived by the North Vietnamese as provocative, that the 2 August incident lasted barely 20 minutes with no damage to the *Maddox* or loss of American life, and that the 4 August "incident" may have been a figment of American imagination, the response was excessive. Basically, the events in the Gulf of Tonkin offered a pretext for demonstrating U.S. resolve and power to North Vietnam. This attempt to intimidate Hanoi was a logical and fateful step in the progression of greater political and military commitment.

By the end of 1964 the United States and North Vietnam thus had moved toward the brink of conflict. Yet in the aftermath of the Gulf of Tonkin incident, both sides anticipated that their objectives might be achieved without war. The North Vietnamese were not intimidated by U.S. air strikes. Rather, still assuming that the political turmoil in the South offered an opportunity for an early victory, the North sent its first regular army unit southward in the fall of 1964. Johnson, in campaigning for the presidency, repeatedly reassured the electorate that he wanted to avoid war and criticized the belligerency of his Republican opponent, Senator Barry Goldwater. Johnson's overriding dream was to build the "Great Society" at home, and he calculated that South Vietnam would survive without military intervention. That depended upon the unlikely propositions that the newest regime in Saigon could build a stable government and that the leaders in Hanoi would abandon the August Revolution's vision of a united, independent Vietnam.

Notes

1. Dulles cited in Charles A. Stevenson, *The End of Nowhere: American Policy in Laos in 1954* (Boston: Beacon Press, 1972), 6.
2. Bernard B. Fall, *The Anatomy of a Crisis: The Laotian Crisis of 1960–61* (Garden City, N.Y.: Doubleday, 1960), 23.

3. McClintock to State Department, 4 July 1954, *Foreign Relations of the United States 1952–54*, vol. 13, *Indochina* (Washington, D.C.: U.S. Government Printing Office, 1982), 1782–84.

4. Dillon to State Department, 24 May 1954, ibid., 1608–10.

5. Hinh cited in Kahin, *Intervention*, 82.

6. *Public Papers of the President: Dwight D. Eisenhower, 1954* (Washington, D.C.: U.S. Government Printing Office, 1960), 949.

7. Tom Dooley, *Deliver Us from Evil*, quoted by Robert Scheer, "The Genesis of United States Support for Ngo Dinh Diem," *Vietnam: History, Documents, and Opinions*, ed. Marvin E. Gettleman (New York: Fawcett, 1965), 243–44.

8. Malcolm Browne cited in Harrison, *The Endless War*, 215.

9. Buttinger, *Vietnam*, 443.

10. Harrison, *The Endless War*, 214.

11. On this point, see Edwin E. Moise, *Land Reform in China and North Vietnam: Consolidating the Revolution at the Village Level* (Chapel Hill: University of North Carolina Press, 1983), 219–22.

12. "The Path of Revolution in the South," November 1956, in Porter and Emerson, eds., *Vietnam*, 187–91.

13. Jeffrey Race, *War Comes to Long An: Revolutionary Conflict in a Vietnamese Province* (Berkeley and Los Angeles: University of Carolina Press, 1972), 110–11.

14. Communist Party Directive, January 1959, cited in Kahin, *Intervention*, 110.

15. Declaration of Former Resistance Fighters, March 1960, in George McT. Kahin and John W. Lewis, *The United States in Vietnam*, rev. ed. (New York: Delta, 1967), 458–61.

16. Le Duan speech cited in Kahin, *Intervention*, 113–14.

17. Resolution of the Third National Congress of the Vietnam Worker's Party cited in Kahin, *Intervention*, 114–15.

18. Martin E. Goldstein, *American Policy toward Laos* (Rutherford, N.J.: Farleigh Dickinson University Press, 1973), 199.

19. Ibid.

20. Eisenhower and Thomas Gates cited in Kahin, *Intervention*, 127.

21. For the text of the Kennedy inaugural address and the writing of the speech, see Theodore Sorensen, *Kennedy* (New York: Harper & Row, 1965), 240–48.

22. David Halberstam, *The Best and the Brightest* (New York: Random House, 1972), 153.

23. As a reflection of this enlarged role, the Military Assistance Advisory Group was replaced by the Military Assistance Command, Vietnam.

24. Kahin, *Intervention*, 140.

25. Roger Hilsman, *To Move a Nation* (New York: Dell, 1967), 442.

26. David Halberstam, *The Making of a Quagmire* (New York: Random House, 1965), 188.

27. Unidentified reporter cited in Bernard B. Fall, *The Two Viet-Nams: A Political and Military Analysis*, rev. ed. (New York: Praeger, 1963), 378.

28. William S. Turley, *The Second Indochina War: A Short Political and Military History, 1954–1975* (Boulder, Colo.: Westview, 1986), 48.

29. Karnow, *Vietnam*, 281.

30. William Bundy cited in Kahin, *Intervention*, 183.

31. George Ball to Saigon Embassy, 23 December 1963, cited in ibid., 193.

32. Karnow, *Vietnam*, 369.
33. *Department of State Bulletin* 61, 24 August 1964.
34. Karnow, *Vietnam*, 374.
35. *Department of State Bulletin* 61, 24 August 1964.
36. Karnow, *Vietnam*, 374.

I was protecting no Sattn

chapter 5

TO TET: THE U.S.–NORTH VIETNAMESE WAR, 1965–1968

In 1965 the United States and North Vietnam went to war. It was a war that neither side may have sought, but it was a war each was prepared to fight in order to achieve its objective.

At the heart of the conflict was the political status of South Vietnam. Both North Vietnam and the United States charged that the other was guilty of "aggression" in the South. In its public defense of U.S. policy, *Aggression from the North: The Record of North Vietnam's Campaign to Conquer South Vietnam*, the State Department in 1965 argued that South Vietnam was "fighting for its life against a brutal campaign of terror and armed attack inspired, directed, supplied, and controlled by the communist regime in Hanoi." That "flagrant aggression" meant that a "Communist government has set out deliberately to conquer a sovereign people in a neighboring state."[1] To the North Vietnamese, American bases and troops amounted to "intervention and aggression" in violation of the Geneva Agreements, thus denying the "peaceful reunification of Vietnam." While the United States persisted in calling South Vietnam an independent nation, the North Vietnamese, referring to the language of the Geneva Agreements, described a country "temporarily divided into the two zones." Just as the United States called upon North Vietnam to abandon its "aggression," so too the Hanoi government said the peace depended upon the Americans ending their "intervention and aggression in South Vietnam."[2]

DECISIONS FOR WAR

As it observed the political turmoil in the South, the leadership in Hanoi calculated in late 1964 that by increasing support for the Viet Cong and by sending North Vietnamese forces into the South, it could bring about

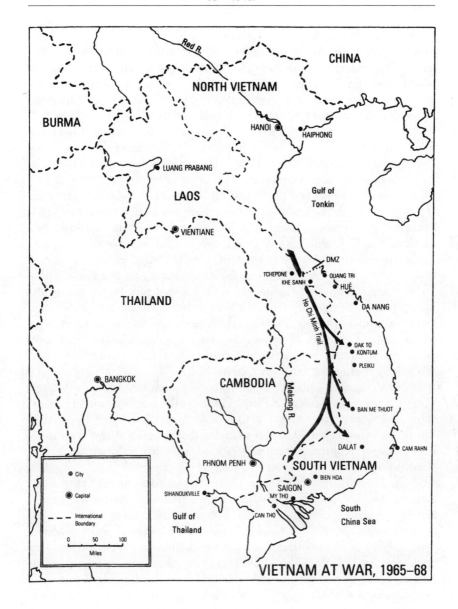

CHINA

NORTH VIETNAM

BURMA

Red R.

HANOI
HAIPHONG

LUANG PRABANG

LAOS

Gulf of
Tonkin

VIENTIANE

THAILAND

TCHEPONE
KHE SANH
DMZ
QUANG TRI
HUÉ
DA NANG

Ho Chi Minh Trail

DAK TO
KONTUM
PLEIKU

BANGKOK

CAMBODIA

Mekong R.

BAN ME THUOT

DALAT
CAM RAHN

SOUTH VIETNAM

PHNOM PENH

BIEN HOA

SAIGON
MY THO

SIHANOUKVILLE

CAN THO

South
China Sea

Gulf of
Thailand

● City

◉ Capital

- - - International
Boundary

0   50   100
Miles

VIETNAM AT WAR, 1965–68

the early collapse of the Saigon government. The first regular unit, which began its trek to the South in October 1964, reached its destination in the central highlands two months later. Although they were concerned about the possibility of American intervention, the North Vietnamese interpreted several events in late 1964 as suggestive that the United States would limit its support of South Vietnam. After the retaliation for the Gulf of Tonkin "attacks," the United States had not reacted with force in the face of several other incidents and impressive Viet Cong victories. On 1 November the Viet Cong attacked the U.S. air base at Bien Hoa; four Americans were killed. There was no U.S. reaction. Later that month Viet Cong units initiated their largest offensive of the conflict and gained control of the heavily populated province of Binh Dinh on the central coast. Again, there was no U.S. reaction. On 24 December in downtown Saigon, the Viet Cong bombed the Brinks Hotel, which housed U.S. officers; 2 Americans were killed and 38 were wounded. Again, there was no American reaction. On 28 December the Viet Cong launched for the first time a division-size attack, hitting an area just 40 miles east of Saigon and overwhelming the South Vietnamese forces. Once again, there was no U.S. reaction. From the perspective of Hanoi, it appeared that President Lyndon Johnson indeed was the "peace candidate" as he had repeatedly portrayed himself in his successful election campaign. Johnson had been forthright, promising that he would not send "American boys to fight a war that I think ought to be fought by the boys of Asia."[3]

North Vietnamese calculations, however, were shattered when the United States reacted to an incident at Pleiku in the central highlands on 6 February 1965. The Viet Cong overran a U.S. airfield and helicopter base. Nine Americans were killed and 130 were wounded; destruction of aircraft was extensive. President Johnson immediately ordered a retaliatory air strike against North Vietnam. Unlike the bombing raids in response to the Gulf of Tonkin incident, this time the retaliation was but a prelude to a sustained program of bombing North Vietnam—Operation Rolling Thunder. As the large-scale bombing became operational, General Westmoreland requested that combat troops be sent to protect U.S. bases. Johnson quickly approved, and on 8 March two batallions of Marines landed at Da Nang. Within days Westmoreland was pressing for more troops, who would engage in offensive military operations. Johnson again approved; on 21 April he authorized the dispatch of a ground-combat force of 40,000 troops. Thus the Pleiku incident marked the beginning of a momentous 10-week period when the United States, through a series of decisions, went to war in Vietnam.

This commitment of American power resulted from the conviction of Johnson and his principal civilian and military advisers that it was the only means to prevent the collapse of the South Vietnamese government. This was a reversal in U.S. policy, for the very weakness of the Saigon regime had earlier been a major reason for avoiding a military commitment. "The major argument against escalation," the historian George Herring wrote, "had become the most compelling argument for it."[4] Changes in the leadership of the military junta in Saigon had failed to end the political crisis. General Khanh, whom American officials had championed, proved no more effective than his predecessors as he imprisoned political opponents and resisted U.S. pressures to relinquish authority to civilian leaders. Moreover, the chronic instability took on increasingly anti-American overtones; rioters destroyed the United States Information Services library in Hué. As militant Buddhists and others called for an end to American intervention in their country's affairs, Americans feared that the South Vietnamese would negotiate with the NLF. Even General Khanh became critical of American interference and made certain conciliatory gestures toward the NLF. The decay of South Vietnam was also evident in the dispirited performance of South Vietnamese troops in battles against the Viet Cong.

Confronting these overwhelming political and military problems, American policymakers decided that South Vietnam had to be held. McGeorge Bundy, Johnson's national security adviser who was in Vietnam at the time of the Pleiku incident, wrote immediately to the president: "Without new U.S. action defeat seems inevitable—probably within the next year or so. There is still time to turn it around, but not much. The stakes in Vietnam are extremely high."[5] The concern was not with the "loss" of Vietnam per se but with the implications of that outcome. The Johnson administration, like its predecessors, accepted a worst-case scenario: that unification of Vietnam under Communist leadership would result in the extension of Communist influence throughout Southeast Asia. That assumption was reinforced by the widely held perception that a militant China would exploit wars of national liberation throughout Asia. Secretary of State Dean Rusk maintained that China's ideology produced "appetitites and ambitions that grow upon feeding."[6] Another high-ranking official wrote in November 1964, "Communist China shares the same internal necessity for ideological expansion today that the Soviet Union did . . . following the Second World War. . . . Our objective should be to 'contain' China for the longest possible period . . . and at the same time strengthen the political and economic structure of the bordering countries."[7] To Rusk and to General Earle Wheeler, chairman of the Joint Chiefs of Staff, American failure in Vietnam would "lose all of Southeast Asia."[8] Hence American policymakers believed that direct military intervention was necessary not only to restrain the Viet Cong and North Vietnam and to bolster South Vietnam but also to prevent Chinese absorption of Southeast Asia.

Underlying this determination to hold the line in Vietnam was the sense of mission that had long characterized the American approach to the world. National creed and history seemed to teach that Americans had a special role to play in fostering democratic institutions and in retarding totalitarian powers. American power, it seemed, was used only for such noble purposes. Having seen themselves in the previous two decades as the guardians of democracy in Greece, Berlin, Korea, and elsewhere, Americans in 1965 saw the burdens of world leadership thrusting a new challenge. In his novel A Rumor of War Philip

Caputo, who was among the first marines sent to Vietnam, reflected, "America seemed omnipotent then: the country could still claim it had never lost a war, and we believed we were ordained to play cop to the Communists' robber and spread our own political faith around the world. . . . We saw ourselves as the champions of a 'cause that was destined to triumph.' "[9]

Optimism, as Caputo's reflections underscore, blended with a sense of superiority, bordering on omnipotence. There was perhaps an underlying racism evident in an approach to Vietnam that assumed that Americans, not Vietnamese, knew what was best for the country and that the Vietnamese would respond to American blandishments or pressures. South Vietnam, of course, owed its survival to the United States. Not only had the Saigon government depended upon American aid for 10 years, but also in 1965 the United States took the position that if the South Vietnamese lacked the resolve to fight themselves and preferred to negotiate with the Communists, it would intervene to save the South Vietnamese from themselves. Besides its paternalistic approach to the South, U.S. policy also assumed that North Vietnam, as an essentially weak and backward nation, would quickly succumb to American pressures. President Johnson privately referred to the enemy as "that little piss-ant country."

Reflecting on the thinking that led the United States to intervene in 1965, one is struck by its casual assumption that Vietnam was another cold war "problem"—like post–World War II Europe—that could be "managed." In that case, the containment policy had been built on strong nationalistic lines, the cultural and economic ties between Western Europe and the United States, and a common perception of the challenge. Those ingredients were lacking in Vietnam. U.S. policy implicitly denied Vietnamese history. Had that history been studied, Americans might have acknowledged the centuries-old Vietnamese resistance to foreign control and manipulation. The Americans were following in the footsteps of the Chinese, French, and others, all of whom had been forced from the country. Had that history been studied, Americans might have realized that the Vietnamese antagonism toward China made it unlikely that they would seek collaboration with their larger neighbor, much less advance its interests in Southeast Asia. Had that history been studied, Americans might have realized the unique circumstances that had enabled the Vietnamese Communist movement to seize the nationalist initiative. It had led resistance to the Japanese, had proclaimed national independence in 1945, and had fought a successful war against the French. That history rendered North Vietnam and the Viet Cong an adversary with much nationalist "legitimacy" and underscored the inherent limitations of the American effort at "nation building" in the South.

OBJECTIVES AND STRATEGIES: WASHINGTON AND HANOI

Since its basic objective was to assure the survival of an independent, noncommunist South Vietnam, the United States sought to use its vast military power to coerce North Vietnam into abandoning support of the insurrection in the South. President Johnson believed that progressively greater use of force would eventually bring North Vietnam to its "threshold of pain"—the point when the material and physical losses became intolerable. U.S. military actions were to probe for that point but were not to go beyond it. "We will do everything necessary to reach that objective [the North's acceptance of a divided country]," Johnson stated publicly in 1965, "and we will do only what is absolutely necessary."[10] Privately, he described his strategy more graphically: "I'm going up old Ho Chi Minh's leg one inch at a time." To Johnson, this strategy had several advantages: it conveyed U.S. determination to Hanoi; it assured him of maximum flexibility; and it also signaled the Soviet Union and China that American power was being used with restraint, thus reducing the prospects of their intervention. This strategy of gradual escalation, however, annoyed many U.S. military officials; Lt. Gen. Phillip Davidson, who served in Vietnam, writes in his history of the war that gradualism "signaled Hanoi . . . [and] forced the United States into a lengthy, indecisive war of attrition—the very kind which best suited Ho and Giap."[11]

Although many analysts predicted that the objectives would not be easily achieved, Americans anticipated that the North Vietnamese could rather quickly be brought to the negotiating table. Men of the first combat unit felt that way. Philip Caputo recalled, "When we marched into the rice paddies on that March afternoon, we carried, along with our packs and rifles, the implicit convictions that the Vietcong would be quickly beaten and that we were doing something altogether noble and good."[12] President Johnson and other officials believed that once America's enormous military potential was brought to bear, the North Vietnamese would yield.

Accordingly, the United States kept applying more pressure on the ground and in the air. U.S. manpower in Vietnam steadily increased. At the time the first combat unit of 3,500 men arrived in the spring of 1965, they joined some 20,000 military advisers in the country. From that modest beginning, escalation followed quickly. By the end of 1965, 180,000 military personnel had been sent to Vietnam; by mid-1966 the number stood at 350,000. Eventually the troop level exceeded 500,000. In the process, the conflict was thoroughly "Americanized" as the United States took over the brunt of the fighting on the ground and unleashed its air power.

Concentrating its resources on a military solution, the United States gave relatively little attention to the political side of the war. The enormous problem of "pacification," that is, securing the loyalty of the rural population to the Saigon government, was obviously vital to U.S. objectives. Despite much rhetoric about "winning the hearts and minds" of the people and although many U.S. officials urged increased concern with pacification, it was not given priority. General Westmoreland and others assumed that after the military operations succeeded, there would be time to focus on such objectives. U.S. officers cynically observed, "Grab 'em by the balls, and their hearts and minds will follow."[13]

Faced with the Americanization of the war, North Vietnam's only effective response was a strategy of protracted war. The Hanoi leadership believed that the United States would be especially vulnerable if forced into such a conflict. "Americans do not like long, inconclusive wars," Premier Pham Van Dong stated, "thus we are sure to win in the end."[14] The only way to defeat the world's most powerful nation, the North Vietnamese leaders concluded, was to outlast it. This was the kind of conflict about which Ho Chi Minh had prophetically warned the French in 1946: "If we have to fight, we will fight. You will kill ten of our men and we will kill one of yours. In the end it will be you who will tire of it."[15]

The North Vietnamese government thus prepared its civilian population and soldiers for a long conflict. Priority had to be given to continuing the struggle in the South, which meant that as more American troops arrived, more men and supplies had to be infiltrated. Toward that end, the North had to preserve its food supply, industry, and transportation system in the face of the systematic American bombing. As that bombing began in 1965, North Vietnamese leaders warned the people that they should be prepared for the total destruction of their country. The soldiers sent to the South were reminded that the war would last many years. Officials told them that "if our generation cannot finish this war, our children and our grandchildren will continue it."[16]

Protracted conflict meant more, however, than just outlasting the Americans. It had two important political requirements: to sustain the support of the rural population in the areas of the South where the Communists had always been strong and to extend their following in other areas. The Viet Cong and North Vietnamese forces, if they were to fight successfully, needed the protection of the Southern peasantry. "This military core, on which the success of the struggle depends," a Communist writer noted during the war, "can be preserved only when it is under constant protection by the popular masses. The latter feed the cadres, hide them in their houses, protect them."[17] Thus while American strategy tended to postpone political activity in the countryside, the North Vietnamese strategy from the beginning stressed the importance of the link between the peasantry and the insurgency.

ROLLING THUNDER: THE AIR WAR AGAINST NORTH VIETNAM

Operation Rolling Thunder, which began in March 1965, had three objectives: (1) strategic—to destroy North Vietnam's war-making capacity and disrupt its communications lines with the South, (2) coercive—to intimidate the leadership of North Vietnam, and (3) political—to reassure the South Vietnamese of American resolve and thus boost the morale of their troops. In line with Johnson's determination that American power be applied gradually, the air war moved through a series of steps of progressively greater bombing.

The first phase of Rolling Thunder, concentrated bombing of the North Vietnamese infiltration routes into the South, continued throughout the subsequent parts of the campaign when other targets were added to the bombing missions. In 1966 U.S. aircraft attacked North Vietnam's petroleum storage facilities, resulting in the destruction of about 70 percent of those facilities. In 1967 the air war intensified as the Rolling Thunder campaign was directed against electrical production plants, the country's only steel plant, its major cement plant, virtually all factories, and targets close to the Chinese border. By the end of that year virtually all military and industrial targets in the North had been destroyed or damaged. As the bombing campaign reached its peak in 1967, the army chief of staff, General Harold K. Johnson, likened the bombing to the "repetitive strokes of a jackhammer. . . . At some point the concrete begins to break up, and . . . [it is] this continuing and unrelenting pressure that will eventually bring us to a conclusion."[18]

The American air war against the North constituted the most intensive campaign of strategic bombing in history. This aerial assault grew from 25,000 sorties in 1965 to 79,000 in 1966 and to 108,000 in 1967. The damage was extensive. According to U.S. estimates, the value of all the facilities destroyed by late 1967 was $340 million. North Vietnamese officials reported that over 300 factories had been destroyed, some having been bombed 80 times. Repeated attacks on the transportation facilities left the country, in the words of a British reporter, "littered with broken bridges and pulverized roads."[19]

Yet for all its destructiveness, Rolling Thunder failed to achieve its strategic and coercive objectives. North Vietnam's war-making capacity survived, and its support of the war in the South actually increased. The leadership in Hanoi was not intimidated. The reasons for the shortcomings of Rolling Thunder reflected inherent limitations of strategic bombing and North Vietnam's capacity to withstand the aerial onslaught.

The concept of strategic bombing was intended for application against highly industrialized societies with large armies requiring massive quantities of weapons and supplies. North Vietnam, however, was an agricultural country with virtually no industry and a primitive transportation system. Its army was relatively small and its needs minimal. The very backwardness of the transportation system facilitated resistance to bombing and repair of damage. Likewise, the limited industry was not vital to the economy or the pursuit of the war in the South. For example, the air attacks by 1967 had virtually eliminated the country's electrical generating capacity, but all of its electrical requirements were less than half those of an American city the size of Cleveland, Ohio. And what electricity was needed for the war effort could be supplied by switching to diesel-driven generators.

Moreover, the North Vietnamese proved remarkably resilient in responding to the damage and in defending their country. To keep its transportation functioning, thousands of people were recruited to repair roads, railroads, and bridges. By 1967, 97,000 people worked full time at this job, and perhaps as many as 500,000 others devoted several days' work each month to transportation repair. The principal repair group was the "Youth Shock Brigade against the Americans for National Salvation." It enlisted young men and women aged 15 to 30, but since most males were in the army, about 60 percent of the Youth Shock Brigade was female. They were paid $1.50 a month but were provided with food, clothing, and housing and were promised attractive jobs after the war. The Youth Shock Brigade worked in small groups throughout the country repairing and rebuilding the targets of American bombing.

These repair crews were almost constantly at work. Along the country's roads one could find piles of tools and cement every mile or two ready for use after the next attack. After the bombing, the crews quickly cleared the rubble, while a couple of its members searched for and defused delayed-action bombs, which the Americans dropped in order to deter repairs.

The maintenance of bridges was especially challenging, since bridges were critical to the movement of supplies and were easy targets for bombers. Destroyed bridges were typically replaced by pontoon bridges constructed of thick bundles of bamboo sticks tied together to form a base for wooden boards. Supplies could then be moved across these floating bridges. For protection during attacks they would be cut loose from one side of the river and covered with branches.

The repair of railroads was more difficult, but because the rail link to China was vital, the North Vietnamese were determined to keep open the lines to the China border. Some 1,000 tons of supplies came by rail daily from China (about one-third of all the country's external aid), and the Hanoi leadership accepted China's offer to provide repair crews. (Keeping open the railroad across North Vietnam was important to China since it was also an important rail connection between southwest and southeast China.)

Besides the massive repair effort, the North Vietnamese also responded to the aerial assault by making greater use of their extensive inland waterway system to transport supplies. Once the United States discovered that more goods were being shipped by boats, the air force began hitting barges and dropping mines into the rivers. The North Vietnamese in turn undertook extensive surveillance of their rivers; spotters warned boats of mines and, when possible, disassembled them.

The movement of supplies southward was treacherous. Trucks, railroad cars, and bicycles were camouflaged. Most travel took place at night; in heavily bombed areas, truck drivers extinguished their lights and were guided along the narrow, bumpy roads by white road posts installed by the Youth Shock Brigades. Bicycles were also vital. A single bicyclist could transport about 150 pounds of supplies over 25 miles per night. It was generally more efficient to put a bamboo frame over the bicycle and push it; that way 600 pounds could be moved but at less than 10 miles a night. The versatility of bicycles made them very useful when other means of transportation were interrupted. When truck or train traffic was stalled while bridges were being repaired, bicycles were loaded with goods and carried or pulled across the river to deliver sup-plies to transportation waiting on the other side.

Besides its determined effort to overcome the devastation of American bombing, North Vietnam also undertook an increasingly active and effective aerial defense. The Soviet Union supplied MiG fighters, antiaircraft guns, and surface-to-air missiles. Although U.S. aircraft generally won dogfights with the small North Vietnamese air force, the occasional MiG attacks challenged the United States' control of the air. Surface-to-air missiles, which at first were of little effectiveness because they were manned by inexperienced sol-diers, increased to some 200 by 1967 and became more deadly. Antiaircraft guns were the principal means of defense; by the end of 1965, some 1,500 guns were in place, and two years later the number had increased to 8,000. By that time they were firing 25,000 tons of ammunition per month at American planes. They seemed to be everywhere; Hanoi, a journalist wrote, resembled "an armed porcupine, with hundreds, probably thousands, of spinny, steel guns sticking out beyond the tops of trees."[20] American pilots thus encountered a very sophisticated defense. One officer stated that the bombing missions against North Vietnam had become the most dangerous ever flown. Another recalled that "ninety-nine per cent of the time as I dropped bombs, somebody was shooting at me." By the end of 1967 more than 700 U.S. aircraft had been shot down. Not only did the flak result in the downing of more and more U.S. aircraft but also it forced others off course, and bombing became less accurate.

The North Vietnamese government also took extensive measures to pro-tect its most important resource, its people. Large numbers of persons were evacuated from the cities. Shelters, totaling some 21 million by 1968, were constructed in Hanoi and Haiphong; single-person shelters dotted all the streets, at intervals of 10 to 30 feet. Deep trenches were built along roads so that persons could quickly take cover in the event of an attack. In the rural areas, peasants constructed tunnels from the villages to their fields so that they could quickly disappear when the bombers appeared. In the heavily bombed area just north of the DMZ, an especially elaborate system of tunnels enabled people to spend most of their time underground. Finally, a civil defense sys-tem—the Home Guard—sprang into action after bombing raids, rescuing per-sons trapped under rubble, administering first aid, and rushing seriously injured persons to hospitals.

The North Vietnamese, while suffering serious problems from the air assault, were able not only to continue but actually to expand their war effort. The infiltration of soldiers moved steadily southward. Some 35,000 troops went to the South in 1965; two years later, despite the intensive U.S. bomb-ing, the number increased to 90,000. Losses to bombing hurt, but did not cripple, the supplying of the South. For instance, in 1967 bombing destroyed supplies, industry, and equipment valued at $139 million, yet the North Vietnamese were still able to move some $98 million worth of supplies south-ward. Losses were offset by increased assistance from Communist allies. By

1967 military and economic aid amounted to more than $1.03 billion. Overland supplies from China and shipments by sea from the Soviet Union and Eastern European countries kept the war material moving to the South and compensated for food and other shortages in the North.

Rolling Thunder also failed to break the determination of North Vietnam. Ever since the beginning of the insurrection in the South, the Communist leadership in Hanoi had been divided between those who favored concentrating on the development of the North (and relying on political struggle to achieve control of the South) and those, pressed by southern leaders, who favored armed revolt in the South and strong northern support of the insurgency. By the time that the United States launched its bombing campaign, Le Duan and other advocates of a major North Vietnamese commitment to support of the war in the South had gained government support for increased infiltration of men and supplies. That commitment had not been easily attained, for other leaders, notably General Vo Nguyen Giap and Truong Chinh, believed that priority should be given to the political struggle and that Southern insurgents should make greater efforts on their own behalf. Yet having begun support of the South, it was difficult for President Ho Chi Minh, Premier Pham Van Dong, and other leaders to alter policy. To yield to American pressure would have threatened the unity of the Communist party in the North and would have precipitated massive Southern disaffection. The Viet Cong believed that the Southerners had been abandoned at the Geneva Conference in 1954 and recalled the slowness with which the North had supported their insurgency. As a result, the North repeatedly assured Southern leaders that it would never abandon them, regardless of the American pressure.

Besides the failure of the air war in terms of its strategic and coercive objectives, it was also costly to the United States financially and morally. In strictly fiscal terms, the "costs" of the air war were more burdensome to the United States than to North Vietnam. By the end of 1967 the United States, as noted, had inflicted damage estimated at $300 million. Yet just the cost of the aircraft lost in combat over North Vietnam to that time amounted to $900 million. The direct cost of the air war—including aircraft operation, munitions (a single B-52 sortie cost $30,000 in bombs), and replacement of losses—totaled $1.7 billion in 1965 and 1966. In terms of cost effectiveness, the bill was staggering: it cost the United States $9.60 for every dollar of bombing damage.

Finally, the air war was costly to the United States in moral terms. The spectacle of the world's most powerful country bombing a backward country troubled many people throughout the world as well as increasing numbers of Americans, including some members of the Johnson administration. Initially, the United States had defended Rolling Thunder on the grounds that it was waged with "surgical precision" against only military targets. North Vietnamese authorities challenged such claims and invited journalists and others to visit their country in order to observe the realities of the bombing. Among those who went to Hanoi was the influential *New York Times* correspondent Harrison Salisbury; his widely read and influential reports from North Vietnam in December 1966 flatly contradicted the "surgical precision" defense and underscored the widespread casualties and extensive damage to civilian property. Secretary of Defense Robert McNamara conceded privately in 1967 his disgust over a bombing campaign that was killing perhaps as many as 1,000 civilians a week.

THE WAR IN THE SOUTH

The struggle for control of the South was a "war without fronts." Unlike conventional wars, in which advancing along fronts is the measure of success, the Vietnam war was fragmented. Countless small actions took place daily in battlefields throughout the country; there were few large battles. While fighting occurred everywhere, the heaviest concentration was in areas where the Communists historically had their greatest strength, that is, in the seven northernmost provinces and in small areas to the west and south of Saigon.

In this confusing situation, the United States steadily brought its air and ground power to force the Viet Cong and North Vietnam troops to abandon their warfare. In 1965 General Westmoreland envisioned a three-year campaign that would culminate in the destruction of the insurgent forces by the end of 1967. The key was integrating two of the United States' greatest strengths—firepower and mobility—through search-and-destroy operations. General Earle Wheeler, chairman of the Joint Chiefs of Staff, saw that such warfare "will enable us to find the enemy more often, fix him more firmly when we find him, and defeat him when we fight him. . . . Our objective will be to keep the combat tempo at such a rate that the Viet Cong will be unable to take the time to recuperate or regain their balance."[21] The measure of success, in this type of warfare, was attrition. Early in the war Westmoreland stated the objective: "Attrit by year's end, Viet Cong and North Vietnamese forces at a rate as high as their capability to put men into the field."[22] This objective as translated to combat troops was blunt: "Find the bastards and pile on." Hence the body count became the instrument for determining "progress": if a large enough number of the enemy was killed, sooner or later their losses could not be replaced and the war would be won.

Toward that end American troops, equipment, and technology took over the war. Americanization was evident everywhere: a network of "firebases" with artillery to protect infantry patrols that were sent out to engage the Viet Cong. Whenever the enemy was discovered, additional forces could be brought in by helicopter and the air force could be called upon to pound enemy positions. When asked what was the answer to insurgency, Westmoreland answered with one word: "firepower." This "pile-on" tactic thus sought to bring massive firepower quickly so that heavy losses could be inflicted. General William Depuy, one of the chief proponents of the search-and-destroy strategy, described the war as follows: "If you wanted to analyze what happened in Vietnam you'd say the infantry found the enemy and the artillery and the air killed the enemy."[23] To find the elusive enemy, advanced technology was employed: portable radar, "people sniffers" that detected the odor of human urine, and other devices were used for tracking. To deprive the Viet Cong of their cover, the air force sprayed herbicides. Over 100 million pounds of chemicals, most notably Agent Orange, covered forests, resulting in the destruction of about one-half of South Vietnam's timberlands.

Much of the war was waged from the air. Indeed, the air war in the South was more extensive and more devastating than that waged against the North. Between 1965 and 1967 the U.S. and South Vietnamese air forces dropped over one million tons of bombs in the South, more than twice the amount dropped on the North. The bombing was directed against Viet Cong–North Vietnamese strongholds, supply routes, and villages that protected and supported them.

During the early months of involvement, U.S. troops secured the area around Da Nang and along the Demilitarized Zone. In the midst of numerous small clashes, one major battle—in the Ia Drang Valley of the central highland in November 1965—seemed to confirm the potential for the search-and-destroy strategy. In pursuit of the Communist forces that had been attacking U.S. bases in the area, a U.S. airborne division engaged a large North Vietnamese unit. Supported by fighter-bombers and B-52s, the American forces inflicted heavy casualties; the North Vietnamese broke off the engagement. The body count estimated two thousand enemy dead; three hundred Americans had been killed. The Ia Drang campaign gave evidence of the effectiveness of using helicopters to rush men into combat and of unleashing massive air power to support ground forces. It clearly indicated the American ability to overwhelm enemy units in open combat. To Westmoreland and the Joint Chiefs of Staff, forcing the North Vietnamese and Viet Cong into such battles was the road to victory.

By late 1966 General Westmoreland decided that U.S.–South Vietnamese forces had attained such numerical superiority (over 1,000,000 troops, including 350,000 Americans, to about 260,000 North Vietnamese–Viet Cong) that by exploiting their firepower and mobility they could seize the military initiative in major offensive operations. His targets were base areas from which the Viet Cong and North Vietnamese launched their warfare. These bases, located in remote regions protected by mountains and jungle, included supply depots, hospitals, training centers, and even rudimentary manufacturing plants. In the base areas, troops were assembled and equipped for guerrilla operations. In preparation for an attack, cadres would carry supplies and hide them near the projected target. Since these base areas were vital to Viet Cong–North Vietnamese operations, U.S. strategists assumed that the enemy would fight to hold them, thus giving American and South Vietnamese forces the opportunity to inflict heavy casualties. "The criticality of the base areas to the enemy," a retired general has written, "would 'fix' him, and United States firepower would 'finish' him."[24] Hence attacks on base areas offered two distinct advantages: the elimination of essential support for offensive operations and the opportunity to inflict heavy casualties.

The principal targets were the Iron Triangle, a Communist base area about 20 to 30 miles northeast of Saigon, and another staging area in War Zone C to the northwest of Saigon near the Cambodian border. In Operation Attleboro, which lasted 72 days in the fall of 1966, 22,000 U.S.–South Vietnamese troops, supported by air strikes and 12,000 tons of bombs, struck a major base area. They killed a large number of enemy troops (1,100) and captured stocks of food, weapons, and supplies. While U.S. commanders proclaimed Attleboro a victory particularly in terms of the 15-to-1 kill ratio achieved, North Vietnamese commanders noted that while their forces had been "depleted," they were not "exterminated" and had not been denied the use of that area. A principal reason that Communist forces withstood the assault was their capacity to control the fighting; as one of the American commanders explained it, "They meted out their casualties and when the casualties were getting too high . . . they just backed off and waited. . . . They were the ones who decided whether there would be a fight."[25] Having survived Attleboro, the Viet Cong quickly resumed control of the region.

Buoyed by the "success" of Attleboro, Westmoreland undertook a still larger operation, Cedar Falls, in January 1967. The objective was to "eliminate the Iron Triangle as a communist base" by obliterating an area of 60 square miles. Some 30,000 U.S. troops were committed to this operation, which began with extensive bombing of the region. Special combat troops were dropped into the villages. Seven thousand people were evacuated from the area. Aircraft and artillery then resumed bombardment before huge bulldozers leveled the dense jungle and villages. Finally, army engineers planted and detonated 10,000 pounds of explosives into the Viet Cong's elaborate tunnel system.

Cedar Falls, which lasted 19 days, was by U.S. criteria a "victory." Seven hundred "enemy" were killed and considerable quantities of supplies captured. The commanding U.S. general proclaimed that Cedar Falls was a "turning point . . . and a blow from which the VC in this area may never recover."[26] Closer examination, however, suggests it failed to accomplish its objective. Communist forces mostly escaped from the area as the operation began. The civilian population, having seen their villages destroyed and having been forced into crowded camps, was left embittered.

Barely had Cedar Falls ended before another large assault, Operation Junction City, sent U.S.–South Vietnamese units back into War Zone C. This two-month operation, which began in late February 1967, again involved massive use of firepower (3,200 tons of bombs and 366,000 rounds of artillery) in support of American–South Vietnamese units. Again, the body count suggested a victory (some 1,800 Viet Cong killed) as did the capture of large amounts of ammunition and food. Yet as in the earlier operations, Junction City failed to secure the area, let alone render the enemy ineffective. "It was a sheer physical impossibility," one American general lamented, "to keep the enemy from slipping away whenever he wished."[27]

All three of these operations demonstrated the potential as well as the limits of search-and-destroy. Massive firepower and assaults enabled the U.S. and South Vietnamese forces to inflict heavy casualties and to capture supplies, but they could not annihilate the enemy. And lacking sufficient troops to occupy the areas permanently, the United States and South Vietnamese left once the operations were proclaimed "victories," assuring the return of Communist control and resumption of the base areas.

These large operations notwithstanding, the conflict remained basically one of small-unit warfare. In those engagements, Communist forces generally held the initiative, determining when and where to attack and to defend against search-and-destroy. The Viet Cong or North Vietnamese initiated nearly 90 percent of the countless battles that were waged throughout the South.

By the end of 1967, after nearly three years of progressively greater involvement in Vietnam and with a troop commitment of nearly 500,000, the United States had failed to achieve its objective of inflicting such heavy casualties that the Viet Cong and North Vietnamese would be forced to abandon their warfare. Westmoreland's attrition strategy overestimated the U.S. capacity to force the enemy into large-scale combat and underestimated the North Vietnamese–Viet Cong capacity to withstand American firepower and technology. Despite substantial losses, the Viet Cong and North Vietnamese not only survived but, in fact, increased in strength. The body count, of course, seemed to provide evidence of winning. Estimates of enemy dead were notoriously inflated, since officers were under pressure to demonstrate success. Yet even allowing for the unreliability of casualty reports, the war of attrition, as defined by Westmoreland, was being won. The kill ratio suggested success: according to the most reliable estimates, about 179,000 North Vietnamese–Viet Cong were killed in combat between 1965 and 1967, more than three times the 53,000 U.S.–South Vietnamese losses. Yet the Viet Cong and North Vietnamese force levels in the South actually increased during that period by perhaps as many as 42,000. This resulted from the Viet Cong's continued success in recruitment, the capacity to control the fighting, and the North's ability to infiltrate more troops to the South. Every year, about 200,000 young men in North Vietnam reached draft age, which provided the basic manpower resource for matching American escalation. In sum, all of American firepower could not "attrit" the enemy at a rate exceeding replacement.

The search-and-destroy strategy had other shortcomings. By placing such emphasis on killing the enemy, the army ignored the importance of gaining control over an area. "While the army killed many VC," one analyst has con-

cluded, "it never denied the enemy his source of strength—access to the people."[28] Time and again, U.S. forces found themselves fighting the same Viet
Cong or North Vietnamese units in the same areas where they had "destroyed"
them earlier. This underscored the chronic unwillingness to devote sufficient
resources to pacification.

Moreover, search-and-destroy actually served the interests of the Communists' strategy of protracted warfare. North Vietnamese and Viet Cong
units were deliberately concentrated in remote areas to draw American forces
away from the more populated coastal areas. By luring Americans into the
mountainous areas close to the Cambodian and Laotian borders, the North
Vietnamese were achieving a central objective of forcing Americans into
inconclusive battles that, the Hanoi leadership calculated, would gradually
reduce U.S. willingness to fight.

SOUTH VIETNAM: THE PRICE OF STABILITY

Although Operation Rolling Thunder and the search-and-destroy
strategies failed to force the North Vietnamese and Viet Cong to abandon
their warfare, the American intervention was instrumental in the survival of
the South Vietnamese government. The revolving door of South Vietnamese
leaders ended in 1965 when Air Vice Marshall Nguyen Cao Ky and General
Nguyen Van Thieu seized power; Ky became prime minister, and Thieu
became commander in chief of the armed forces. At first, few expected the
new leaders to last longer than their several predecessors, but Ky and Thieu
managed to hold the backing of the generals. Ky and Thieu also took a strong
anticommunist stance and, unlike some of their predecessors following Diem's
overthrow and unlike much of the Buddhist leadership, they disavowed any
suggestion of negotiation with the North. Impressed by these developments
and determined to bring political stability to the South, the United States
strongly supported Ky and Thieu.

The American commitment to the Ky-Thieu regime was dramatized in
early 1996 when President Johnson summoned Prime Minister Ky to meet
him in Honolulu. Johnson took the occasion to exhort Ky and other South
Vietnamese officials to win the war ("nail the coonskins on the wall" as he put
it) and to pursue reform. Ky promised a "social revolution" that would improve
the lives of all South Vietnamese. When Ky finished, an elated Johnson told
him, "Boy, you speak just like an American."[29]

Despite the promises of reform, Ky-Thieu government's policies resembled
those of the Diem regime. But whereas the United States had eventually disavowed Diem's repressive measures, it stood by the new leadership. The
change in the American approach was especially evident in 1966 when the
Buddhist renewed their demands for reforms and elections. The Buddhist
unrest intensified when Ky fired a prominent Buddhist general, Nguyen
Chanh Thi, who had much influence over central Vietnam. The Buddhist

protest was led by Tri Quang, the monk who had also led the opposition to Diem three years earlier. Protests in several cities demanded not only reform but also an end to foreign intervention. Demonstrators in Hué and Da Nang carried signs that read "End Foreign Domination of Our Country." U.S. facilities, including the consulate in Hué, were attacked. The demonstrations and rioting were reinforced by nine instances of self-immolation. Troops in Hué and Da Nang, who remained loyal to General Thieu, supported the protest. It seemed that South Vietnam was coming apart. One U.S. official explained American frustration succinctly: "What are we doing here? We're fighting to save these people, and they're fighting each other."[30]

Yet unlike 1963, when similar protests led the United States to intervene and eventually bring about Diem's downfall, this time it stood by the Saigon government. Whatever the weaknesses of Ky and Thieu, American officials feared that any alternative leadership, especially those active in the Buddhist protest, would likely negotiate with the North. Thus when the South Vietnamese responded with force, the United States supported the action. Charging that his opponents were under Communist control (which was not the case), Ky personally led an assault to "liberate" Da Nang and Hué. His troops were transported there by U.S. aircraft, and supported by armored units, they eventually crushed the opposition. In response, at least 10 Buddhist nuns and monks protested through acts of self-immolation. The spectacle of South Vietnamese forces fighting among themselves, which went on for several weeks and cost many lives, undermined the American promises of "progress" and illustrated the fact that South Vietnamese "nationhood" remained an elusive, if not impossible, goal. Military strength and mass arrests temporarily quieted the Buddhist movement but did not resolve the fundamental problems of the Saigon government.

The shallowness of the South Vietnamese leadership's commitment to reform was evident in its implementation, under American prodding, of "democratic" changes. Elections for a constituent assembly in early 1967 were manipulated in ways that precluded participation of the opponents of the Saigon government. The Buddhist leadership boycotted the elections. The resulting constitution provided for representative institutions and individual liberties, but the president was given virtually dictatorial powers in case of a national emergency, which he had the authority to declare. Communists and "neutralist sympathizers" were ineligible to hold office. With the new constitution in place, elections were held in September 1966. Beforehand, rivalry between Thieu and Ky, each of whom led cliques within the ARVN officer corps, threatened the fragile unity of the Saigon regime. To the consternation of Ky, Thieu decided to seek the presidency. Ky, whose flamboyant lifestyle and political histrionics troubled many of his Vietnamese and American supporters, yielded to pressure and reluctantly agreed to be the vice presidential candidate. Thieu, in the judgment of most U.S. officials, was a leader of more substance and sounder political instincts than the somewhat mercurial Ky.

The elections, however, underscored once again the shallowness of the Saigon government's support. Controlling the electoral apparatus and with Communists and "neutralist symphatizers" ineligible to participate, Thieu and Ky were expected to win overwhelmingly in a field of 11 presidential–vice presidential slates, of which none of the other candidates was widely known. Despite considerable fraud and intimidation on their behalf, the Thieu-Ky ticket received only 35 percent of the popular vote. Finishing second with 17 percent of the vote was an obscure lawyer, Truong Dinh Dzu, who advocated negotiations with the Viet Cong. Dzu, as a "neutralist sympathizer," should not have been on the ballot, but he outmaneuvered the government by keeping his political views to himself until he had managed to have his candidacy validated. Despite the narrowness of the Thieu-Ky victory, the United States claimed that the election gave them a mandate. The election, however, was better described by the journalist Robert Shaplen as "an American-directed performance with a Vietnamese cast."[31]

The democratic facade could not conceal the Thieu-Ky government's unsavory side. Political repression went beyond denying "neutralists" the opportunity to hold office. Thousands of political opponents were imprisoned and tortured; there was evidence as well that some critics were assassinated. For instance, as soon as the 1966 election was over, the regime arrested its unexpectedly popular rival, Truong Dinh Dzu. At a time when young men were needed for military service, the government concentrated resources on building up its police force so that political surveillance and control was even more extensive than under the Diem government.

For officials of the South Vietnam government, corruption was a way of life. Large amounts of American aid were siphoned off in a variety of ways. Military assistance, for instance, intended for the South Vietnamese army was often paid to "phantom" soldiers. South Vietnamese officials typically charged the United States excessively for goods and services, pocketing the difference from the actual costs. In many cases, Americans paid for imaginary goods; it was suggested, for instance, that all the cement charged to the United States would have paved the entire country. Large amounts of American supplies, including rifles, ammunition, and flak jackets, were stolen and sold openly on the streets of Saigon.

Morale problems plagued the army. Young men resisted military service; in 1966 only one in seven of draft age reported. More and more soldiers fled from the army; fully 100,000 young men—constituting one-third of the army—deserted each year.

Fueling the corruption and declining morale was the massive American presence. The firepower and defoliation of the countryside drove peasants from their villages into the cities; American military operations made refugees of four million persons—one of every four South Vietnamese. The overflowing cities faced enormous economic and social problems. The refugees were forced to live in squalid, disease-ridden conditions, and many, to survive, became beggars. The disinherited living on the streets became increasingly alienated and an obvious target of Viet Cong recruitment. Family life disintegrated as young men and women, tempted by the lure of making easy money from the Americans, abandoned filial loyalty and became part of the booming economy that served the American military. A young woman could make more money in a week as a prostitute than her peasant father could earn in a year.

The infusion of American troops and other personnel shattered much of the traditional social structure. To accommodate the Americans, bars and brothels lined the city streets and grew up around the base areas. Saigon was overwhelmed by the influx of American personnel, goods, and supplies. Large numbers of South Vietnamese civilians became engaged in businesses that were directed toward serving Americans. In addition, the dollars spent by Americans fueled inflation; prices increased by 170 percent between 1965 and 1967.

Underlying the political, social, military, and economic problems of South Vietnam was the increased dependency on the United States. It seems ironic, but as the U.S. commitment deepened, relations between Americans and South Vietnamese became more strained. U.S. military officers and enlisted men distrusted ARVN not only because it had been infiltrated by the Viet Cong but, more important, because its units were often reluctant to fight. Time and again, Americans contrasted the indifference of ARVN with the fighting qualities of the enemy.

If Americans thought more deeply about the situation, however, the lack of morale among ARVN forces was understandable. The war, after all, was no longer "their" war; it seemed that the United States would persevere, thus eroding incentive for military risks. This situation breeded considerable resentment against Americans, not only in the military but also throughout Vietnamese society. American military tactics may have seemed essential to gaining the initiative, but the bombing, defoliation, and firepower campaigns not only dislocated hundreds of thousands of peasants but also were the cause of mounting disenchantment. The U.S. military was, after all, destroying much of the fabric of rural life; in a culture where the self-contained village was a central social entity and where ancestral lands were revered, people came to see the Americans as a corrosive force. The large American mission intended to "save" South Vietnam was, in a very real sense, destroying that country militarily, economically, and socially.

The American-Vietnamese drama was played out in many encounters between military units and peasants. Americans understandably distrusted villagers, as the villagers often harbored the Viet Cong. Moreover, they could not identify the enemy; the Viet Cong was everywhere but nowhere. The villager who was seemingly friendly by day might be part of the Viet Cong by night. The peasants working in the rice paddies might be waiting for an opportunity to attack an unsuspecting American patrol. The peasants always seemed to know where the Viet Cong had planted bombs and traps against American and ARVN forces; as they walked along paths and roads, they carefully side-stepped those spots where they obviously knew that mines had been left. That sense of widespread peasant collusion with the Viet Cong added to the insecurity of American forces. This tension created situations in which Americans came to resent, if not hate, Vietnamese.

It was an atmosphere that made indiscriminate killing a means of survival. "I saw cruelty and brutality that I didn't expect to see from our people," one American soldier recalled. "It was almost impossible to know who the enemy was at any one time. Children were suspect, women were suspect. Frequently the ARVNs themselves were on two payrolls. . . . It's very easy to slip into a primitive state of mind, particularly if your life is in danger and you can't trust anyone."[32] Such a mind-set helps to explain the atrocity at the village of My Lai in March 1968 when a U.S. company under Lieutenant William Calley murdered more than 200 civilians, including women and children.

TET: NORTH VIETNAMESE CALCULATIONS

By 1967 the Vietnam War was at a stalemate. The United States had prevented the North Vietnamese and Viet Cong from taking control of the South, but it could not force them to abandon their struggle. The situation was fulfilling the Communist projections of a "protracted struggle." Time thus seemed to be on their side, for conventional military wisdom taught that in fighting insurgents "you lose if you do not win."

The North Vietnamese leadership calculated that circumstances favored a bold move. In an extended analysis in the fall of 1967, General Vo Nguyen Giap argued that North Vietnam should exploit certain American vulnerabilities. The United States seemed to be overextended, and further escalation in Vietnam would be detrimental to its domestic economy and to meeting its obligations in other parts of the world. Moreover, the U.S. relationship with South Vietnam, Giap realized, had inherent tensions as dependency fostered resentment. A major military offensive thus offered an opportunity to exploit these weaknesses: it would remind the American public and leaders of the costs of continuing the war, and it would demonstrate the limits of American power to the South Vietnamese, thus driving a wedge in the alliance. The offensive, it was anticipated, would cause such confusion that President Johnson would be forced to stop bombing of the North and to negotiate. The protracted struggle, as defined by Communist strategies, would then move into its next stage—fighting while talking.

Guided by such thinking, the North Vietnamese decided to launch a series of simultaneous attacks, to be manned principally by the Viet Cong, against South Vietnam's principal cities. By taking the war from the jungles and villages to the cities, which American and South Vietnamese officials considered to be secure, they would demonstrate that all parts of the country were vulnerable. To a large extent, everyday life in the cities had not been greatly affected by the war beyond its considerable social and economic impact; the real hardship of fighting, pain, and suffering were part of the experience of peasants, not urbanites. The most optimistic North Vietnamese projection was that the offensive would so demoralize the people of the cities and the ARVN forces that there would be a popular demand for Thieu to relinquish power to a coalition government. The idea of stimulating a popular uprising in the cities was not new; the inspiration for it was the August Revolution of 1945, when the people of the cities had rallied behind Ho Chi Minh's call for national independence. Communist strategists in both the North and South believed that attacks on the U.S.–South Vietnamese strongholds would bring ultimate victory. The attacks were set for the end of January 1968 during the lull in the fighting that accompanied the Tet, or lunar New Year, holidays.

The offensive had two important preliminary tactical steps—one conciliatory and the other diversionary—launched in the fall of 1967. As part of the effort to undermine the South Vietnamese attachment to the United States, North Vietnam and the NLF softened their approach to negotiation. The most important gesture was Hanoi's explicit assurance that it would enter into discussions once the United States stopped its bombing of the North.

At the same time, the Communist forces attacked a number of remote American outposts near the Demilitarized Zone and along the Laotian and Cambodian borders. The objective was to draw American resources and attention away from the cities. These well-coordinated assaults were repulsed, after intense fighting that lasted for weeks, by the massive use of firepower, which inflicted heavy losses on the North Vietnamese and Viet Cong forces. American commanders regarded these assaults, as the North Vietnamese hoped, as indicative of a concentrated effort to gain control of the northernmost sector of South Vietnam. That American assumption seemed to be verified when reports indicated that the North Vietnamese were moving troops into place for a major offensive against the American base at Khe Sanh, located in South Vietnam's northwest corner.

Westmoreland and other U.S. military and civilian leaders, including President Johnson, looked upon the Khe Sanh assault as a repetition of the battle of Dien Bien Phu 14 years earlier, when Communist forces had besieged French defenders in the decisive battle of the French–Viet Minh War. The parallels seemed unmistakable: just as Dien Bien Phu had enabled the Communists to grab territory that enhanced their bargaining position at the Geneva Conference, so it seemed that the assault on Khe Sanh was part of a plan to seize the northern provinces on the eve of possible negotiations. The lesson was simple: the Americans had to hold Khe Sanh. Accordingly, Westmoreland ordered reinforcement of Khe Sanh and prepared for large-scale air warfare to defend the remote outpost. Johnson became obsessed with

Khe Sanh; he told the Joint Chiefs of Staff, "I don't want any damn *Din Bin Phoo*."

Thus, by the time the North Vietnamese finally attacked Khe Sanh on 21 January, the Americans were prepared for a major battle. In a struggle that was destined to go on for more than two months, the United States unleashed artillery, bombs, and napalm to an extent unparalleled in the conflict. Some fifty thousand U.S. troops were tied down at Khe Sanh or in its defense. That concentration of manpower in fact was what the North Vietnamese intended. Contrary to Westmoreland's projections, the Khe Sanh assault was diversionary. The U.S. marine commander at Khe Sanh later called it a "trap . . . to force you into the expenditure of an absolutely unreasonable amount of men and matériel to defend a piece of terrain that wasn't worth a damn."[33]

Fundamental to the calculations of North Vietnamese planning for the Tet Offensive was the element of surprise. American interpretations of the military situations and developments of late 1967 created a mind-set that discounted North Vietnamese capabilities. Mounting casualties and the destructiveness of the bombing, American military leaders believed, were eroding enemy morale. U.S. commanders generally interpreted the attacks on the remote outposts in the fall as an act of despair. When Westmoreland returned to the United States for a brief visit in November 1967, he assured Americans that the "enemy's hopes are bankrupt" and "we have reached an important point where the end begins to come into view."[34] And since American leaders had become convinced that Khe Sanh would be the decisive battle of the war, they were disinclined to consider the possibilities of important assaults elsewhere. Noting that President Johnson and his advisers were "mentally in the trenches" at Khe Sanh, General Dave Richard Palmer has reflected that "it is hard to keep an eye on the big picture while hunkering in a bunker. . . . The war in Vietnam that fretful January of 1968 was seen through a microscope focused on Khe Sanh."[35]

As that month began, Radio Hanoi broadcast a poem from the ailing 77-year-old Ho Chi Minh in which he exhorted his followers:

> This spring outshines previous springs.
> Of triumphs throughout the land come happy tidings.
> Forward!
> Total victory shall be ours.[36]

Toward that end, the Viet Cong surreptitiously moved cadres and supplies into towns and cities throughout the South. They became part of the migration into the cities that was part of the Tet holidays. Viet Cong joined with the peasants headed toward the cities on buses and bicycles. Some dressed in ARVN uniforms and hitched rides on American trucks. Weapons were smuggled in various ways: in beds of flowers, in truckloads of fruits and vegetables, and even in caskets. By the time that the holiday truce began, the Communist forces were in position for their surprise attacks.

THE TET OFFENSIVE

Beginning shortly after midnight on 30 January, the North Vietnamese and Viet Cong broke the Tet truce by suddenly launching an offensive of astonishing scope. Attacks by some 84,000 troops touched every part of South Vietnam from the Demilitarized Zone to the southern tip. They assaulted the six largest cities, 36 of the 44 provincial capitals, and some 50 hamlets. Throughout the country, the assaults were not only sudden but also brutal, often killing government officials and other civilians indiscriminately.

The Tet Offensive caught the American command by surprise. Convinced that the Khe Sanh assault was the principal effort of a desperate enemy, U.S. officials discounted reports of infiltration into the cities. Although expecting an offensive somewhere, they could not conceive of an attack of the magnitude of what occurred during the Tet holiday. An American officer conceded that "if we'd gotten the whole battle plan, it wouldn't have been credible to us." A military history textbook would later state that "the first thing to understand about Giap's Tet Offensive is that it was an Allied intelligence failure. . . . The North Vietnamese gained complete surprise."[37]

Nowhere was the surprise greater than in Saigon and Hué. Both were hit the second morning of the offensive. The Tet celebrations had continued in Saigon and Hué since people believed that those cities were invulnerable from the attacks that had been launched elsewhere. In Saigon the most daring assault was undertaken by the 20 Viet Cong who, in the early morning hours of 31 January, drove a truck and taxi through the city's empty streets to the U.S. embassy. They blew a hole in the embassy compound wall and poured through it. From their position in the courtyard they threatened the embassy's main buildings. American reinforcements quickly arrived, however, and the attackers were doomed. Within four hours of the attack the embassy had been secured and all of the invaders had been killed. Yet the assault upon a symbol of the U.S. presence had accomplished an important psychological objective for the Communists. Elsewhere in Saigon, Viet Cong units attacked the Tan Son Nhut airport, the presidential palace, the South Vietnamese army headquarters, the air base at Bien Hoa, and other targets.

Simultaneously with the assault on Saigon, Viet Cong units also attacked Hué, which was destined to be the scene of the most prolonged battle of the Tet Offensive. They overran the older part of the city, called the Citadel, once the home of the Annamese emperors, and hoisted the Viet Cong flag over the Palace of Peace.

Despite the surprise of the attack, U.S. and ARVN forces fought back quickly and effectively in battles waged across South Vietnam. Fully exploit-

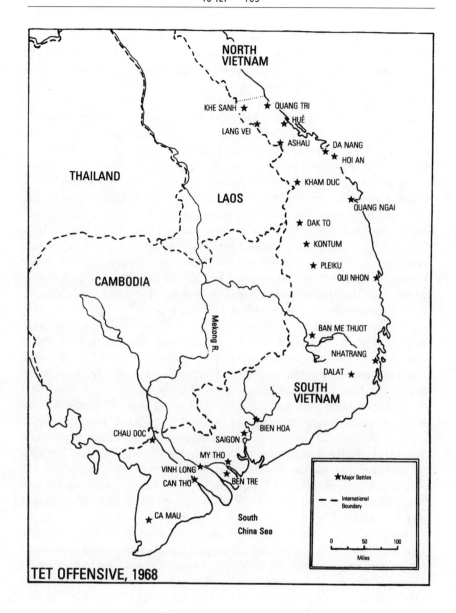

TET OFFENSIVE, 1968

ing superior mobility and firepower, they were able to force Viet Cong and North Vietnamese from the cities. Generally, the Viet Cong and North Vietnamese did not have time to establish strong defensive positions, and they received only scant support from the people. In most cases, the offensive came to an abrupt end, with Communist forces suffering heavy losses. Saigon was typical: American and South Vietnamese forces quickly regained control, so that within six days of the startling attacks the city had been largely secured. At Hué, on the other hand, intense fighting dragged on for three weeks. Human and material losses were devastating: some 500 U.S. and ARVN troops and about 5,000 North Vietnamese and Viet Cong were killed, as well as large numbers of civilians. The homes of over 100,000 persons were destroyed. And in perhaps the worst atrocity of the war, the Viet Cong summarily executed as many as 5,000 persons—mostly officials, school teachers, intellectuals, priests, nuns, and foreigners—the bodies of most of the victims later being discovered in mass graves outside the city. By the time the Communist forces finally abandoned Hué on 23 February, General Palmer writes, the "beautiful city of twenty-five days ago was a shattered, stinking hulk, its streets choked with rubble and rotting bodies."[38]

The Tet Offensive was over, and President Johnson proclaimed the Communist effort a "complete failure." Tet indeed was, in many ways, a U.S.–South Vietnamese victory. In their futile assaults, the Viet Cong–North Vietnamese suffered enormous losses. Perhaps as many as 40,000 men, nearly half of the troops who had been thrown into the attacks, were killed, and thousands of others were made disabled. The Viet Cong, which absorbed the brunt of the fighting, was badly crippled and never again was an effective fighting force. In addition, the South Vietnamese acquitted themselves much better than the Hanoi leadership had anticipated. The ARVN forces generally fought effectively, and the civilian population, however fragile its ties with the Saigon government, did not rally to the Viet Cong. A confidential North Vietnamese document acknowledged that "the people's spirit for uprising is still very weak."[39]

Yet in another and ultimately more important sense, the North Vietnamese achieved a victory. Giap had calculated that the offensive would remind the Johnson administration of the costs of continuing the war, and in that respect his projections proved accurate. In terms of its political consequences, the most important aspect of the Tet Offensive was in the United States, not Vietnam. The impact upon the American public, who had been led to believe by favorable body counts and Westmoreland's promises that the enemy was on the verge of defeat, was devastating. The sheer magnitude and complete surprise of the offensive staggered the American public. The extensive television coverage of the Tet battles added to the public's incredulity and disenchantment with the war. Reports of the occupation of part of the U.S. embassy compound led one cartoonist to draw a picture of the startled President Johnson on the telephone asking, "What the hell's Ho Chi Minh doing answering the Saigon embassy phone?" The respected newscaster Walter Cronkite allegedly reacted to the embassy raid by asking, "What the hell is going on? I thought we were winning the war."[40] Other images added to the public confusion. Television cameras and news photographers captured the gruesome scene on the streets of Saigon when General Nguyen Ngoc Loan, the chief of South Vietnam's national police, summarily executed a Viet Cong suspect. When the sequence of General Loan pointing his pistol at the prisoner's head and then pulling the trigger was shown on television, NBC commentator John Chancellor told the audience, "There was awful retribution. Here the infamous chief of the South Vietnamese National Police, General Loan, executed a captured VC officer. Rough justice on a Saigon street as the charmed life of the city of Saigon comes to a bloody end."[41] And then there was the war's classic statement of doublethink. After leveling a town in the Mekong Delta, an American officer explained that "we had to destroy the town to save it." That statement, the historian George Herring has observed, "seemed to epitomize the purposeless destruction of the war."[42] And as Johnson was claiming victory, Cronkite returned from a visit to Vietnam and told television viewers that it seemed "more certain than ever that the bloody experience of Vietnam is to end in a stalemate."[41]

Tet dramatically reinforced discontent with the war. Public opinion polls indicated a sharp increase in opposition to Johnson's conduct of the war. The growing disenchantment found expression in the campaign of Senator Eugene McCarthy, an avowed antiwar candidate, for the Democratic presidential nomination. The tumultuous events in Vietnam gave vitality to McCarthy's challenge to Johnson, whose followers told voters in New Hampshire (the scene of the first presidential primary) that the Communists in Vietnam were watching the New Hampshire primary. Despite such suggestions that a vote for McCarthy was unpatriotic, McCarthy stunned the nation by almost defeating Johnson in the New Hampshire voting. A few days later, Senator Robert Kennedy of New York, a far more illustrious critic of Vietnam policy, announced his candidacy for the Democratic nomination.

Thus, as a consequence of forces unleashed by Tet, the Johnson administration was forced to reevaluate objectives and strategy in Vietnam. Given the pressures on Johnson, there was only one logical step to take—toward negotiations. The North Vietnamese had calculated correctly. The popular disenchantment with the war indicated that more and more Americans disapproved of its conduct, but there was no consensus on alternatives; some favored withdrawal, while others sought a more aggressive approach to secure victory even at the risk of war with the Soviet Union or China. From the beginning of U.S. involvement, Johnson had ruled out military actions that would threaten a wider war. Within the administration, Westmoreland's request for an additional 206,000 troops touched off intense debate about the war effort. The new secretary of defense, Clark Clifford, led the opposition to the request. To Clifford and other dissidents within the administration the troop request showed the bankruptcy of the U.S. position, since all that

Westmoreland and the Joint Chiefs of Staff could promise was more of the same strategy but with no assurance that the additional men would be sufficient to force the North Vietnamese to negotiate on U.S. terms. Johnson himself reluctantly came to the same conclusion.

The redefinition of U.S. policy found expression in President Johnson's nationally televised address on the evening of 31 March. He began, "I want to talk to you about peace in Vietnam," and announced that U.S. bombing of almost all of North Vietnam would be ended; the exception was the area below the 20th parallel, the staging area for attacks across the Demilitarized Zone. He indicated a willingness to negotiate at any time and in any place and named the respected diplomat W. Averell Harriman as the U.S. representative whenever negotiations did begin. And finally, he announced that he would not be a candidate for another term as president.

Thus the Tet Offensive was a powerful reminder to the American public and leadership of the stalemate in Vietnam. In accentuated trends in public opinion and gave impetus to dissidents within the administration. Johnson's 31 March speech, when contrasted with Westmoreland's assurances of four months earlier that the war was being won, underscored a fundamental shift in U.S. policy. Having denied the request for additional troops and having curtailed virtually all of the bombing of North Vietnam, Johnson had taken the first steps toward de-escalation of U.S. involvement. To reverse that direction was not inconceivable, but it was bound to have serious political repercussions in the United States.

For the moment, fighting was relatively limited, but the siege of Khe Sanh continued for a few more days. There, as Westmoreland stated, "the amount of firepower . . . exceeded anything that had been seen before in history by any foe, and the enemy was hurt, his back was broken."[44] Over 115,000 tons of American bombs, rockets, and napalm left this once verdant eight-square-mile area "absolutely denuded. The trees were gone . . . everything was gone. Pockmarked and ruined and burnt . . . like the surface of the moon."[45] Having suffered heavy casualties (ten thousand killed or seriously wounded, by U.S. estimates) but also having forced a major American commitment to defend Khe Sanh, the North Vietnamese withdrew.

Barely had the United States proclaimed victory at Khe Sanh than it planned to abandon its base there. American forces withdrew from Khe Sanh, with all remnants of the base, according to orders, "buried by bulldozer, burned or blown up."[46] The withdrawal from Khe Sanh to concentrate forces at a more secure and mobile base, however sensible in logistical terms, seemed incomprehensible to those who had heard just a few weeks earlier that it was of such overriding importance that it had to be held at any cost. By the time that Khe Sanh was abandoned in June 1968, however, Westmoreland had left Vietnam and General Creighton W. Abrams was in command of U.S. forces. Implicit in the change of command was the search for a more effective means of waging war.

Hence the North Vietnamese, despite their enormous losses and disappointments in the Tet Offensive, had forced the United States to the "talking while fighting" stage of protracted warfare. Moreover, the tumultuous events of early 1968 left the American public confused about the purpose of the war and civilian and military officials uncertain about how the power of the United States could be effective in Vietnam.

Notes

1. Introduction to U.S. Department of State White Paper, 1965, in Kahin and Lewis, *U.S. in Vietnam*, 479–82.

2. Speech by Pham Van Dong, 8 April 1965, in Kahin and Lewis, *U.S. in Vietnam*, 489–95.

3. Johnson cited in Philip B. Davidson, *Vietnam at War: The History, 1946–1975* (Navato, Calif.: Presidio, 1988), 327.

4. George C. Herring, *America's Longest War: The United States and Vietnam, 1950–1975*, 2d ed. (New York: Knopf, 1986), 127.

5. *Pentagon Papers: The Defense Department History of United States Decisionmaking on Vietnam* (Boston: Beacon, 1971), 3:309–10.

6. Ibid., 3:724.

7. Ibid., 3:644.

8. Ibid., 3:194.

9. Philip Caputo, *A Rumor of War* (New York: Holt, Rinehart, Winston, 1977), xii.

10. Address at Johns Hopkins University, 7 April 1965, *Public Papers of the Presidents of the United States: Lyndon B. Johnson, 1965* (Washington, D.C.: U.S. Government Printing Office, 1966), 395.

11. Davidson, *Vietnam at War*, 339.

12. Caputo, *A Rumor of War*, xii.

13. Karnow, *Vietnam*, 435.

14. Cited in John M. Van Dyke, *North Vietnam's Strategy for Survival* (Palo Alto, Calif.: Pacific Books, 1972), 30–31.

15. Harrison, *The Endless War*, 263.

16. Van Dyke, *North Vietnam's Strategy*, 28–31.

17. Harrison, *The Endless War*, 263–64.

18. Van Dyke, *North Vietnam's Strategy*, 22.

19. Ibid., 27.

20. David Schoenbrum cited in ibid., 64.

21. Wheeler cited in Andrew F. Krepinevich, *The Army and Vietnam* (Baltimore, Md.: John Hopkins University Press, 1986), p. 166.

22. Westmoreland cited in Thomas C. Thayer, *War without Fronts: The American Experience in Vietnam* (Boulder, Colo.: Westview, 1985), 89.

23. Depuy cited in Krepinevich, *Army and Vietnam*, 197.

24. Davidson, *Vietnam at War*, 422–23.

25. Depuy cited in Krepinevich, *Army and Vietnam*, 190.

26. Depuy cited in Bernard Williams Rogers, *Cedar Falls–Junction City: A Turning Point* (Washington, D.C.: U.S. Army Center of Military History, 1974), 78.

27. Krepinevich, *Army and Vietnam*, 191.

28. Ibid., 197.

29. Karnow, *Vietnam*, 443–44.

30. Ibid., 445–46.

31. Robert Shaplen, *The Road from War: Vietnam, 1965–1970* (New York: Harper, 1970), 151.

32. Al Santoli, *Everywhere We Had: An Oral History of the Vietnam War by Thirty-Three American Soldiers Who Fought It* (New York: Ballantine, 1981), 69.

33. General Lowell English cited in Karnow, *Vietnam*, 542.

34. *Department of State Bulletin* 64, 11 December 1967, 786–88.

35. Dave Richard Palmer, *Summons of the Trumpet: A History of the Vietnam War from a Military Man's Viewpoint* (New York: Ballantine, 1978), 217.

36. Karnow, *Vietnam*, 535.

37. D. R. Palmer, *Summons of the Trumpet*, 228–29.

38. Ibid., 247.

39. Ibid., 256.

40. Cronkite cited in Don Oberdorfer, *Tet!* (Garden City, N.Y.: Doubleday, 1971), 158.

41. John Chancellor quoted in George A. Bailey and Lawrence W. Lichty, "Rough Justice on a Saigon Street: A Gatekeeper Study of NBC's Tet Execution Film," *Journalism Quarterly* 49 (1972): 222.

42. Herring, *America's Longest War*, 192.

43. Cronkite cited in Karnow, *Vietnam*, 547.

44. Robert Pisor, *The End of the Line: The Siege of Khe Sanh* (New York: Ballantine, 1982), 223.

45. Ibid., 221.

46. Ibid., 231.

chapter 6

TO THE FALL OF SAIGON: THE END OF A WAR AND
FULFILLMENT OF A REVOLUTION, 1968–1975

The momentous events of 1968, beginning with the Tet Offensive, altered the American position in Vietnam. In the United States, the discrediting of the Johnson administration over the war, the deep divisions within the Democratic party between critics and supporters of Johnson, and the racial and political turmoil that culminated in the violence on the streets of Chicago during the Democratic convention led to the defeat of Vice President Hubert Humphrey, the Democratic presidential candidate. The triumphant Richard Nixon campaigned on the promise that he had a "secret plan" to end the war. The new administration quickly brought changes to U.S. policy.

Nixon's approach to Vietnam was an integral part of an effort to redefine America's global strategy. Henry Kissinger, who became Nixon's national security adviser, played a major role in formulating the new U.S. policy. Envisioning a world in which the major powers would uphold international stability, Nixon and Kissinger worked to improve relations with the Soviet Union and to break the 20 years of hostility between the People's Republic of China and the United States. This "grand design" of the new administration assumed that through various incentives and pressures, the United States could encourage the Soviet Union's cooperation in maintaining order. Nixon and Kissinger also calculated that the Soviet Union and China could be induced to influence North Vietnam to compromise. The change in the U.S. approach to the major Communist powers took shape slowly before reaching its peak in 1971 and 1972. While developing the global "grand design," the Nixon administration had to grapple with the intractable problems of the war in Vietnam.

As the new administration took office on 20 January 1969, it was determined to end the war. Kissinger described Vietnam as the "bone in the nation's throat," and Nixon vowed that he would not allow the war to overwhelm his presidency as it had that of his predecessor. However anxious they were to extricate the United States from Vietnam, both leaders eschewed any approach that would appear to sell out the Saigon government. Nixon was no more prepared than his predecessors to accept defeat. His stated objective was "peace with honor," and over the next four years his administration worked toward that vague, if not elusive, goal.

Nixon and Kissinger inherited a negotiating process that had dragged on for more than eight months without substantial progress. Formal meetings between American and North Vietnamese representatives had begun in Paris on 13 May 1968, but fundamental differences between the two sides and the South Vietnamese opposition to a negotiated settlement undermined the process. The North Vietnamese refused to negotiate until the United States agreed to a total cessation of bombing. Meanwhile, General Thieu and other leaders of South Vietnam feared that negotiations would lead to a coalition government in Saigon, a change that would place the National Liberation Front in a position to achieve political dominance. To reassure Thieu, President Johnson had met with him at Honolulu in July 1968 and promised that the United States would not approve the establishment of a coalition government in the South and that Thieu's government should be represented in the negotiations. After six months of "negotiating to negotiate," the United States and North Vietnam reached an "understanding." Most important, the United States accepted the North Vietnamese negotiating stipulation; on 31 October President Johnson announced a total halt of air and naval attacks on North Vietnam. It was also agreed that both the Saigon government and the National Liberation Front were to be included in the negotiations; the North Vietnamese disavowed plans for large-scale attacks on the major cities of the South. Distrustful of the outgoing Johnson administration and expecting stronger support from the incoming Nixon, the South Vietnamese then engaged in three months of procedural wrangling. This meant that it was not until 25 January 1969—five days after Nixon's inauguration—that substantive four-party negotiations began.

To achieve a settlement that would be satisfactory not only to the United States and North Vietnam but to the Thieu government as well constituted the basic challenge to "peace with honor." At the heart of the U.S.–North Vietnamese conflict remained the status of South Vietnam. The North Vietnamese insisted, as they had since the early stages of the war, on the elimination of the Saigon government and on inclusion of the National Liberation Front in a new South Vietnamese government; the United States insisted, as it had since the early stages of the war, that the legitimacy of the existing Saigon government be recognized. Tied to the issue of the postwar government was the question of the presence of American and North Vietnamese troops in South Vietnam. The United States, which held to the "two Vietnams" concept, sought a mutual withdrawal of forces from the South, while the North Vietnamese—who never admitted to the presence of their troops in the South and who held, in any event, to the proposition that Vietnam was a single, not a divided nation—called for the withdrawal of only U.S. forces. The death of Ho Chi Minh in September 1969 occasioned a renewal of North Vietnam's commitments. His heirs—Premier Pham Van Dong, General Vo Nguyen Giap, Truong Chinh, Le Duan, and other veterans of the August Revolution—disseminated Ho's last testament that called for more sacrifices to withstand "U.S. aggression" and to "win total victory."

To achieve U.S. objectives the Nixon administration relied on a strategy that integrated "Vietnamization" with the element of military surprise. Vietnamization involved the gradual withdrawal of U.S. troops, the buildup of the South Vietnamese military, and renewed efforts at nation building. At the same time, Nixon was prepared to use U.S. power in bold ways by eliminating certain restrictions imposed by Johnson on the conduct of the war. Nixon's objective was to achieve not only strategic gains but also to intimidate the North Vietnamese. He wanted Hanoi to think of him as a "madman" who was prepared to throw caution to the wind in order to achieve his objectives.

Nixon's Vietnamization and military surprise tactics were carefully orchestrated. Although the Nixon approach gave somewhat greater coherence to U.S. strategy than had been true between 1965 and 1968, it had inherent limitations. To strengthen ARVN and the Saigon government and to coerce the North Vietnamese into accepting U.S. peace terms required, in addition to efficient and judicious use of U.S. resources, time. Nixon, however, did not have that luxury. The events of 1968 and the steadily decreasing popular support for the war underscored the American public's limited patience. Nixon recognized that if he was to be reelected in 1972, he needed to bring the war, or at least U.S. participation in it, to an end by that time. In a closed meeting with a congressional committee in 1969, the secretary of the army stated bluntly, "Time is running out on our side in Vietnam."[1]

VIETNAMIZATION

In implementing troop withdrawals and Vietnamization, American officials followed the advice of Sir Robert Thompson, a British counterinsurgency expert who emphasized that "troop withdrawals must be balanced against a declining enemy capability and a rising South Vietnamese capability; they must not be so fast that they allow the North Vietnamese to stage an all-out offensive before the South Vietnamese are ready to cope with it; they must not be so slow they encourage the South Vietnamese to think the American combat forces will be around forever."[2] The objective was to build a strong South Vietnamese force that would be capable of holding its own against the North Vietnamese.

In June 1969 Nixon announced the first troop withdrawals; it began modestly with the return of 25,000 of the 550,000 U.S. troops in Vietnam. By the time Nixon's first year in office ended, the number of troops had been reduced to 475,000; a year later, the American force totaled 335,000. Troop withdrawals were, of course, popular at home and enabled Nixon to defuse much of the antiwar protest. Yet the phased withdrawals also reduced American options, because they could not be reversed without a substantial political price. For that reason, some officials were skeptical; Kissinger remarked that troop withdrawals were addictive: once started, they could not be stopped.

Meanwhile, the size of the South Vietnamese Army steadily increased, from 820,000 soldiers in 1968 to about 1,000,000 by 1970. The United States equipped the South Vietnamese with the most sophisticated weaponry. It provided nearly a million M-16 rifles, 12,000 M-60 machine guns, 40,000 M-79 grenade launchers, and 2,000 heavy mortars and howitzers. This meant that for the first time, the South Vietnamese were better equipped than the North Vietnamese. Accompanying this massive effort at equipping the South Vietnamese was an enormous training program under American auspices. Such a large, well-trained, and well-equipped army, U.S. leaders assumed, would discourage large-scale North Vietnamese military actions and would encourage serious negotiations.

Vietnamization was facilitated by changes in the level and intensity of the fighting, which Americans defined as a "lull." The substantial Communist losses during the Tet Offensive reduced the size of their forces in the South, made it more difficult to recruit rural youths to their ranks, and disrupted their political structure. In North Vietnam, military leaders acknowledged that the revolution in the South had been forced "temporarily" into a defensive position necessitating some retrenchment. Yet the revolution was not, as some Americans conjectured, "withering on the vine." The lull in fighting also reflected differences in U.S. strategy. General Creighton Abrams, who succeeded Westmoreland as commander of U.S. forces, shifted from the big-unit search-and-destroy operations to small-unit patrolling and pacification. This meant that American forces were no longer engaged in the same levels of massive-firepower warfare that had characterized the Westmoreland era. Moreover, most of the fighting after 1969 involved small units in South Vietnam's more remote areas. The North Vietnamese forces controlled that warfare; they initiated most of the combat and imposed heavy casualties on the South Vietnamese army. While U.S. combat deaths decreased from 1969 onward, South Vietnamese casualties remained high. ARNV battlefield deaths exceeded 20,000 per year from 1969 to 1971.

Vietnamization, despite all of the American dollars that supported it, failed to remedy the chronic political and military problems of South Vietnam. ARVN remained an inept instrument riddled with political intrigue and corruption. "Vast amounts of military aid, training, and on-the-spot advice," one scholar has written, "cannot transform a politicized army into an effective fighting force."[3] Officers were promoted on the basis of favoritism, corruption, and bribery. A Defense Department study acknowledged that "without major reforms . . . it is unlikely that [ARVN] will ever constitute an effective political or military counter to the Viet Cong."[4] Unwilling to reform the army, the Thieu government was also indifferent to the need to develop a strategy for fighting without U.S. support.

The nation-building side of Vietnamization likewise brought minimal results. A variety of programs, mostly funded by the United States and using American as well as South Vietnamese personnel, endeavored to broaden Saigon's control and to rally popular support on its behalf. Whereas the search-and-destroy strategy had minimized the importance of securing the rural areas, a program of "accelerated pacification" sought to establish control over contested territory. Rural development teams were sent into the countryside to organize village administration and to start construction projects. The "open arms" project offered amnesty to Viet Cong–North Communist defectors. A large-scale land reform program, "Land to the Tiller," sought to blunt the Communists' appeal to the peasantry by reducing the size of maximum landholdings, redistributing excess lands, and returning powers to the traditional village councils.

The most controversial operation was the Phoenix Program, which was intended to eliminate the Communists' political structure: Organized by the CIA in collaboration with South Vietnamese officials, this effort sought to identify Viet Cong agents and supporters who would then be "neutralized" (arrested or killed). Official estimates claimed that in its first year, Phoenix resulted in the "neutralization" of some 20,000 "Communists" (about one-third of them killed). Many critics of U.S. policy in Vietnam were appalled by what seemed to be a widespread program of organized murder. Whatever the moral considerations in this undertaking, Communist leaders in the South later acknowledged that the Phoenix Program had undermined their recruitment efforts. Despite claims that the Phoenix Program eventually "eliminated" some 60,000 "Communists," it was riddled with corruption and inefficiency. Local officials were under pressure to meet quotas, which led to indiscriminate arrests of innocent villagers. Any Vietnamese killed in any skirmish were routinely identified as Viet Cong. Among those arrested, nearly 90 percent were free within 90 days, most of them simply bribing their captors to regain their freedom. A Defense Department study in 1971 concluded that Phoenix was "only marginally effective . . . a fragmented effort, lacking central direction, control and priority." A CIA participant stated it more succinctly: Phoenix "was thought of by geniuses and implemented by idiots."[5]

Regardless of various indicators of progress, the entire pacification effort suffered from two related flaws: it was a belated "quick fix" that lacked the time to confront fundamental problems, and it could not surmount—indeed, it reflected— the weaknesses of the South Vietnamese government. Considering the extent to which the Saigon government had been isolated from the rural population and the years of Communist activity in the villages, it was late in the game to under-take such a massive operation, however badly it was needed. Success, consider-ing the odds facing the Saigon government, required years of careful planning and patient working with the peasantry, but with the U.S. gradually withdraw-ing militarily, pacification had to achieve its objectives quickly.

The corruption and intrigue that plagued the army undermined pacifica-tion as well. The rural development teams were composed principally of urban youth who used such service to evade the draft. They were, by definition, out-siders in the villages that they were supposed to be serving. The "open arms" program was riddled with corruption. Officials were offered rewards for rally-ing Communists to support the South Vietnamese government: that of course, provided an incentive for bribery. Hence, of the 47,000 "Viet Cong defectors" claimed in government reports for 1969, many if not most were pro-Saigon civilians who shared in rewards. According to one estimate, only one in five of the Communist defectors under this program was genuine. Land reform was perhaps the best example of "too little too late," for it merely redressed the long-standing inequities of the rural "reforms" of Ngo Dinh Diem in 1956. The effect of the land reform effort of 1970 was also limited by corruption, as officials in some areas engaged in widespread profiteering.

THE CAMBODIAN INVASION, 1970

While Vietnamization and U.S. withdrawal signaled a drastic reduction of American military involvement, Nixon's strategy also included the calculated use of American military power in ways that exceeded earlier limits. This so-called big-play or madman approach had three related pur-poses: to weaken the North Vietnamese capacity to wage war in the South, to embolden the South Vietnamese by reassuring them of U.S. support, and to intimidate the Hanoi government into accepting U.S. terms for ending the war. Extension of the war into neighboring Cambodia was the first and most important example of Nixon's determination to employ the "big-play" tactic. Many critics of the earlier emphasis on search-and-destroy find in Nixon's actions a much more appropriate use of U.S. power. "Actually a solution had been there all along," General Dave Richard Palmer argues, "but it had been laid aside in favor of the concept of graduated response. The solution was to carry the war to the enemy, to hit him in his vulnerable and vital sanctuar-ies."[6] That is what Nixon sought in the Cambodian attack.

Until 1970 Cambodia, under the leadership of Prince Sihanouk, had main-tained an uneasy neutrality in the conflict that was being waged in Vietnam. Despite difficulties in dealing with shifts in the policy of the mercurial Sihanouk, American policymakers assumed that U.S. interests were best served by Cambodian neutrality.

Having led the Cambodian nationalist movement that brought indepen-dence from the French, Sihanouk, after the withdrawal of the French in 1954, built upon his considerable popularity to consolidate his political power. Strongly anticommunist in his domestic policies, Sihanouk repressed the small Cambodian Communist movement, leaving it in disarray. In his foreign policy, Sihanouk's professed neutrality in the cold war enabled him to draw economic and military aid from both the United States and its allies as well as from the Communist bloc. Thus during the early years of Cambodian independence, foreign assistance flowed from Western nations, principally the United States and France, as well as from the Soviet Union, China, and other Communist countries. Neutrality seemed the only way for this small country—which had been subjected historically to intrusions by its larger neighbors, Thailand and Vietnam—to return its independence.

By the early 1960s, as the United States became more and more deeply involved in Vietnam, Cambodian neutrality rook on an anti-American tone. Protests and pressures from resurgent leftists led Sihanouk, who always was inclined to preempt the ideology of his critics, to denounce the United States. Claiming that the Americans were plotting against him (he later wrote a book titled *My Wars with the CIA*), Sihanouk rejected U.S. military aid in 1963 and severed diplomatic relations in 1965.

Such gestures, however, failed to appease all of Sihanouk's critics. In 1966 the reinvigorated Cambodian Communists, known as the Khmer Rouge and led by Pol Pot, urged armed resistance to Sihanouk. Brutal suppression by Sihanouk's army only temporarily stemmed the insurgency, which gradually regained strength.

At the same time, the North Vietnamese extended the Ho Chi Minh Trail through Cambodian territory; men and supplies moved across eastern Cambodia as a vital part of their war in South Vietnam. With the tacit approval of Cambodian authorities, North Vietnamese used the port of Sihanoukville (Kompong Som) as a major supply base; trucks carried goods from the port to the Cambodian–South Vietnamese border, where the North Vietnamese constructed supply depots and staging areas. Sihanouk, who was determined to avoid antagonizing the North Vietnamese, tolerated this violation of Cambodian sovereignty. In return for his cooperation, the North Vietnamese did not support the Khmer Rouge. Thus, neutral Cambodia had become an accomplice in the North Vietnamese war effort.

The Johnson administration in turn tolerated this situation. Johnson rejected requests to attack the North Vietnamese sanctuaries in Cambodia, for he feared the consequences of broadening the war. In particular, he wanted to keep Sihanouk in power as a means of limiting North Vietnam's influence in Cambodia. U.S. intervention would weaken Sihanouk's stature and would invite North Vietnamese collaboration with the Khmer Rouge.

Despite U.S. tolerance, Sihanouk's delicate maneuvering was becoming unraveled. To many of his traditional supporters he seemed impotent in the face of the mounting Khmer Rouge insurgency and the Vietnamese incursions. So in still another reversal, Sihanouk sought accommodation with the

United States; he privately indicated a willingness to permit U.S. "hot pursuit" of Communist forces into Cambodian territory "to liberate us from the Vietcong" and pleaded for understanding of Cambodia's position. "We are a country caught between the hammer and the anvil," he told an American correspondent, "a country that would very much like to remain the last haven of peace in Southeast Asia."[7]

While Sihanouk could speak eloquently of his country's plight, he was in some ways more a dilettante than a leader. Rather than confront the mounting problems of his country, Sihanouk spent much of his time engaged in frivolous activities—producing and starring in motion pictures, endlessly criticizing his opponents, blaming the Vietnamese for the Cambodian Communist uprising, and traveling overseas. It was not until mid-1969 that Sihanouk realized that the situation was getting out of hand, and trying to appease his critics, he named General Lon Nol as premier of a "Salvation Government." It was, however, probably too little too late to salvage Sihanouk's position.

By that time Nixon had taken his first military step into Cambodia, an act that further complicated the country's political situation. In March 1969 Nixon authorized a bombing campaign against the North Vietnamese sanctuaries. Over the next 14 months, Operation Menu resulted in over 3,600 B-52 bombing missions, dropping altogether over 100,000 tons of bombs on Cambodian targets. Recognizing that this extension of the war would meet with strong criticism from Congress and the public, the Nixon administration went to elaborate lengths to construct a veil of secrecy around the bombing campaign. While Americans were ignorant of Operation Menu, it was, of course, known to Cambodians. Many military and political leaders were emboldened by this sign of U.S. resolve. Indeed, Cambodia provided intelligence to the Americans on the sanctuaries, restricted North Vietnamese access to Sihanoukville, and, in a significant shift, resumed diplomatic relations with the United States. Critics of Sihanouk's deference to the North Vietnamese now pressed for a vigorous anti-Vietnamese campaign.

Cambodia had thus reached the point by 1970 where it had to decide whether to support the U.S. effort or resume its neutral position. It was a critical moment for that small and vulnerable country. Yet no matter how serious the situation in Cambodia, Sihanouk took an annual extended vacation on the Riviera as a "cure" for his obesity. It was during his 1970 sojourn that the Cambodian National Assembly removed him as chief of state. Lon Nol, who headed the new government, called for an end to foreign intrusions and for a policy of "strict neutrality."

In fact, the coup increased both Vietnamese and American influence in Cambodia. The North Vietnamese, not prepared to abandon their bases, solidified control over their Cambodian sanctuaries. In a reversal of their position during the Sihanouk era, the North Vietnamese now collaborated with the Khmer Rouge in its bid for power. The political changes in Cambodia gave impetus to the renewed requests of U.S. military commanders that the war be extended to attack the North Vietnamese sanctuaries. The Nixon administration, which welcomed the overthrow of Sihanouk, responded quickly on 14 April when a desperate Lon Nol appealed for help. Beyond assistance to Lon Nol's government, Nixon decided to carry the U.S. war effort into Cambodia. The principal targets were 14 major North Vietnamese bases just inside Cambodia, which had been off-limits to American and South Vietnamese forces. Also hidden somewhere in the jungle was the NLF's headquarters: Central Office for South Vietnam (COSVN).

In a dramatic move, Nixon authorized a large-scale cross-border operation. This would disrupt the North Vietnamese war effort, thus buying time for Vietnamization and warning Hanoi that Nixon would not be bound by the limits of the past. Who could predict, so the reasoning went, what the "madman" might do next? In a televised address to the American public on the evening of 30 April, Nixon justified the Cambodian incursion as necessary to uphold American credibility and international stability. "If when the chips are down," Nixon stated, "the world's most powerful nation, the United States of America, acts like a pitiful helpless giant, the forces of totalitarianism and anarchy will threaten free nations and free institutions throughout the world."[8]

As Nixon spoke, a U.S.–South Vietnamese force of 20,000 soldiers, supported by U.S. air power, was crossing the Cambodian border. The results of the incursion were mixed. Militarily, the outcome resembled the Iron Triangle campaign of 1967. The extensive bombing, followed by the U.S.–South Vietnamese ground assault, leveled some 1,700 acres of heavy jungle and destroyed 800 bunkers. The Americans and South Vietnamese captured large quantities of supplies and weapons and disrupted North Vietnamese military operations. "At a time when North Vietnam sorely needed a victory," General Dave Richard Palmer writes, "it received instead a jolting setback."[9] Indeed, the invasion achieved much of its purpose. South Vietnam gained a measure of security. Moreover, the South Vietnamese forces fought well; Palmer observes that the "incursion was a benchmark in the maturing of ARVN, the point where confidence and spirit caught up to ability."[10] Yet even those participants and historians who consider the incursion as a military success also acknowledge that it failed to impose a decisive defeat on the North Vietnamese; their use of Cambodian territory was interrupted but not ended. And COSVN turned out to be disappointing, little more than a few huts in the jungle. (U.S. forces were removed by 29 June; South Vietnamese troops, by then totaling 34,000, remained.)

Politically, the results were even more mixed. In terms of the overall Nixon objective of "peace with honor," the Cambodian incursion bought time: for Vietnamization, for the staged withdrawal of U.S. forces, and for the South Vietnamese nation-building program. On the level of negotiations, however, the North Vietnamese had not been coerced into making concessions; they remained as uncompromising as earlier. Moreover, within Cambodia the invasion added to political instability and committed the United States to another weak ally. The U.S.–South Vietnamese attack forced the North Vietnamese troops into the more populated areas of Cambodia and into closer collaboration with the Khmer Rouge. In response, the Lon Nol government became dependent on U.S. support for its survival as it became involved in what proved to be a prolonged and ultimately futile civil war. In sum, by the spring of 1970 the United States had two client states in Indochina. The compromised neutrality of Sihanouk's Cambodia was preferable—not only for Cambodians but for the United States as well—to the tragic Cambodian warfare that began in 1970.

The most devastating political effect, however, was in the United States, where the Cambodian attack touched off the most extensive, and ultimately most tragic, antiwar protests. Nixon's contention that the assault would hasten the end of the war found little support. He badly misjudged public sentiment. Many Americans felt, in a word, betrayed. Having been promised that the war was winding down, they saw instead an extension of that war into a neutral country. War weariness and disillusionment touched off protests at universities, sometimes leading to violent confrontations. It was a volatile situation. At Kent State University in Ohio protest turned to tragedy when on 4 May National Guardsmen gunned down four young persons. A few days later a protest at Jackson State College in Mississippi ended in the police slaying of two students. Evidencing a remarkable insensitivity, the Nixon administration blamed the nation's discontent on disloyal and rebellious youth—"bums," as the president described them. Throughout the country that somber "Cambodian spring," the increasingly strident antiwar protests and demonstrations and fear of further violence led hundreds of colleges and universities to close their doors. On the other side, many Americans supported the Cambodian attack and resented the evident radicalism of the antiwar protesters. A consensus on Vietnam policy now eluded Nixon just as it had his predecessor.

The domestic reaction to the Cambodian invasion, while divided, effectively reduced Nixon's options. Clearly the American public would no longer tolerate expansion of the war or new missions for U.S. ground troops; this meant that henceforth the big-play tactic could be employed only in limited ways. More important, the wave of protests in the spring of 1970 gave unmistakable expression to a widespread determination that the war had to be brought to an end.

INCURSION INTO LAOS: OPERATION LAM SON, 1971

The American's public's war weariness and disapproval of any expanded U.S. ground combat did not prevent a second expression of the surprise strategy—an incursion into Laos in 1971—but did force a limited U.S. role. Again, the principal objective was to buy time for Vietnamization by disrupting North Vietnamese supply lines and staging areas. The target was the town of Tchepone, about 20 miles inside Laos. The assault was code-named

Operation Lam Son 719, taken from the name of the village where the Vietnamese had withstood a Chinese invasion in 1427.

Although the 1971 incursion into Laos dramatized the U.S. willingness to engage in bold ventures, it was, in fact, an extension of substantial U.S. warfare in that country. Laotian sovereignty had long been violated by the North Vietnamese and the United States, as both sought to control that country. North Vietnam assumed that sooner or later it would control its sparsely populated neighbor, while U.S. policy sought to uphold Laotian independence. After the 1962 agreement providing for the neutrality of Laos under the leadership of Prince Souvanna Phouma, the United States provided military and economic assistance to the royal government. Such support did not deter the Communist-led Pathet Lao's warfare against the royal government, and in fact, the Pathet Lao gradually increased its influence. The struggle for power within Laos was entwined with the war in Vietnam. The Ho Chi Minh Trail moved across the remote, mountainous region of eastern Laos. Besides stationing troops in Laos to facilitate the movement of men and supplies along the Ho Chi Minh Trail, the North Vietnamese also supported and trained the Pathet Lao.

The United States, for its part, engaged in secret but extensive warfare, much of it under CIA auspices. Besides officially backing the Souvanna Phouma government and its army, the United States, through the CIA, trained and equipped mountain tribesmen, principally the Hmong (or Meo) to fight against the Pathet Lao. In addition, the United States bombed North Vietnamese positions in Laos. These bombing missions, officially described as "aerial reconnaissance," had begun in 1964 and over the next four years resulted in the dropping of 455,000 tons of bombs. Under Nixon, the Laotian bombing intensified; indeed, in each of the first two years of his administration, the bombing surpassed the total of the period from 1964 to 1968. Thus, when the U.S.-supported South Vietnamese invading force crossed into Laos in 1971, it was taking the warfare in that country to a new level.

The attack into Laos had the same objective as that on Cambodia, but it differed significantly in that U.S. combat troops and advisers did not accompany the South Vietnamese into battle. In the aftermath of the Cambodian invasion, Congress enacted legislation that prohibited U.S. ground forces from entering Cambodia or Laos. This meant that for the first time the South Vietnamese forces would be fighting on their own. They would, however, still have the benefit of U.S. air support. In addition, the Laotian campaign differed from that undertaken in Cambodia in that it involved entering an area where the North Vietnamese had long been established and had built an extensive logistical lifeline. Attacking isolated sanctuaries in Cambodia was not the same as moving into a region where the North Vietnamese had some twenty thousand troops, including 19 antiaircraft battalions, 12 infantry units, a tank regiment, and an artillery regiment. And the North Vietnamese were close to home, facilitating their capacity to rush reinforcements into the battle.

Such considerations, however, did not deter U.S. and South Vietnamese officials, who were determined to reduce North Vietnamese infiltration. Intelligence reported a heavy North Vietnamese stockpiling in base areas inside Laos, which suggested that the enemy might be planning an assault on the two northernmost provinces of South Vietnam. Whether they planned to attack in 1971 or 1972 (which, to Americans, seemed more likely because it could influence the presidential election), the U.S. and ARVN commands assumed that an assault on Laos, however risky, would prevent greater dangers in the future. The operation had to take place before the rainy season, and time seemed of the essence for if the attack were delayed until 1972, the steady U.S. withdrawal would reduce support for the South Vietnamese assault force.

Operation Lam Son 719 began on 30 January 1971 when U.S. forces began securing the approaches to Laos on Route 9 and reopening the firebases at Khe Sanh that had been abandoned after the bitter siege of 1968. Khe Sanh was to be the major forward supply point for the operation. On 8 February South Vietnamese troops, with American air support, crossed into Laos. The assault followed Route 9 through a narrow valley surrounded by mountainous jungles. The advance was covered by a series of leapfrogging air assaults to the north of the road and by airmobile infantry to the south. At first the invasion went easily, but within a few days North Vietnamese resistance slowed the South Vietnamese and antiaircraft defense limited U.S. air support. Yet the South Vietnamese force, which totaled 21,000 soldiers, slowly continued its advance, and on 6 March it captured Tchepone, which had been reduced to rubble by U.S. bombing. After destroying the remaining North Vietnamese facilities nearby, the South Vietnamese, their mission thus far largely a success, determined to return home. That decision was made, rather than the alternative of advancing toward other base areas, because mounting North Vietnamese artillery attacks and troop reinforcements indicated that a large counterattack was imminent.

As the South Vietnamese began their withdrawal, Operation Lam Son 719 became unraveled. General Giap and other leaders in Hanoi believed that with a force of now 36,000 troops, the North Vietnamese could achieve a decisive victory that would completely discredit Vietnamization. Accordingly, they ordered massive assaults on the South Vietnamese. "Orderly withdrawal under enemy pressure," the military historian Shelby Stanton writes, is the "quickest undoing of an unfinished army."[11] The "unfinished" character of the South Vietnamese army quickly became evident. Most of its units panicked, and Route 9 was littered with bodies (some 2,000 South Vietnamese were killed in the Laotian campaign) as well as with abandoned tanks, vehicles, equipment, and artillery. The debacle included some of the South's most highly regarded units, including the "elite" airborne division and a marine batalion. Only U.S. air power enabled the remnants of the demoralized forces to return to South Vietnam.

Operation Lam Son 719 brought, at best, a marginal benefit to the Americans and South Vietnamese. The military historian General Dave Richard Palmer claims that its "most important result was to delay for nearly a year the possibility of an invasion. . . . Saigon had gained still more time to develop and to prepare. Vietnamization would not have to face its test that year."[12] In another and more important sense, however, the Laotian operation was, in fact, a test of Vietnamization, and one that suggested its limitations. The South Vietnamese army had not performed well on its own, and only U.S. air power had prevented the annihilation of the withdrawing ARVN force. Shelby Stanton concludes that for the Saigon government, Lam Son 719 "turned out to be a sour defeat, exposing grave deficiencies in planning, organization, leadership, motivation, and operational expertise. . . . Vietnamization had not brought the South Vietnamese military to the point where it could safely challenge [North Vietnamese Army]–defended base territory."[13]

Although President Thieu proclaimed a victory in Laos and President Nixon assured Americans that "Vietnamization has succeeded," the reality of the "sour defeat" was not lost among the South Vietnamese and Americans. In Saigon and other cities, much of the educated elite openly worried about their country's ability to survive without American support. Vietnamization itself became a target of criticism, and anti-U.S. demonstrations in Saigon underscored growing resentment and apprehension. One poster showed Nixon standing above a pile of dead South Vietnamese soldiers with a message that Vietnamization meant the sacrifice of Vietnamese by the United States.

In the United States, the Laotian campaign was a catalyst to renewed antiwar protests. Most notably, disillusioned Vietnam veterans, under the banner of Vietnam Veterans against the War, gathered in Washington to publicly denounce the war and their role in it and to throw away their medals. Former navy officer John Kerry spoke for many when he said it was time to "reach out and destroy the last vestige of this barbaric war."[14]

Lastly, Operation Lam Son 719 had important lessons for the North Vietnamese. They had suffered heavy losses—perhaps as many as 10,000 dead—yet they had routed a well-equipped South Vietnamese army, which suggested that the military situation had shifted in their favor. A North Vietnamese military historian later recalled that Lam Son 719 was "proof that the [North Vietnamese] could defeat the best [South Vietnamese] units. We had not been certain we could do this before. 'Vietnamization' did create a strong South Vietnamese army. . . . Our army had to learn how to organize large-scale battles. So 1971 was a big test."[15]

THE NORTH'S EASTER 1972 OFFENSIVE

If the Cambodian invasion ultimately forced the Nixon administration to recognize the imperative to end the war, the spring 1972 invasion of

South Vietnam eventually brought the same message home to the leadership in Hanoi. The outcome of the invasion fell considerably short of North Vietnam's objectives.

The North Vietnamese leadership calculated that the spring of 1972 was an opportune moment to launch a major attack. The decision reflected several assumptions: (1) that the United States could not mount an effective military response, since political restraints in the United States would prevent Nixon from reversing the withdrawal of U.S. troops; (2) that the North Vietnamese could make significant political gains that Nixon, under pressures to end the war before the presidential election, would be forced to accept in a negotiated settlement; and (3) that South Vietnam was vulnerable in view of the disillusionment and casualties resulting from the attack on Laos.

Hanoi was also driven to seek an early end to the war by the changing international situation. The improved relationship between the United States and the Soviet Union, which would be dramatized in Nixon's visit to Moscow in the spring of 1972, left Communist leaders in Vietnam wary. Recalling how the Soviet Union had been slow to support their struggle against the French and had accepted the division of Vietnam in 1954, the North Vietnamese feared that the Soviets might reduce assistance or pressure them to accept U.S. terms for ending the war. Equally, if not more, upsetting to Hanoi was the American opening to China, beginning with Kissinger's visit to Beijing in 1971 and followed by Nixon's journey there in February 1972. Since China clearly looked to the United States as a counterweight to its tensions with the Soviet Union, it was susceptible to U.S. pressures on the Vietnam situation. China also was deeply suspicious of the ties between the Soviet Union and Vietnam and wanted the United States to play a prominent role in Southeast Asia as a means of balancing the Soviet Union's power in Asia. Although Chinese leaders officially declined American overtures that they act as an intermediary in ending the war, China's interests pointed in the direction of a negotiated settlement. The Chinese suggested to the North Vietnamese that reunification might still be a distant goal. Thus, as a result of the Nixon administration's pursuit of a new world order, North Vietnam, which for a decade had been able to exploit the Sino-Soviet split to its advantage, now felt pressures from both of the major Communist powers to compromise its basic objectives. It seemed like a repetition of the 1954 settlement. The Easter 1972 Offensive thus offered an opportunity, perhaps the last, for North Vietnam to force a settlement on its own terms.

As in the Tet Offensive, the North Vietnamese had maximum and minimum objectives. At its best, the 1972 attack would result in the defeat of the South Vietnamese army, the overthrow of Thieu's government, and the withdrawal of the United States. At the least, the 1972 offensive would cause further loss of military and civilian morale, undermine Vietnamization, and enhance the North's bargaining position. Toward those ends, the North Vietnamese, diverting their slender resources from economic reconstruction, committed a dozen infantry units with substantial armored and heavy artillery support. If the attack was successful, it would complete what the Tet Offensive had begun.

Beginning 30 March, some 120,000 North Vietnamese regulars and thousands of Viet Cong guerrillas assaulted South Vietnam's northern provinces, the central highlands, and the area northwest of Saigon. The attack, like the Tet Offensive, caught the United States by surprise. As in 1968, the U.S. command in Saigon discounted North Vietnam's military capability, assuming that the North lacked the resources to engage in anything more than small-unit warfare. Just a few days before the attack, Secretary of Defense Melvin Laird stated that a large-scale invasion was "not a serious possibility." Even after the invasion began, Americans were still disbelieving; General Westmoreland, now the army chief of staff in Washington, remarked that the "staying power of the enemy is not great."[16]

Despite such predictions, North Vietnamese forces took much territory, especially in the northern provinces. They overran Quang Tri province and advanced on Hué. In the central highlands, another wave of the offensive moved on the key town of Kontum, while a third force moved across the Cambodian frontier and threatened to take An Loc, 60 miles north of Saigon.

The United States responded quickly. Ending the restrictions on U.S. bombing that had been in place since November 1968, Nixon ordered air attacks on North Vietnam, including raids on Hanoi and Haiphong. He also ordered the mining of Haiphong and other harbors, a step that the United States had previously declined to take since it risked confrontation with the ships of the Soviet Union and other countries. Operation Linebacker, the renewed air assault on the North, exceeded previous air warfare as round-the-clock missions bombed supply lines, depots, factories, power facilities, and virtually all targets of any military value. The bombing was made all the more devastating by the first use of "smart bombs," which were guided with precision to their targets by computers acting on laser or television signals. Linebacker effectively destroyed the fuel and ammunition depots and much of the supply lines on which the North Vietnamese army depended. Besides the air war on the North, the United States also employed wide-scale bombing in the South to support the beleaguered South Vietnamese forces. American support was vital to the South Vietnamese army as it withstood the attacks on Kontum and An Loc.

The major engagement of the Easter 1972 Offensive was fought in Quang Tri province, with the most intense battle waged over its capital, Quang Tri City. After being taken early in the offensive by the North Vietnamese, Quang Tri became the principal objective of the South Vietnamese after they had held off the attack on Hué. The South Vietnamese assault on Quang Tri brought massive firepower to bear—each day some 25,000 rounds of artillery were fired, and American bombers flew 40 missions. Unable to dislodge the North Vietnamese through firepower, General Thieu ordered a marine assault, which took five days of intense fighting before finally forcing the North Vietnamese to abandon the city. On 15 September—after 10 weeks of fighting—the South Vietnamese recaptured Quang Tri. Arnold Isaacs, a journalist who witnessed the battle, recalls, "When it was finally recaptured Quang Tri was no longer a city but a lake of shattered masonry. . . . The destruction was equally complete elsewhere. Only charred skeletons remained of the villages. . . . It was another case—on a larger scale than before—of destroying Vietnam to save it."[17]

To the North Vietnamese, however, the results of the Easter 1972 Offensive were disappointing. "They had severely miscalculated both the fighting ability of the South Vietnamese Army and the ability of the United States to react," Col. Harry Summers has written. "Their attempt to mass [their forces] had proven disastrous—again over 100,000 battle deaths."[18] The evidence of loss was everywhere: North Vietnam had been subjected to the most sustained bombing of the war, and its army had suffered enormous losses. Moreover, the Soviet Union and China, although continuing their material support, gave priority to improving relations with the United States. Their protests against renewed U.S. bombing and the mining of Haiphong harbor had been perfunctory. The North Vietnamese especially resented the Soviet Union's grandiose hosting of Nixon in the name of détente at the very time U.S. bombing raids were devastating their country. On several occasions the North Vietnamese Communist party newspaper criticized the behavior of the large Communist powers; for instance, it spoke disparagingly of "those who are departing from the great, invincible revolutionary thoughts of the time and are pitifully mired on the dark and muddy road of unprincipled compromise. . . . We Communists must persevere in the revolution and not compromise with our adversaries."[19]

Frustrated in their military-political objectives and fearing that the international changes would leave them isolated, the North Vietnamese leadership decided that the circumstances dictated the necessity to reach a settlement quickly. They calculated that the prospects for reaching an agreement with the United States were better prior to, rather than after, the 1972 presidential election. With these various considerations in mind, North Vietnam backed away from its insistence that the Thieu government be removed.

The effect of the invasion on the South was difficult to assess. The success of the South Vietnamese army in withstanding the assault and in forcing most of the Northern armies to retreat led many U.S. officials to conclude that South Vietnam was at last capable of standing on its own. Still, the South Vietnamese army's success depended, to a large extent, on U.S. support.

That point was not lost to the South Vietnamese leadership and public. Indeed, morale was undermined by the offensive, for after nearly four years of small-unit warfare concentrated in remote areas, the North had again demonstrated its capacity to recover from losses and to launch a large-scale attack. The steady withdrawal of U.S. forces and Nixon's pursuit of improved relations with the Soviet Union and China further unnerved the South Vietnamese. Just as the North Vietnamese feared that their allies could no longer be counted on, so too the South Vietnamese feared that the American commitment would be sacrificed in the interest of major-power cooperation. Above all, the intensity of the fighting and the renewal of large-scale U.S. bombing in the South contributed to an almost palpable war weariness among the South Vietnamese population. More and more frequently people talked about the imperative to end the war, even if it meant Northern or Communist control. A South Vietnamese officer told an American at the time, "If this were truly a patriotic war, everybody would be willing to fight. But we do not want to kill other Vietnamese. We do not want victory. We want only peace."[20] As his comment underscored, South Vietnam, after nearly 20 years of U.S. support on an unparalleled scale, had still not achieved the kind of national identity that would lead people to see themselves waging a "patriotic war."

In sum, the North Vietnamese invasion and South Vietnamese counterattack underscored to both of the Vietnamese sides the senselessness of continued warfare. "In the final analysis," the historian George Herring has observed, "the furious campaigns of the summer of 1972 merely raised the stalemate to a new level of violence."[21] Similarly, the journalist Arnold Isaacs reflected, "The battle [of Quang Tri] was a wholly accurate image of the Vietnam war of 1972, the symbol of the hopeless, endless, bloodsoaked stalemate that the war had become."[22]

TALKING AND BOMBING FOR "PEACE," 1972–1973

The Cambodian incursion of 1970, the Laotian invasion of 1971, and the Easter 1972 Offensive contributed, each in its own way, to the political situation that finally led to a treaty ending the war. The United States and North Vietnam had independently reached the same conclusion: military and political circumstances required compromise in their bargaining positions. Although both sides still held to their fundamental objectives with respect to the status of South Vietnam, each had at least realized that those objectives could not be immediately achieved. Since any compromise in the U.S. commitment to South Vietnam's independence threatened its very existence, the Thieu government, its military vulnerability having been so graphically evident in the 1971 and 1972 campaigns, resisted the movement toward a settlement.

In Paris, the long stalemate quickly ended during the resumption in July 1972 of the private talks between Kissinger and Le Duc Tho, the high-ranking member of the North Vietnamese Politburo with whom Kissinger had met intermittently since 1970. The United States had previously signaled its willingness to back away from its initial insistence that both U.S. and North Vietnamese troops be withdrawn from the South. That critical concession reflected reality; having failed militarily to force the North Vietnamese from the field, the United States could not hope to achieve that objective diplomatically. The North Vietnamese now backed away from their long-standing insistence that the United States end support of the Thieu government and that it be replaced by a coalition government that would include representatives of the Provisional Revolutionary Government (PRG), as the National Liberation Front was redesignated. On 8 October Le Duc Tho presented a draft agreement that provided for a cease-fire in place, with the armies of each side remaining in areas under their control. This was to be followed by the withdrawal of all U.S. troops within 60 days, the exchange of prisoners of war, and negotiations between the Thieu government and the PRG. Those negotiations were to arrange for democratic elections under the supervision of a Council of National Reconciliation and Concord, which would represent the Saigon government, PRG, and neutrals. Finally, the draft treaty called for eventual reunification of the South and North "through peaceful means" and for an American contribution to "healing the wounds of war and to post-war reconstruction." Jubilant over the North Vietnamese concessions, Kissinger exclaimed to an aide, "We have done it!" The drafting of a final settlement quickly went forward.

The South Vietnamese leaders, however, were outraged by what they saw as the height of American arrogance. From Saigon's perspective, the United States had arbitrarily negotiated a settlement, thereby effectively abandoning an ally without even consulting that ally. Thieu and others were indignant over the infringement on South Vietnamese sovereignty inherent in the provisions that permitted Northern troops to remain in the South and affirmed the objective of reunification. They saw the Council of National Reconciliation and Concord as another name for a coalition government, which they had consistently opposed. The settlement, Thieu recognized, rendered his government more insecure than ever.

Hence the most critical obstacle to an American exit from Vietnam became the U.S.-created and -sustained government in Saigon. Indeed, Thieu's bitter denunciation of the treaty unraveled the process. He stated that "peace will come when I sign the agreement. . . . Any signatures, even ten signatures, without mine will be completely of no value."[23] The North Vietnamese became annoyed over Thieu's recalcitrance; believing that Thieu would never act independently of the United States, they blamed the Americans for using Thieu to sabotage the settlement. Thus Hanoi publicly charged that the United States was reneging on the terms it had agreed to during the Paris negotiations. An exasperated Kissinger tried to get the process back on track when he stated publicly on 31 October that "peace is at hand."

But it was not quite at hand. Nixon, following his overwhelming reelection a few days after Kissinger's statement, cajoled the South Vietnamese. A massive airlift of U.S. weapons and equipment (Project Enhance Plus) gave the South Vietnamese hundreds of aircraft (making it the fourth largest air force in the world), over 200 tanks, over 100 armored personnel carriers, nearly 2,000 trucks, and other matériel. Besides this effort to build up the South Vietnamese military, Nixon promised Thieu that the United States would seek revision of the draft agreement to meet Thieu's objections but warned that not all could be met. Nixon wanted a settlement and would not allow Thieu to veto an agreement; as he said privately, "The tail cannot wag the dog." Yet to make the agreement tolerable, Nixon assured Thieu that "you have my assurance of continued assistance in the post-settlement period and that we will respond with full force should the settlement be violated by North Vietnam."[24]

That "swift and retaliatory action," in fact, came before a final settlement was reached. Following three weeks of tense and unproductive U.S.–North Vietnamese negotiations principally over the South's objections to the draft treaty, the Nixon administration blamed the delay on Hanoi. In what was perhaps a classic instance of blaming the other side for problems that were of his own making, Kissinger told Nixon that the North Vietnamese leaders were "just a bunch of shits. Tawdry, filthy shits."[25] Nixon responded to the breakdown in negotiations by a renewed bombing campaign against the North, Operation Linebacker 2.

Launched on 18 December, Linebacker 2—which become commonly called the Christmas Bombing—was a final and devastating evidence of Nixon's willingness to unleash U.S. power. He instructed the Joint Chiefs of Staff to undertake massive air attacks on military and communications facilities in the Hanoi area as well as on the docks, shipyards, and other installations at Haiphong. "I don't want any of this crap about the fact that we couldn't hit this target or that one," Nixon admonished. "This is your chance to use military power to win this war, and if you don't I'll hold you responsible."[26]

The Christmas Bombing was an 11-day assault in which B-52 bombers and other aircraft dropped over 40,000 tons of bombs principally in the 60-mile Hanoi-Haiphong corridor. It was the most devastating bombing campaign of the entire war. Typical of the assault were the simultaneous B-52 raids on the night of 29 December, when 72 bombers hit Hanoi from four different directions, at the same time that 18 bombers attacked the rail center north of the city and another 30 bombers struck Haiphong.

Like so many U.S. actions during the war, this last burst of U.S. power brought mixed results. It reduced North Vietnam's military capacity and its access to outside assistance. The extensive bombing damage, when added to the blockage initiated earlier in 1972, disrupted the supply lines from China and the Soviet Union; military estimates contended that North Vietnam could now receive only about 20 percent of the outside supplies available earlier. The Christmas Bombing was also a stark warning to North Vietnam that Nixon might reintroduce U.S. air power if it violated the final treaty. Finally, this signal of U.S. resolve served to reassure the South Vietnamese and to bring Thieu into line.

Yet the price of the bombing campaign was also considerable. The North Vietnamese unleashed nearly 1,000 surface-to-air missiles against the U.S. aircraft, with the result that the United States suffered its heaviest air losses of the war: 26 aircraft, including 15 B-52s, and 92 crew members were shot down. The assault also brought strong criticism throughout the world. European allies and much of the press in Europe condemned the American action. Pope Paul VI described the bombing as the "object of daily grief." The Chinese, despite their recent infatuation with Nixon, organized a massive demonstration against the bombing. And in the United States, the reaction to the Christmas Bombing underscored once again the public's opposition to any broadening of the war; just six weeks after his overwhelming reelection, Nixon's "approval rating" dropped to 39 percent—a direct consequence of public disenchantment over intensifying a war when peace was supposedly "at hand."

Much of the criticism of the Christmas Bombing charged that the United States was terrorizing the people of North Vietnam. In fact, the bombing campaign, although directed against the most populous area of North Vietnam, took a relatively small toll of civilian lives (about 1,600) when measured against other massive bombing assaults. Anticipating a renewal of the air war, the North Vietnamese government had evacuated large segments of the civilian population from Hanoi and Haiphong. More important, the U.S. command took extraordinary steps to direct the bombing against only military targets, and bombing crews often took risks to bomb accurately. Of course, some bombs went astray and hit some residential areas as well as a hospital, but overall, the Christmas Bombing was carried out with extraordinary precision.

In the end of the Christmas Bombing must be evaluated in terms of whether it forced North Vietnamese concessions in the search for an end to the war and whether it altered the long-term political-military balance between the North and South. Few analysts accept the Kissinger and Nixon contention that the bombing brought the recalcitrant North Vietnamese back to the bargaining table prepared to make important concessions. "Nixon's dynamic bombing campaign had been superfluous," Stanley Karnow writes, "at least as an instrument of diplomacy."[27] The historian George Herring concurs that the "bombing did not produce a settlement markedly different from the one the United States had earlier negotiated. . . . The changes from the October agreement were largely cosmetic."[28]

The basic terms of the final settlement negotiated by Kissinger and Le Duc Tho in January 1973 indeed followed closely the draft agreement of October 1972. The Thieu government still had to be coerced into going along with this Paris Agreement. Among the few changes in the agreement was inclusion of a reference to the Demilitarized Zone, a provision which the South Vietnamese had insisted upon as an affirmation of the division of the country. Yet in deference to the North's vision of a united Vietnam, the article regarding the Demilitarized Zone was followed by a clause stating that it was "only provisional and not a political or territorial boundary."[29]

Such incongruous language about the DMZ typified this fundamentally flawed treaty, which left unsettled the basic issue over which the United States and North Vietnam had fought: the status of South Vietnam. Who would rule in the South had been the point of contention between Washington and Hanoi ever since the "temporary" division of Vietnam nearly 20 years earlier. The Thieu government remained, but the provisions for a National Council of Reconciliation and Concord and for representation of the PRG meant that implementation of the settlement would reduce its claims to legitimacy. The presence of North Vietnamese troops in the South—to which Thieu had most vehemently objected—and the withdrawal of the remaining U.S. forces left South Vietnam vulnerable.

In the end the settlement reflected military and political realities. For domestic and international reasons, the United States was not prepared to continue its fighting, and the Paris Agreement provided for a graceful exit from an intractable conflict. Nixon could boast that he had achieved "peace with honor," for the U.S. was able to withdraw, have its prisoners of war returned, and see Thieu still in power in Saigon. Yet such claims disingenuously ignored that fact that, having been unable to force the North Vietnamese to abandon their warfare in the South, the United States had no choice but to tolerate the continued presence of their troops in the South. Likewise, the Hanoi leadership, having seen their country battered by nearly a decade of bombing and having absorbed devastating losses in men and matériel, preferred a settlement to continued fighting. Although abandoning their insistence that Thieu be removed, the North Vietnamese did not compromise their ultimate objective: national unification. The settlement, with its cumbersome political process in the South and with its anticipation of eventual unification, reflected the essential objectives of the North Vietnamese.

No one, however, expected that the political terms of the 1973 settlement would ever be implemented. The still unresolved question of political power in the South—which could not be settled diplomatically because of the fundamental military stalemate—would almost certainly be settled by force.

As the American forces completed their withdrawal and the North Vietnamese released U.S. prisoners of war, the Vietnamese in both the North and South were embittered by the way that the United States was ending its military involvement. "By any fair standard," Arnold Isaacs notes, "Nixon and Kissinger had treated their Vietnamese ally with contemptuous disregard, and their Vietnamese enemy with bad faith and brutality."[30] While Nixon reassured Thieu that the United States would retaliate if North Vietnam violated the agreement, the South Vietnamese government believed that it had been betrayed and was skeptical about Nixon's promises. The North Vietnamese, although relieved that the United States was withdrawing the last of its troops, bitterly resented the Christmas Bombing and distrusted American intentions more than ever. If "peace with honor" meant leaving Vietnam with the respect of friend and foe, then the Nixon-Kissinger policy must be judged a failure.

THE UNENDING STRUGGLE, 1973–1974

The Paris Agreement, as anticipated, accomplished nothing except U.S. disengagement. The vague political provisions required the good faith and trust of two sides that had irreconcilable differences. The status of the southern half of Vietnam still had to be settled, and both Hanoi and Saigon realized that arms, not negotiations, would be the means.

The Thieu government appeared to be in a strong position, in that it could claim control over 75 percent of the territory and 85 percent of the population of South Vietnam. Its army, including reserves, totaled about one million troops, nearly 10 times the estimated strength of Viet Cong and North Vietnamese units in the South. The last-minute infusion of U.S. military assistance added to an advantage that Thieu sought to exploit. Believing that time was of the essence, he ordered ARVN forces to seize as much territory as possible. The South Vietnamese not only regained many areas that Communists had seized just before the cease-fire but also contested Viet Cong control in other areas where the Communists had long been dominant.

As the South Vietnamese army took the initiative in 1973, the leadership in Hanoi was marshaling its resources for a long-term campaign. With many of the Communist units in the South in disarray and suffering from shortages of food and ammunition, the North Vietnamese decided to build "a base for the task of liberating South Vietnam and unifying the nation."[31] That base was methodically constructed. Communist forces in the South avoided engagements with ARVN units except for cases where they enjoyed clear superiority. Meanwhile, the North infiltrated about 100,000 troops into the South, thus increasing the combined North Vietnamese–Viet Cong strength to about 230,000 (and reducing the ARVN advantage to about a four-to-one margin). The North Vietnamese improved their logistical position in the South by constructing a road link into the central highlands and extending petroleum pipelines into the northern provinces. Thus reinforced, they became more resourceful in late 1973 and early 1974 and recaptured their traditional strongholds in the Mekong Delta. The North Vietnamese, however, still avoided an all-out assault. Among their reasons was the belief that the Saigon government's economic and political problems would work to their long-term advantage.

Indeed, the evidence of the Thieu's government's strength was, as the North Vietnamese calculated, quite misleading. Like so many signs of U.S. "progress" in Vietnam, the Thieu government's control over the South and initiative of 1973 concealed fundamental flaws. "Control" over the countryside and population was often ephemeral. Countless villages continued to be only nominally under Saigon's authority. In other places, South Vietnamese authorities might govern by day, while the Communists held power at night. Most important, the Saigon government's "control" did not mean its acceptance by the villagers. In fact, the peasantry's distrust of the government intensified. Thieu, like every leader in Saigon since 1954, refused to undertake the kinds of rural reforms that were essential to winning the support of the peasantry. Instead, Thieu, who depended upon the military for his power, put army officers in charge of his administration, reaching all the way to the district and village levels. The officer corps, which came predominantly from the old aristocracy and from the urban business and commercial class, were estranged culturally from the villagers.

The Thieu government suffered, above all, from internal decay. Graft and corruption pervaded it at all levels. Money bought everything: exemptions from military service, government positions ranging from police officer to provincial chief, exit visas, false death certificates. In one way or another, money was extracted for virtually all government services. Nowhere was the corruption more notorious than in the military. Affluent soldiers avoided combat by purchasing safe assignments. Promotions and command positions were available to the highest bidders. Pilots were known to demand bribes before agreeing to fly missions on behalf of besieged ground forces. Likewise, the quartermaster corps demanded bribes before sending food and supplies for the troops. Military convoys were "taxed" by local officials as they entered provinces that their forces had been sent to defend. High-ranking officers siphoned millions of piasters from the military payroll; they took the pay of "ghost soldiers" (men who had been killed or deserted but whose names still appeared on the payroll) and "flower soldiers" (draftees who held civilian jobs and "gave" their military pay to officers in return for avoiding military service). At the top of this sordid situation were Thieu and other top military officers who lived luxuriously. It was a system that Thieu, who never enjoyed wide popularity, had fostered in order to survive. The political scientist William Turley observes that "corruption had become the glue that held the Thieu regime together."[32]

The corruption was made even worse by the crippling effects of urban unemployment and inflation. The withdrawal of U.S. forces caused serious dislocations; hundreds of thousands of jobs had depended upon the large American presence. Saigon and other cities that had enjoyed a facade of prosperity by catering to the Americans suddenly were crippled by soaring unemployment. Rising world prices, combined with the ending of means by which the United States had controlled inflationary pressures, produced an astounding 65 percent rate of inflation in 1973. This meant that the vast majority of civil servants and soldiers were not receiving enough pay to meet basic needs. And, of course, these economic problems simply added to the incentives for graft and bribery.

Perhaps the ultimate expression of the decay of South Vietnam was the widespread black market with the Communist forces. The Viet Cong and

North Vietnamese forces were able to get many essential items—food, fuel, medicine, radios—from areas under South Vietnamese government control. To be certain, many of these goods were passed along by Viet Cong sympathizers, but most were sold by Southerners whose only motive was profit.

By 1974, as this situation became more and more desperate (the inflation rate hit 90 percent that year), opposition to the Thieu government became widespread. The Buddhist leadership again took the initiative in opposing a government that, as in 1963 and 1966, still had no mandate. Even the Catholic clergy, whose anticommunism had traditionally made it tolerant of the Saigon regime's abuses, criticized the widespread corruption and called for a thorough cleansing of the government.

Lastly, the army—on which Thieu depended for power—was coming unraveled. On top of its crippling corruption, ARVN'S military capability steadily eroded. Whatever the merits of Thieu's objective of securing control over as much territory as possible, the effect was to leave ARVN widely dispersed. Each advance in 1973 meant that ARVN was stretching itself more and more thinly. About half of the army was tied down in the South's northernmost provinces. The army's capacity to hold areas, let alone continue the initiative, was undermined by attrition. Heavy casualties resulting from battles against an enemy that still could choose the time and place of battle, combined with a high rate of desertion, meant that losses were exceeding replacements. Each year about 90,000 young men reached draft age and entered the service (another 60,000 bought their way out annually), but that did not match the total number of deaths, casualties, and desertions. Moreover, the army suffered from the faulty underlying strategic assumption that it could fight as the United States had done. Mobility and massive firepower were essential to ARVN's plans to hold the South, but to sustain the South Vietnamese army in such operations would have required $3 billion a year in U.S. military assistance, which was not politically feasible in view of the widespread disenchantment in Washington over military spending in Vietnam. Instead U.S. aid dropped sharply, from about $2.3 billion in 1973 to $1 billion in 1974. In the United States, the Watergate scandal engulfed Nixon, whose assurances of U.S. support had encouraged Thieu's land-grabbing initiative. After Nixon resigned the presidency in August 1974, Kissinger urged another $1.5 billion in military assistance, but Congress cut the authorization to $700 million. This reduction in U.S. assistance limited ARVN's military capacity, as it suffered from shortages of gasoline, ammunition, spare parts, and other essentials.

As a result of the massive corruption, the evident demise of the army, and the substantial reduction of U.S. aid, the always fragile South Vietnamese political structure disintegrated. Popular disillusionment with the government became pervasive. The Buddhist and Catholic protests mounted, and more and more of the educated classes talked of reaching an accommodation with the Communists. Perhaps most ominously, a loss of morale plagued the armed services; some 240,000 men deserted the army in 1974. After two decades of U.S. support, the government of South Vietnam still did not represent any genuine sense of nationhood.

A REVOLUTION COMPLETED: THE HO CHI MINH CAMPAIGN

The long war ended with an abruptness that startled both sides. Having marshaled their resources and having built an elaborate line of supply into the South, the North Vietnamese leaders were confident of ultimate victory. Seeking to exploit the chronic weakness of the South Vietnamese government, they calculated that a successful frontal assault on ARVN would lead to a popular uprising against the Saigon government. As Hanoi in late 1974 planned for an offensive the following spring, it set 1976 as the target date for a decisive victory. That the North Vietnamese did not anticipate the crumbling of the South Vietnamese military, which would in fact occur in 1975, was hardly surprising, for in 1974 the war had been waged so long and with so few significant military gains that a sudden breakthrough seemed inconceivable. The North Vietnamese also were uncertain about the reaction of the United States to an offensive; would the United States save its ally? Premier Pham Van Dong, in a meeting with other officials, predicted that the Americans would not return; he reasoned that the United States might resume bombing (which the North Vietnamese could survive), but never again would it send ground troops.

The North Vietnamese launched their campaign in the central highlands, where ARVN forces were notably thinner than in the northern provinces. In mid-December 1974 Communist troops attacked in Phuoc Long province and, after seizing a key junction, moved on to seize the capital city of Phuoc Binh on 6 January 1975. Shortly afterward the entire province was in their hands. In Saigon, South Vietnamese officials were stunned by the defeat and by the American indifference to this first important North Vietnamese offensive in three years. Emboldened by their success, the North Vietnamese attacked another central highlands target, the city of Ban Me Thout, capital of Darlac province. Beginning on 1 March with a diversionary move toward Pleiku that led the South Vietnamese to concentrate on defense of that city, the North Vietnamese forces captured Ban Me Thuot in 10 days.

Within two months the North Vietnamese captured much of the central provinces—the most substantial shift in the military balance in nearly two decades of fighting. A desperate General Thieu abruptly altered his strategy. He decided to "lighten the top and keep the bottom." Abandoning the commitment to hold as much territory as possible, he ordered his forces to withdraw from the northern provinces and concentrate on maintaining control of the coastal cities. Thieu's order, rather than leading to an effective defense, touched off a panic. His undisciplined army was responsible for much of the ensuing chaos, as military commanders often abandoned their armies and troops joined civilians in fleeing from the advancing Communist forces. Nearly one million refugees overwhelmed Da Nang, rendering impossible Thieu's order that the city be held. South Vietnamese troops fought not against the North Vietnamese but against civilians for places on airplanes and ships that evacuated thousands of persons. On 26 March North Vietnamese troops took Hué, and four days later they marched into Da Nang without opposition.

As the fall of Da Nang was followed quickly by the hasty retreat of the South Vietnamese army from the coastal provinces, attention shifted to Saigon. North Vietnamese military and political strategists, meeting near Ban Me Thuout in early April, decided to undertake an immediate offensive on Saigon: The Ho Chi Minh Campaign. Time was of the essence, for the campaign had to succeed before the arrival of the rainy season. Time was of the essence in another sense as well, for the North Vietnamese believed that the people of Saigon were so demoralized by the collapse of Saigon's authority in the northern provinces that they would not defend the South Vietnamese capital. That assumption was correct, for in Saigon there was no rallying to support the government; no one rushed to enlist in an army from which others were fleeing, and no official summoned the populace to prepare for combat. Instead, political leaders and generals plotted against Thieu, who resigned on 21 April, telling his people in a radio address, "I resign but I do not desert."[33] In fact, he left Vietnam four days later.

By the time that Thieu was leaving, North Vietnamese troops were advancing on Saigon. They encountered their only significant opposition during the 1975 campaign in a two-week battle northeast of Saigon, near Bien Hoa. Once that line of defense was broken, the North Vietnamese moved rapidly toward the capital, where U.S. helicoptors belatedly evacuated some seven thousand American personnel, along with South Vietnamese officials and families who had been closely associated with United States. As the chaotic evacuation ended, North Vietnamese units reached the outskirts of Saigon on the evening of 29 April.

The next morning the remnants of South Vietnamese authority ended not with a bang but a whimper. Thousands of ARVN troops shed their uniforms and raced for their homes in their underwear. In government offices, small numbers of civil servants, who had been secretly working for the Communist cause, announced that they were taking power. A North Vietnamese tank lumbered through the streets of Saigon toward Independence Palace and bashed down its gates. Moments later inside the palace, the ranking North Vietnamese officer, Colonel Bui Tin, met General Duong Van Minh, who had led the plot against Diem 12 years earlier and who had been placed in the presidency after Thieu's departure. The exchange was simple but direct. Minh offered to transfer authority, but Bui Tin retorted that he had none to hand over: "Your power has crumbled. You cannot give up what you do not have."[34]

Winners and losers saw the tumultuous events of the spring of 1975 from widely differing historical perspectives. Its international stature tarnished by the war, the United States nonetheless remained a global power with the luxury of casting aside concern with Vietnam. Indeed, Americans moved quickly to forget about the war. President Gerald Ford stated that "Americans can regain the sense of pride that existed before Vietnam. But it cannot be achieved by refighting a war that is finished. . . . These events, tragic as they are, portend neither the end of the world nor of America's leadership in the world."[35] Secretary of State Kissinger was more blunt: "Vietnam was a great tragedy. We should never have been there at all. But it's history."[36]

That abandonment embittered those who had become dependent on the United States. Even allowing for the corruption and ineptitude of the South Vietnamese government, General Thieu, in his often hysterical resignation speech, was not entirely unreasonable in his indictment of American arrogance: "Kissinger didn't see that the agreement led the South Vietnamese people to death. . . . I never thought that a man like Mr. Kissinger would deliver our people to such a disastrous fate. . . . The United States has not respected its promises. It is unfair. It is inhumane. It is not trustworthy. It is irresponsible."[37]

And for the victorious Communist forces, the collapse of the South Vietnamese government meant the completion of a revolution begun 30 years earlier. The Ho Chi Minh Campaign marked the fulfillment of Ho's assertion of national independence in 1945; a unified Vietnam would now be realized for the first time since before the arrival of the French. Bui Tin expressed such patriotic sentiments to General Minh: "Between Vietnamese, there are no victors and no vanquished. Only the Americans have been beaten. If you are patriots, consider this a moment of joy. The war for our country is over."[38]

Notes

1. Stanley Resor cited in Murray Marder, "Our Longest War's Tortuous History," in Allan R. Millett, ed., *A Short History of the Vietnam War* (Bloomington: Indiana University Press, 1978), 33.

2. Sir Robert Thompson cited in Palmer, *Summons of the Trumpet*, 283.

3. Allen E. Goodman, "The Dual-Track Strategy of Vietnamization and Negotiation," in John Sclight, ed., *Second Indochina War Symposium* (Washington, D.C.: Department of the Army, 1986), 149.

4. Ibid., 148.

5. Both cited in Arnold R. Isaacs, *Without Honor: Defeat in Vietnam and Cambodia* (Baltimore, Md.: Johns Hopkins University Press, 1983), 108.

6. D. R. Palmer, *Summons of the Trumpet*, 291.

7. Karnow, *Vietnam*, 590.

8. *Public Papers of the President of the United States: Richard M. Nixon, 1970* (Washington, D.C.: U.S. Government Printing Office, 1971), 405–10.

9. D. R. Palmer, *Summons of the Trumpet*, 300.

10. Ibid., 301.

11. Shelby L. Stanton, *The Rise and Fall of an American Army: U.S. Ground Forces in Vietnam, 1965–1973* (New York: Dell, 1985), 336.

12. D. R. Palmer, *Summons of the Trumpet*, 308.

13. Stanton, *Rise and Fall of an American Army*, 337.

14. Kerry cited in Karnow, *Vietnam*, 632.

15. Interview with Col. Hoang Co Quang, cited in Turley, *The Second Indochina War*, 138.

16. Laird and Westmoreland cited in Karnow, *Vietnam*, 640.

17. Isaacs, *Without Honor*, 26.

18. Harry G. Summers Jr., *On Strategy: A Critical Analysis of the Vietnam War* (Novato, Calif: Presidio, 1982), 134–35.

19. *Nhan Dan* cited in Isaacs, *Without Honor*, 20–21.

20. Ibid., 27.

21. Herring, *America's Longest War*, 249.

22. Isaacs, *Without Honor*, 240.

23. Thieu cited in ibid., 46.

24. Nixon to Thieu, 5 January 1973, in William Appleman Williams, Thomas McCormick, Lloyd Garden, and Walter LaFeber, eds., *America in Vietnam: A Documentary History* (Garden City, N.Y.: Doubleday, 1985), 308–9.

25. Kissinger cited in Karnow, *Vietnam*, 652.

26. Nixon cited in ibid.

27. Ibid., 654.

28. Herring, *America's Longest War*, 255.

29. For the important parts of the treaty's text, see John Clark Pratt, ed., *Vietnam Voices: Perspectives on the War Years, 1941–1982* (New York: Penguin, 1984), 551–54.

30. Isaacs, *Without Honor*, 62–63.

31. COSVN Directive, 19 January 1973, cited in Turley, *The Second Indochina War*, 160.

32. Ibid., 167.

33. Pratt, ed., *Vietnam Voices*, 612.

34. Karnow, *Vietnam*, 669.

35. Ibid., 667.

36. Isaacs, *Without Honor*, 485.

37. Pratt. ed., *Vietnam Voices*, 611–12.

38. Karnow, *Vietnam*, 669.

chapter 7

TO RECONCILIATION: CAMBODIA, MIAS, AND DIPLOMATIC RECOGNITION, 1975–1995

For two decades after the Communist victory ended the long war in Vietnam, hostility continued between the United States and Vietnam. Wartime hatreds and sacrifices always make it difficult for former enemies to reconcile, but the postwar adjustment between Americans and Vietnamese was unusually strained and extended. It was also extraordinary in that normally it is the victorious power that determines the postwar relationship and must decide whether to treat the defeated enemy generously or punitively. Despite its failure in Vietnam, the United States remained a military and economic superpower while the reunified Communist Vietnam, which was officially named the Socialist Republic of Vietnam (SRV) in 1976, remained among the world's poorest countries, a condition aggravated by the dislocations and costs of decades of warfare.

Holding the upper hand, the United States sought to isolate Vietnam diplomatically and economically. Continuing a policy that dated back to 1945, when American officials ignored Ho Chi Minh's request for diplomatic recognition of his fledgling government, the United States declined to recognize the SRV. In addition, the United States imposed a trade embargo and pressured its allies in Europe and Asia to avoid economic ties with Vietnam. On the other side, Vietnam sought the "normalization" of relations with the United States (meaning formal U.S. diplomatic recognition of the SRV, which would bring with it the exchange of ambassadors and agreements on trade, investments, and other forms of communication), relations that were economically and strategically important to Vietnam.

Bitterness over its loss in Vietnam accounted principally for the initial postwar hostility of the United States toward its former enemy. To some

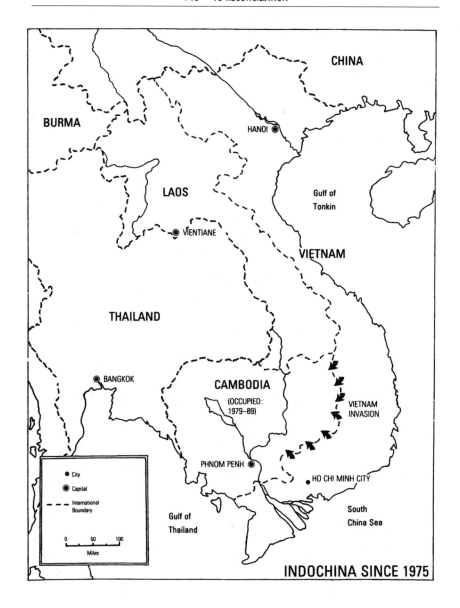

CHINA

BURMA

LAOS

Gulf of
Tonkin

HANOI

VIENTIANE

VIETNAM

THAILAND

BANGKOK

CAMBODIA

(OCCUPIED:
1979–89)

VIETNAM
INVASION

PHNOM PENH

HO CHI MINH CITY

South
China Sea

Gulf of
Thailand

● City

◉ Capital

– – – International
Boundary

0   50   100
Miles

INDOCHINA SINCE 1975

extent, the United States' concern with its evolving relationship with the People's Republic of China, where a process leading toward normalization was well under way by the time the war in Vietnam ended, limited accommodation since China preferred a weak Vietnam. Eventually two developments unforeseen in 1975—Vietnam's invasion and occupation of Cambodia and the hardening of the U.S. demand for a "full accounting" of Americans listed as missing-in-action (MIAs) from the war—prolonged the American-Vietnamese impasse.

THE COMMUNIST ASCENDANCY IN LAOS AND CAMBODIA

Contrary to the predictions of many American officials during the war in Vietnam, the Communist victory in Vietnam did not notably erode U.S. influence throughout Asia. Eight months after the Communist victory, President Gerald Ford visited Japan, China, Indonesia, and the Philippines and reasserted U.S. commitments as he issued a six-point Pacific Doctrine, which included a "continuing stake in stability and security in Southeast Asia."[1] By this time, the Association of Southeast Asian Nations (ASEAN)—which had been established in 1967 and included Thailand, the Philippines, Indonesia, Malaya, and Singapore (Brunei joined in 1984)—was emerging as a vital economic and political force. Closely tied to the Western capitalist system, ASEAN's members were determined to enhance regional stability.

American "losses" beyond Vietnam were limited to Laos and Cambodia, which had always been pawns in the struggle for control of Vietnam. In the spring of 1975, the Communist ascendancy in Vietnam was paralleled by the victories of the Communist forces in Laos (the Pathet Lao) and Cambodia (the Khmer Rouge). This was not, however, a monolithic Communist triumph, for national rivalries, exacerbated by China's influence, dominated the interaction among the Indochina states. The Vietnamese Communists' relationship with their neighbors differed, for the Pathet Lao had always been tied to and supported by the Vietnamese while the Khmer Rouge represented traditional Cambodian suspicion of Vietnamese influence and looked to China for leadership. These differences were evident in the circumstances that brought the Pathet Lao and Khmer Rouge to power.

The Pathet Lao's victory was anticipated. Throughout their years of supporting the Pathet Lao and using the jungle trails of eastern Laos as a major part of the Ho Chi Minh Trail, the North Vietnamese had assumed that their victory would also bring Communist control over Laos. To prevent that eventuality, the United States had also been been deeply involved in Laos; it had supported the neutralist Royal Laotian Government headed by Prince Souvanna Phuoma, had covertly armed and trained Hmong and other hill tribes to fight against the Pathet Lao, and had engaged in extensive secret bombing against the Ho Chi Minh Trail and the Pathet Lao.

Since the U.S. objective of denying control of Laos to the Communists had been derived from its commitment in Vietnam, the gradual American withdrawal from Vietnam was paralleled in Laos. As the United States moved toward a settlement in Vietnam, it also urged Souvanna Phuoma to negotiate with the Pathet Lao. With the Pathet Lao having steadily gained ground over the years and with the Americans withdrawing, the parties reached a ceasefire agreement in February 1973 that established a Pathet Lao–dominated coalition government. Two years later as the Communists were unifying Vietnam, the Pathet Lao simply seized total power.

The Communist victory in Laos was relatively bloodless when compared with the final stages of the conflicts in Vietnam and Cambodia, but it too had a cruel side. The Pathet Lao sent some 20,000 officials and supporters of the Souvanna Phuoma government to "reeducation camps," and the Hmong tribesmen, now abandoned by the Americans, were attacked and eliminated as a political threat. The remnants of the Hmong fled the country, with some 100,000 of them eventually migrating to the United States.

In Cambodia the triumph of the Khmer Rouge ended a devastating five-year civil war in which the United States had played a pivotal role that was driven by political and military considerations in Vietnam. President Richard Nixon's secret bombing of North Vietnamese positions in Cambodia, which had begun in 1969, had emboldened opponents of Prince Sihanouk's policy of precarious neutrality toward the war being waged in Vietnam. In early 1970, the army, headed by General Lon Nol, deposed Prince Sihanouk and sought U.S. assistance. The American–South Vietnamese invasion of North Vietnamese sanctuaries in Cambodia in May 1970 solidified the U.S. tie with Lon Nol's government, which was officially named the Khmer Republic. The invasion drove the North Vietnamese from the remote border areas into the more populated parts of Cambodia and forced them into collaboration with the Khmer Rouge, the small Cambodian Communist movement. Given the traditional animosity between Vietnamese and Cambodians, this was an uneasy partnership. Nonetheless, circumstances necessitated cooperation, and the North Vietnamese trained and equipped the Khmer Rouge. Meanwhile, Prince Sihanouk, now in exile in China, also allied himself with the Khmer Rouge. As it supported the Khmer Republic, the United States thus found its new ally facing increasingly strong opposition from the Khmer Rouge, which was supported by the North Vietnamese and which enjoyed the blessings of the deposed Prince Sihanouk, who was still Cambodia's most widely known and respected leader.

The U.S.–Khmer Republic coalition duplicated the U.S.–South Vietnamese relationship. Lon Nol—like General Thieu and his predecessors in Saigon—lacked political stature, relied on repressive tactics to hold power, and headed a government that suffered from widespread corruption. As in South Vietnam, the Cambodian army squandered much of the U.S. military assistance, which totaled some $400 million between 1970 and 1972, and never became an effective fighting force.

In the meantime the Khmer Rouge's power grew steadily and controlled much of the Cambodian countryside. To stem the tide, the United States, as it had throughout its prolonged involvement in Indochina, called on its air power and in the first half of 1973 engaged in extensive bombing of North Vietnamese and Khmer Rouge positions in Cambodia. Only an act of Congress in August 1973 ended the Cambodian bombing campaign.

By then the aerial assault, whatever its effects on Communist military capability, had contributed to the disintegration of Cambodian society. Over two million refugees—about one-fourth of Cambodia's population—fled from the villages into the country's few cities, which could not meet the need for food, supplies, and social services, most notably medical facilities. Phnom Penh grew from 600,000 people to over 2,000,000, quickly becoming a city of the poor and malnourished.

The Khmer Rouge's drive to power was accompanied by a terrifying fanaticism, as its forces engaged in systematic brutality against their fellow Cambodians. In January 1975 they laid siege to Phnom Penh. Three months later Lon Nol and other high officials as well as U.S. personnel fled the capital, and the Khmer Republic collapsed. When the Khmer Rouge took control, it ordered the residents of Phnom Penh to leave under the pretext that the Americans were going to bomb the city, but the real reason was to begin the Khmer Rouge's social revolution. The agony of Cambodia had not ended; it was, in fact, just moving to another and ultimately more tragic stage.

VIETNAM'S STRUGGLE, 1975–1978: THE FAILURE OF ACCOMMODATION WITH AMERICA

In Vietnam, the triumphant Communist leadership faced enormous problems as it shifted priorities from war to reconstruction. The political and economic integration of a country that had been divided for generations would have been difficult under any circumstances, but in Vietnam it was aggravated by the effects of devastating warfare. American firepower had destroyed much of the best agricultural lands and uprooted the peasantry. Half of the rural population in the former South Vietnam had been forced from their lands and were now living in slums that surrounded Saigon, Da Nang, Hué, and other cities. Defoliation had killed large segments of forests, leaving extensive soil erosion, in addition to uncertain effects on the health of peasants. The social dislocations resulting from the American presence were only exacerbated by the American departure. The southern cities were filled with victims of the war: 400,000 amputees, 500,000 prostitutes, 100,000 drug addicts, and 800,000 orphans. Two decades of dependence upon American expenditures and economic assistance had created an artificial economy that left the South without a strong commercial or industrial base.

To launch economic rehabilitation and development, the SRV in 1976 put forth an ambitious Five-Year Plan that envisioned the creation of a socialist state and "de-Westernizing" the South. In the rural areas the Communist leadership, building upon the popularity of land reform measures associated with their struggle against the French and Americans, redistributed land and moved toward collectivization of agriculture. To increase agricultural production and to reduce urban population pressures, the SRV established New Economic Zones (NEZ) in the rural areas and subsidized migration from the cities for development of land in those zones.

Besides its ambitious economic goals, the Communist leaders also sought to purge the institutions and groups associated with the now defunct South Vietnamese state. A 1976 party document stated that "the exploiting classes remain and the poisons of the enslaving culture and the social evils caused by U.S. neo-colonialism as well as the influence of bourgeois ideology in society remain potent. . . . The negative aspects of capitalism . . . are still to be overcome."[2] Many high-ranking officials of the former Saigon government and its army's officers were executed, and hundreds of thousands of others were placed in "reeducation" camps.

Besides its internal problems, the Vietnamese also confronted external threats from China to the north and Cambodia to the southwest. China curtailed its assistance to Vietnam once the war ended, pressed its claims to long-disputed areas along the Sino-Vietnamese border and to disputed mineral-rich areas in the South China Sea, and became the principal supporter of the avowedly anti-Vietnamese Khmer Rouge regime in Cambodia.

To rebuild its war-devastated society and to balance China's influence, Vietnam needed economic and technical assistance, trade, foreign investment, and ties with another major power. The preferred source of such benefits was its former enemy.

Indeed for a brief moment in 1977, Americans and Vietnamese moved toward accommodation. When Jimmy Carter became president that year, he and Secretary of State Cyrus Vance envisioned an opening to Vietnam as a way of bringing closure to the war. Accordingly, the new administration sent a mission, headed by United Auto Workers president Leonard Woodcock, to Hanoi for discussions with high-ranking SRV officials. The Woodcock mission's progress led to subsequent meetings between U.S. and Vietnamese officials in Paris.

Two issues—MIAs and reconstruction assistance—divided the two governments. The United States was principally concerned with gaining assurances that Vietnam would assist in accounting for MIAs, but the issue had not yet taken on strong emotional overtones. Vietnam's overriding interest was reconstruction assistance, which it believed the Americans had a moral and legal obligation to provide. In the 1973 Paris Agreement ending the war, the United States had promised to assist in postwar reconstruction, and President Nixon had subsequently written a letter to Prime Minister Pham Van Dong specifying that such assistance would "fall in the range of 3.25 billion dollars of grant aid over five years."[3] To Americans, however, Hanoi had violated the

Paris Agreements and thus could make no claims in their name. Moreover, any proposal for assistance to Vietnam was bound to be controversial in Congress and among the American public. Carter indicated a willingness to consider reconstruction assistance after relations were normalized, but he declined to make such a commitment as part of the process leading to normalization. So while the Vietnamese linked their "good faith" on MIAs with a commitment to assistance, the Americans insisted on separating the issues and would not base normalization on "bones for dollars."

The negotiations slowed. Both sides were to blame. The Vietnamese overplayed their hand and made their demands public, including the text of Nixon's letter. They evidently expected popular support in the United States, but in fact their action added to congressional and public criticism, already strong among conservatives, of normalizing relations with the former enemy. Moreover, within the Carter administration, key officials, notably National Security Adviser Zbigniew Brezizinski, argued to defer the talks with Vietnam so as not to complicate the delicate normalization negotiations with the People's Republic of China. The United States, as promised, supported Vietnam's successful bid for United Nations' membership in the fall of 1977 but otherwise backed away from the pursuit of accommodation with Hanoi.

Vietnam's failure to gain external assistance came as its economic problems worsened. Disappointing harvests led to food shortages. Peasants of the Mekong Delta, accustomed to owning their land and selling products in a free market, resisted collectivization of agriculture. The NEZ program failed to attract many urban dwellers. In early 1978 the government clamped down, restricting the activities of the large private traders, who were mostly ethnic Chinese. As a result a large segment of the Chinese community and others who felt threatened began fleeing the country. Going by sea to Hong Kong and other noncommunist countries, these "boat people"—totaling between 400,000 and 1,000,000 persons—elicited much sympathy in the West where their migration was typically seen as evidence of the harshness of Communist rule in Vietnam.

THE RULE OF THE KHMER ROUGE: THE CAMBODIAN HOLOCAUST, 1975–1978

One can only conjecture about how different the recent history of Southeast Asia might have been if Cambodia had been spared the three years of the Khmer Rouge's reign of terror. After the Khmer Rouge took power in 1975 and proclaimed Democratic Kampuchea, Cambodia became the principal source of regional instability and of U.S.-Vietnamese differences.

When the heavily armed, youthful Khmer Rouge forces, dressed in peasant black, took control of Phnom Penh, the capital, and Battambang, the second largest city, they forced some 3.5 million people into the rural areas and sealed the country's frontiers so that their revolution could be accomplished without outside interference. The forced ruralization of the population marked the beginning of a brutal program to achieve self-sufficiency by rapidly increasing agricultural production so that export earnings from crops would finance the building of an industrial society. Supervised by Khmer Rouge cadres, Cambodians of all ages were mobilized to work from dawn to dusk.

Although proclaiming a "super great leap forward," the Khmer Rouge built a backward-looking world. They eliminated private lands and enterprises, money, telegraph, telephone, and even postal services. The Khmer Rouge radically transformed all aspects of Cambodian life, destroying schools and Buddhist temples, separating members of families, imposing puritanical rules of social behavior, and engaging in endless indoctrination of a hapless people.

The Khmer Rouge was led by Pol Pot, who became premier, and Khieu Samphan, the chief of state. They had similar backgrounds. Both had become Communists while studying in France in the late 1940s and, upon returning to Cambodia, had joined the small group that resisted Vietnamese domination of the Cambodian Communist party. Their inspiration to convert Cambodia into a socialist agrarian society came from the ideology that Mao Tse-tung had followed in revolutionizing Chinese society. China in turn championed the Khmer Rouge's program; Mao promised that his nation would fight "shoulder to shoulder" on behalf of Democratic Kampuchea's "revolutionary cause."[4]

The Khmer Rouge revolution quickly became a tragedy of immense proportions. Malnutrition was endemic, as Khmer Rouge cadres, in order to obtain targeted "surpluses," reduced the public's food rations. Malnutrition, accompanied by overwork, meant that disease became commonplace, and with the Khmer Rouge having repudiated Western medicine, hundreds of thousands of persons died of malaria and other diseases. Executions took a staggering number of lives, as the Khmer Rouge eliminated those groups—like army officers, civil servants, intellectuals, writers, and teachers—who were identified with the old order. Likewise, anyone resisting the forced relocation or rural work was summarily executed. Later Pol Pot and his associates turned against suspected enemies within the Khmer Rouge itself, as thousands of alleged dissidents were executed after being tortured and forced to confess to treason. And as Cambodians fled in increasing numbers to neighboring Thailand and Vietnam, the Khmer Rouge responded with even more terror. Again, tens of thousands were executed as they tried to leave the country. The most reliable estimate of the total human losses—victims of disease, starvation, and execution—indicates that about one million persons (out of a 1975 population of 7.3 million) died during the nearly four years of the Khmer Rouge rule.

Much of the terror was carried out by teenaged soldiers. Dith Pran, whose experiences formed the basis for the powerful motion picture *The Killing Fields*, described the youthful cadres: "Their minds have nothing inside except discipline. They do not believe any religion or tradition except Khmer Rouge orders. That's why they killed their own people, even babies, like we might kill a mosquito."[5]

The tragedy of Cambodia under the Khmer Rouge can only be described as genocide. Even among the horrors of the twentieth century, the Cambodian holocaust was unique in that a country's leaders systematically eliminated their own people. Jean Lacouture, a renowned French scholar of Southeast Asian history, observed that "ordinary genocide (if one can ever call it ordinary) usually has been carried out against a foreign population or an internal minority. The new masters of Phnom Penh have invented original, auto-genocide. After Auschwitz and the Gulag, we might have thought this century had produced the ultimate in horror, but we are seeing the suicide of a people in the name of revolution—worse, in the name of socialism."[6]

Reports of the Cambodian holocaust eventually reached the outside world. In particular, a powerful 1978 book *Murder of a Gentle Land* used the stories of refugees to indict Khmer Rouge rule. Yet such accounts initially elicited little sympathy for the Cambodian people. The reasons were varied. In the United States, many former critics of the American war in Vietnam dismissed stories of the Cambodian genocide as propaganda from Thailand and other pro-American countries. The Carter administration, which was avowedly dedicated to upholding human rights throughout the world and did denounce violations in many countries, virtually ignored the situation in Cambodia. The principal reason was the priority given to the normalization of relations with the People's Republic of China; since China was the Khmer Rouge's principal supporter, the United States chose not to risk Sino-American rapprochement by questioning the integrity of China's ally.

One of the few prominent leaders to challenge official indifference was Senator George McGovern, who had been the Democratic Party presidential nominee in 1972. He urged that the international community intervene to stop the mindless killing. Stating that the Khmer Rouge made the "Nazis look very tame by comparison," McGovern asked: "do we sit on the sidelines and watch a population slaughtered or do we marshal military force and put an end to it?"[7]

VIETNAM'S INVASION AND OCCUPATION OF CAMBODIA, 1979–1989

McGovern's question was answered by the intervention not of the international community but that of Vietnam acting unilaterally. Strategic, not humanitarian, considerations prompted its action, however. By the late 1970s, Vietnam felt threatened by the impact of the Khmer Rouge on its territory and by the Khmer Rouge–China connection. Claiming to "liberate" regions of Vietnam that were populated predominantly by Cambodians and that had once been part of Cambodia, the Khmer Rouge's troops repeatedly attacked along the Vietnam border, touching off clashes with Vietnamese forces. China encouraged and equipped the Khmer Rouge's aggressiveness along the Vietnam frontier.

The intermittent border warfare and the human tragedy of the Khmer Rouge revolution had a devastating effect on the already-crippled Vietnamese economy and society. Some 375,000 Cambodians sought sanctuary in Vietnam, while roughly 500,000 Vietnamese living along the Cambodian frontier fled from their homes to escape the Khmer Rouge's incursions that typically included atrocities against Vietnamese civilians. This influx of refugees added, of course, to the pressures on Vietnam's already-overflowing cities.

Vietnam exploited the mounting Cambodian discontent with the Khmer Rouge. Within its borders, the nucleus of a pro-Vietnamese Cambodian Communist movement took shape. During the early 1970s, Pol Pot had attempted to purge the Khmer Rouge of those Cambodian communists (known as the Khmer-Vietminh) who had traditionally looked to Vietnam's Communist movement for leadership, prompting many to flee to Vietnam. By 1978 they were joined by many second-level officials of the Khmer Rouge who had become disillusioned with the excesses of the revolution and broke from Pol Pot's leadership. The most notable was Heng Samrin, who sought sanctuary in Vietnam after leading a large but abortive uprising in Cambodia's eastern provinces against the Khmer Rouge in early 1978. Heng Samrin and other disillusioned Khmer Rouge officers who made their way to Vietnam had long been active in the Cambodian Communist movement, particularly the Khmer-Vietminh segment. The SRV leadership saw in Heng Samrin and other dissident Cambodian Communists the basis of an anti–Khmer Rouge revolution.

From the perspective of the leaders in Hanoi, the Chinese, in collaboration with the Khmer Rouge, were threatening to encircle their country. "When we look at Cambodia," a Vietnamese official said, "we see China, China, China."[8]

The mounting Cambodian crisis forced Vietnam to end its independent foreign policy and seek external military assistance. In early 1978 Vietnam decided that it would intervene in Cambodia but realized that this step would alienate China, as the Khmer Rouge's principal benefactor, and Thailand, which had a long history of fearing Vietnamese expansion. These circumstances necessitated support of a major power. Since 1975 the SRV had resisted the Soviet Union's pressures to enter into a collective security pact and to side with the Soviets in their differences with the Chinese. The suspension of Chinese assistance to Vietnam, however, led to Hanoi's decision in June 1978 to join the Council for Mutual Economic Assistance (COMECON), the Soviet-dominated economic bloc.

That step notwithstanding, Vietnam again signaled its interest in establishing diplomatic relations with the United States. In view of the continuing American official and popular hostility toward Vietnam, the abortive 1977 effort at establishing diplomatic relations, and the U.S. pursuit of its opening to China, Vietnam's prospects for developing the American connection were remote.

Despite the slim prospects, the SRV still gave priority to seeking U.S. support. Thus, in the fall of 1978, Foreign Minister Nguyen Co Thach spent three weeks at the United Nations' meeting in New York in the hope that contacts with American officials might lead to a reversal of U.S. policy. Thach dropped the earlier insistence on economic rehabilitation assistance that had undermined the 1977 discussions. The United States was under some pressure from the ASEAN countries to normalize relations with Vietnam in the belief that it would help to stem the tide of "boat people" fleeing Vietnam. More important in American calculations, however, was the plan to establish full diplomatic relations with China, which would have been put at risk by any sign of friendship with Vietnam. The Thach mission thus failed.

When Thach left the United States, he went directly to Moscow, and within days he concluded the Soviet-Vietnamese Treaty of Friendship. The Vietnamese thus enhanced security at an especially desperate moment. In return for increased levels of Soviet assistance, the Vietnamese permitted Soviet control over the naval base at Cam Ranh Bay.

On 25 December 1978, Vietnamese forces invaded Cambodia, where they were generally welcomed as liberators. Their armies used heavy artillery and air bombardment to smash the Khmer Rouge forces. On 7 January 1979, the Vietnamese captured Phnom Penh, and control of Cambodia passed from one Communist government to another. Democratic Kampuchea of the Khmer Rouge was replaced by the People's Republic of Kampuchea (PRK) under the leadership of Heng Samrin and Hun Sen. The remnants of Pol Pot's army took refuge in sanctuaries in the densely forested areas along the Cambodian-Thai border. An agreement between Heng Samrin's government and the SRV permitted the stationing of Vietnamese troops in Cambodia; a force of 140,000 Vietnamese was concentrated on the Khmer Rouge–infested Cambodian frontier with Thailand.

China's reaction to the invasion of Cambodia came swiftly. In early 1979 Chinese forces attacked six provinces in northern Vietnam for the avowed purpose of punishing Vietnam. In intense fighting the Vietnamese army held its own, and after a month the Chinese withdrew. The Chinese had caused considerable destruction, but they had failed to intimidate the Vietnamese, much less divert them from their campaign in Cambodia. Besides that show of strength, China also played a critical role in the survival of opposition to the People's Republic of Kampuchea. China provided sanctuary for Khmer Rouge leaders and funded the Khmer Rouge's continuing warfare against the PRK.

Vietnam's invasion alienated not only China but also the United States and the members of ASEAN, all of whom condemned Vietnam for "aggression" and "imposition" of an "alien regime" on Cambodia. The opposition of ASEAN was especially significant since it deprived Vietnam of contacts with a flourishing economic unit. In addition, under pressure from the United States, Japan and several Western countries ended modest economic assistance programs to Vietnam. To the Vietnamese, this international response ignored the extent to which the Khmer Rouge had provoked Vietnam. Hanoi saw itself acting in self-defense. An authority on recent Cambodian history has written that "there is ample evidence that the [Khmer Rouge] were primarily responsible for the overt hostilities that led to war."[9]

The Vietnamese-imposed PRK government, led by Hun Sen as prime minister and Heng Samrin as chief of state, terminated the terror of the Khmer Rouge and rebuilt Cambodia's society and economy. It ended forced ruralization, freeing people to return to the cities (Phnom Penh, whose population had shrunk to 20,000, was resurrected as over 400,000 people flocked back to the capital). The new government also stabilized the villages and facilitated a more effective means of food production and distribution. Private Western relief agencies helped to reduce the serious food shortages. With abundant crops by the early 1980s, the hardships of the Khmer Rouge became a thing of the past. Indeed the PRK devoted much time to reminding Cambodians of the suffering caused by the Khmer Rouge rule, including the macabre collection and display of massive collections of the skeletons of its victims.

However important in terms of guaranteeing its security and rehabilitating Cambodia, Vietnam paid a considerable price for its occupation of Cambodia. The unrelenting opposition of China, the United States, and ASEAN left Vietnam isolated and dependent upon the Soviet Union. The "collusion between the chieftain of imperialism [i.e., United States] and Chinese expansionism and hegemonism," a report at the Vietnamese Communist Party Congress of 1982 stated, "necessitated solidarity and cooperation with the Soviet Union."[10]

Extensive Soviet assistance—which included food, heavy machinery, oil, communications systems, and above all, military weapons and equipment—left Vietnam deeply in debt (amounting to $14.5 billion by 1990), a situation made worse by its unfavorable balance of trade. Vietnamese resented their dependency. They blamed their chronic food shortages and lack of consumer goods on the Soviet Union and sarcastically referred to the thousands of Soviet officials and advisers in their country as "Americans without money."

FROM REAGAN TO CLINTON: COMING TO TERMS WITH VIETNAM

Vietnam's problems were of little concern to the United States as both public opinion and official policy toward Vietnam became more hostile during the 1980s. The United States made normalization contingent upon Vietnam meeting two conditions: a withdrawal of its forces from Cambodia and a "full accounting" of MIAs.

Its resolute opposition to Vietnam's presence in Cambodia led the United States to support a loose coalition of Cambodian groups that opposed the PRK. This included the armies and followers of the Khmer Rouge, Prince Sihanouk, and former prime minister Son Sann. Although Prince Sihanouk was the titular head of this coalition and each of the three groups had its own armies along the Thai-Cambodian frontier, the Khmer Rouge—with its army of 40,000 men—held the greatest influence. International support for the coalition included China, which was principally responsible for arming the Khmer Rouge, and ASEAN. The United Nations recognized the coalition as representing Cambodia in that organization.

Besides its insistence on Vietnam's withdrawal from Cambodia, the United States, especially during the administration of Ronald Reagan, took a hard line on the MIA issue, which became an increasingly emotional and politically charged concern to many Americans. The MIA crusade broadened to include demands for return of POWs (prisoners of war allegedly being held by the Vietnamese). Not only were Americans insisting on an accounting of the missing through the return of the remains of Americans killed in Vietnam but now they increasingly believed that some of their fellow countrymen were still being held in captivity. As part of his vigilant anticommunism and reassertion of national pride, Reagan recast the Vietnam War, calling it a "noble cause," as he gave prominence to the MIA issue. Speaking to a Memorial Day audience in 1984, Reagan stated: "Today, a united people call upon Vietnam with one voice: Heal the sorest wound of this conflict. Return our sons to America."[11] Reagan's implication that Americans were still being held played to popular emotions that were already being exploited by the media, as several television programs and motion pictures, especially the adventures of the fictional Rambo, conveyed the impression that Americans were still imprisoned in Vietnam. This fiction defied logic and evidence. Reports of occasional "sightings" of Americans in Indochina were invariably found to be inaccurate if not fraudulent. Nonetheless, a national public opinion survey showed that 82 percent of Americans believed that fellow countrymen were being held against their will in Vietnam.

Missing combatants were not unique to the Vietnam War, but the American insistence on accounting for them was unprecedented. The Defense Department listed 1,750 Americans as missing in Vietnam (and 2,387 for all of Indochina). It discounted the reports of Americans being seen in Vietnam and considered all but one of the MIAs to be legally dead. The exception was maintained for the symbolic reason of demonstrating official interest in forcing a Vietnamese accounting for the MIAs.

What made the concern with MIAs even more striking was their relatively small number. The percentage of MIAs in Vietnam, when compared with total casualties, is much less than in other wars. Casualty lists of World War II still include 80,000 combatants classified as missing, and from the Korean War the number is 8,000. The missing represent 20 percent and 15 percent respectively of the confirmed dead in those conflicts. In the case of the Vietnam War, the missing constituted about 4 percent of those known to be killed. In Vietnam the military's efficiency in removing wounded men from combat areas (thanks mostly to the widespread use of helicopters) reduced the number of casualties who were left behind.

The persistence of the MIA issue, it seems, resulted from the bitterness of the loss in Vietnam, especially acute among conservatives whose influence increased in the 1980s. Moreover, it became difficult for any leader or group to oppose the demand for full accounting so long as more information might be forthcoming. The historian Terry Anderson, a veteran of the Vietnam War, observed that "MIAs are only important when the United States loses the war. The real 'noble cause' for [the Reagan] administration is not the former war but its emotionally impossible crusade to retrieve 'all recoverable remains.' "[12]

Reagan's position found strong support from various groups, most notably the National League of POW/MIA Families, which was especially vigilant in forcing the accountability objective. In 1988 Reagan addressed the League's annual national meeting and took the occasion to warn Vietnam that the "deep pain" felt by Americans on the MIA issue poisoned the prospects for an improved relationship with the United States. While speaking principally about the need for Vietnamese cooperation in accounting for MIAs and returning remains, Reagan also addressed the possibility of Americans being held. "Until our questions are fully answered," the president said, "we will assume that some of our countrymen are still alive."[13]

Vietnam's leaders came to accept the necessity of accommodating the United States on the MIA issue. While repeatedly denying holding any Americans, they invited Defense Department officials to visit Vietnam for the purpose of recovering unidentified remains of war victims. Between 1985 and 1987 the remains of 88 persons were taken from Vietnam. Meanwhile, the National League of POW/MIA Families joined with other groups, most notably the Vietnam Veterans of America (VVA), in pressuring the Reagan administration to work with Vietnam on the MIA and other issues. The VVA served as an important unofficial link between the Vietnamese and American governments. When a VVA delegation visited Vietnam in early 1987, it met with Foreign Minister Nguyen Co Thach, who expressed strong interest in direct conversations with U.S. officials on a wide range of issues. Although the State Department objected to such informal diplomacy, VVA president Robert O. Muller justified the group's role as "providing a bridge to Vietnam, a conduit to dialogue"—a purpose that the VVA realized.[14] In August 1987 President Reagan dispatched a special mission to Hanoi to discuss the MIA issue. Headed by General John W. Vessey Jr. (a veteran of the Vietnam War and former chairman of the Joint Chiefs of Staff) and including among its members several officials as well as representatives of the National League of POW/MIA Families, the mission led to an understanding with Vietnam, which agreed to an accelerated effort at accounting for MIAs. Over the next two years, this program of cooperation between Vietnamese and American officials resulted in over 100 sets of remains being transported to the United States. (Not all remains brought from Vietnam have been Americans, as the final determination of identity is not made until the remains reach the U.S. Army's Central Identification Laboratory in Hawaii.)

In addition to its effort to satisfy U.S. demands on the MIA issue, Vietnam also ended its occupation of Cambodia. On 5 April 1989, Hanoi announced that its remaining troops (estimated at 60,000 men) would return to Vietnam within six months. The Vietnamese thus terminated an occupation that, besides its detrimental effect on Vietnam's international position, had become excessively costly, absorbing half of its military expenditures and adding to its dependency on an increasingly less reliable Soviet Union.

Vietnam's withdrawal was also encouraged by developments—in which the United States played an important role—that indicated the Khmer Rouge would not return after Vietnam's departure, allaying the long-held fear of many Cambodians, Vietnamese, and others. In October 1988 the United Nations General Assembly passed a resolution declaring that Cambodia must not return to "the universally condemned policies and practices of the past." Passed by a margin of 122 votes to 19, the resolution was supported by both the United States and China. The U.S. ambassador stated that "we must assure that Hanoi's withdrawal will not lead to the return of the Khmer Rouge, a contingency to which the United States and the international community are unutterably opposed."[15] (After the Vietnamese withdrawal from Cambodia, the United Nations assumed responsibility for the stabilization and democratization of Cambodia, which led to the adoption of a new constitution and nationwide elections in 1993 that established a coalition government.)

Vietnam's withdrawal from Cambodia facilitated its adaptation to a changing international environment. The treaty with the Soviet Union, which had outlived its usefulness, was finally rendered obsolete by the demise of the Soviet Union itself. As two of the few remaining Communist states in the world and with the status of Cambodia no longer a dividing issue, Vietnam and China moved toward a cautious rapprochement. Both the ending of the cold war and the Vietnamese withdrawal from Cambodia facilitated the opening of badly needed foreign capital investment and economic assistance. Japan, for instance, resumed its aid program, while the World Bank and International Monetary Fund (with the approval of the United States) removed longstanding restrictions on lending to Vietnam. To pull the economy out of its doldrums, the Vietnamese government accelerated market-driven reforms that attracted foreign investors. As a result, the Vietnamese economy showed significant growth in the early 1990s, though poverty remained endemic.

By the early 1990s, the U.S. policy of economic and diplomatic isolation of Vietnam had lost both its rationale and most of its domestic support. To an increasing number of Americans, Vietnam's withdrawal from Cambodia and its continuing "good faith" effort to recover and return the remains of MIAs met the conditions for normalizing relations. The influence of the MIA activists lessened as commercial interests argued that the embargo was preventing Americans from moving into the Vietnam market. Meanwhile, European and Japanese investors were pouring capital into Vietnam. Under such pressure, in 1991 President George Bush moved cautiously away from the hard-line policy, authorizing an informal agreement with Vietnam on a number of steps that were intended to lead to diplomatic ties. Bush, however, never publicly endorsed normalization, and he left office with the process still incomplete.

For his successor, Bill Clinton, normalization presented some political problems. During the 1992 presidential campaign, his activities as student protester and his avoidance of serving in a war he "opposed and despised," while not unusual for college youth of his generation, had become an issue. So any steps he took toward normalization were bound to generate more than the usual criticism from those groups that were still determined to press Vietnam more vigorously on the MIAs.

Despite his political liabilities, Clinton moved decisively toward ending the impasse in American-Vietnamese relations. In February 1994, after the Senate had passed a nonbinding resolution urging an end to the embargo, Clinton took that step. In the next few months, a number of American corporations—including Mobil Oil, Citibank, Bank of America, General Electric, Boeing Aircraft, Singer Sewing Machine, and Hilton Hotels—entered into arrangements with Vietnamese authorities to do business in that country. The Vietnamese sponsored a trade fair in America, and American businesses did the same in Vietnam, which stimulated further interest in expanding economic opportunities. The U.S. Chamber of Commerce and other groups called upon Clinton to normalize relations as a step toward a bilateral trade agreement and allowing U.S. agencies like the Export Import Bank and the Overseas Private Investment Corporation to help American companies in Vietnam. The promise of expanding economic opportunities coincided with a tempering of public attitudes toward Vietnam. By this time public opinion polls indicated that most Americans had come to favor normalizing relations. Finally, Clinton's decision for recognition was facilitated by the support of some veterans' groups as well as politically prominent individual veterans.

A half century of antagonism between the United States and the Communist government of Vietnam ended on 11 July 1995 when Clinton extended full diplomatic recognition to the Socialist Republic of Vietnam. Standing behind him as he made that dramatic announcement at the White House were four Senators who were Vietnam veterans: John Kerrey, Charles Robb, Bob Kerry, and John McCain. Especially important was the support of McCain, a prominent Republican who as a navy pilot 30 years earlier had been shot down over North Vietnam and had spent five years imprisoned in the notorious "Hanoi Hilton."

Evoking words used by Abraham Lincoln at the end of the Civil War, Clinton stated that "this moment offers us the opportunity to bind up our own wounds. They have resisted time for too long. We can now move onto common ground."[16] Thus 50 years after Ho Chi Minh had futilely appealed for American recognition of the fragile government that he and his followers had established through the August Revolution, the United States finally accepted its legitimacy.

Notes

1. *Department of State Bulletin* 72, 29 December 1975, 36.

2. Vietnamese Communist Party, *4th Congress National Documents* (Hanoi: Foreign Language Publishing House, 1977), 42.

3. Nixon–Pham Van Dong message cited in Isaacs, *Without Honor*, 133.

4. Mao Tse-tung statement cited by John H. Esterline and Mae H. Esterline, *How the Dominoes Fell: Southeast Asia in Perspective* (London: Hamilton House, 1986), 91.

5. Sydney H. Schanberg, *The Death and Life of Dith Pran* (New York: Viking, 1985), 48.

6. Jean Lacouture cited by William Shawcross, *Quality of Mercy: Cambodia, Holocaust, and Modern Conscience* (New York: Simon and Schuster, 1984), 63.

7. George McGovern cited by Shawcross, *Quality of Mercy*, 68.

8. Vietnamese official cited by Karnow, *Vietnam*, 45.

9. Michael Vickery, *Cambodia, 1975–1982* (Boston: South End Press, 1982), 195.

10. Hanoi Domestic News Science, 27–29 March 1982, cited in Carlyle A. Thayer, "Vietnam's New Pragmatism," *Current History* 82 (April 1983): 183.

11. *New York Times*, 31 May 1984.

12. Terry H. Anderson, "The Light at the End of the Tunnel: The United States and the Socialist Republic of Vietnam," *Diplomatic History* 12 (Fall 1988): 450.

13. *New York Times*, 30 July 1988.

14. Ibid., 22 April 1987.

15. Ibid., 4 November 1988.

16. Ibid., 12 July 1995.

EPILOGUE: REFLECTIONS ON A WAR

From 1965, when the conflict in Vietnam was Americanized, until 1973, when direct U.S. military involvement ended, Vietnam policy was the central political issue in the United States. To the American leaders and public, the war became a virtual obsession. The military frustrations led to debates not only about U.S. policy in Vietnam, but also about the overall American approach to world affairs. Ultimately the popular disillusionment over the war destroyed the Johnson presidency. Nixon's effort to limit the U.S. role through Vietnamization won popular support, but his decision to send forces into Cambodia led to criticism and protest, which increased the pressures on him that led to the controversial agreement of January 1973.

To both Americans and Vietnamese, the human and material costs of the war were staggering. Nearly 59,000 Americans were killed in fighting a conflict that drained the nation's resources. The direct cost amounted to about $155 billion, eroding support for domestic programs, reducing U.S. defense capabilities elsewhere, and triggering a high rate of inflation. As tragic as the American losses, they pale by comparison with those of the Vietnamese. Vietnamese deaths—in the North and South, combatants and civilians—have been estimated as approaching two million. The war left additional millions of Vietnamese unaccounted for or wounded, including hundreds of thousands of invalids. In terms of direct human costs in relation to total population, the Vietnamese war stands as one of the most destructive conflicts of the last 200 years. In addition, the massive use of American firepower meant that thousands of villages suffered serious damage. Throughout the country, but mostly in the South, some 38,000 square miles of land and 20,000 square miles of forest were partially or completely destroyed from bombing and defoliants. The bombing left the Vietnamese countryside a land of craters—26 million, by one estimate.

The intensity of the American-Vietnamese encounter from 1965 to 1973 seems strange when viewed in the context of the historic pattern of negligible interaction between the two countries. When Vietnam was part of French Indochina prior to World War II, U.S. interest in the French colony was limited to a modest trade. During the French–Viet Minh War of 1946–1954 and the subsequent division of Vietnam, the American public had at best a hazy awareness of Vietnam as a "trouble spot," but it was only one in a world of problems confronting the United States. U.S. officials, of course, had been concerned with developments in Vietnam since the end of World War II, and their decisions during the French–Viet Minh War led to steadily greater U.S. involvement in Vietnamese affairs. Yet it was not until the early 1960s that the intractability of the problems facing the United States in Vietnam—in particular the emergence of the Communist-led insurgency and the mounting Buddhist hostility to the Diem government—forced persistent high-level attention to what had become an ongoing crisis.

Then after the intensity of the war period, Vietnam abruptly became again a country of minimal concern to the United States. The withdrawal of the last U.S. troops and the release of the POWs meant that Vietnam—aside from the Communist victory in 1975 and depictions of the plight of the boat people—faded from the public's consciousness. There has been immense popular interest—as evident in motion pictures, novels, television programs, military histories, and accounts of participants—in the U.S. war in Vietnam, but that has not included concern about the Vietnamese as a people or until recently about the postwar U.S.-Vietnamese relationship. The extent to which the MIA issue stirred emotions underscored the extent to which the war shaped American attitudes long after it ended. The normalization of relations and increased Vietnamese-American interaction promise, in the long run, to bind up the old wounds.

While the United States has been able to indulge in a pattern of negligible involvement–massive intervention–neglect in dealing with Vietnam, Vietnam has not been able to ignore the United States. From 1954 to 1975 the United States, by its actions as well as its inactions, was the dominant external force in Vietnam. Even before that, in the decade after World War II, the United States began to influence Vietnamese developments in significant ways. In 1945 Ho Chi Minh sought American support of the August Revolution, for he recognized that only the United States could provide the diplomatic leverage and assistance that would enable his fledgling government to survive. When the United States did commit its resources to Vietnam, it did so in opposition to the Viet Minh; U.S. financial backing was vital to the continuation of the French war effort after 1950. As the French–Viet Minh War reached its tragic conclusion at Dien Bien Phu in 1954, American denial of desperate French appeals for support assured the Viet Minh victory. That did not mean, however, that the United States was prepared to accept the Viet Minh's claim to nationalist legitimacy. Instead it fostered the division of the country, making a major commitment of its resources on behalf of a South Vietnamese government headed by Ngo Dinh Diem. In the process, the United States alienated the Communist leadership in Hanoi and the Southern opponents of Diem. It also initiated a pattern of South Vietnamese dependency that encouraged Diem and his successors to assume that the United States would never abandon them.

Having committed resources and prestige, the United States became more and more deeply involved politically and militarily. The search for a strong non-communist leader who could rally the disparate elements of South Vietnamese society led to persistent American manipulation of Southern politics. To achieve the survival of the fragile South Vietnamese government, the United States intervened with massive military power, including an air war that left Vietnam the most heavily bombed country in history. When events finally forced the United States to disengage from Vietnam, it did so in ways that embittered both its enemy and its ally. Yet after the unification of Vietnam, the victorious Communists again looked to the United States for support—to fulfill promises for rehabilitation assistance, to provide security in the face of Chinese hostility, and to preclude dependency upon the Soviet Union. Despite continuing American hostility, a major objective of Hanoi's leadership remained the opening of diplomatic contacts with the United States.

Reflecting on the American experience in Vietnam, two questions linger: How did Vietnam become so important to the United States? Why did the United States fail to achieve its objectives? Both raise difficult issues and divide former policymakers, participants in the war, journalists, and scholars. No definitive answers may yet be possible, but each question needs to be addressed in any effort to come to terms with the most devastating diplomatic-military setback in American history.

HOW DID VIETNAM BECOME SO IMPORTANT TO THE UNITED STATES?

Vietnam's importance was derived from the global strategy of containment, which for two decades after the Communist victory in China in 1949 held that Vietnam was the key to the future of Southeast Asia. If Vietnam came under Communist control, so the reasoning went, the stability of the rest of the region—Laos, Cambodia, Thailand, Burma, and Malaya on the mainland, and even the Indonesian and Philippine archipelagoes—would be threatened. The loss of Southeast Asia to Communist movements, either under the control of or closely tied to the Soviet Union and China, would have contributed a major shift in the world's geopolitical balance. The loss of Southeast Asia would have deprived the United States and its European allies as well as Japan of access to one of the major sources of raw materials and one of the most potentially profitable markets in the world.

Communist control of Vietnam per se thus was not the threat; rather it was the fear that Vietnam would be just the first of a series of dominoes to collapse.

That a Communist victory in Vietnam would have any implications beyond that country was uncertain, but U.S. leaders refused to risk that it would not. The worst-case scenario dictated U.S. decision making. In a message to the American public in 1965, President Lyndon Johnson stated the ambiguities and imperatives of the domino theory: "I cannot tell you tonight as your President—with certainty—that a Communist conquest of South Vietnam would be followed by a Communist conquest of Southeast Asia. But I do know there are North Vietnamese troops in Laos. I do know that there are North Vietnamese–trained guerrillas in northeast Thailand. I do know that there are Communist-supported guerrilla forces operating in Burma. And a Communist coup was barely averted in Indonesia."

Having set forth a description of the turmoil in several countries—which assumed linkage among the various Communist activities (and which ignored U.S. military and/or covert operations in the region)—Johnson moved to the worst-case outcome, Communist domination of Southeast Asia: "So your American President cannot tell you—with certainty—that a Southeast Asia dominated by Communist power would bring a third world war much closer to terrible reality. One would hope that this would not be. But all that we have learned in this tragic century suggests to me that it would be so. As President of the United States, I am not prepared to gamble on the chance that it is not so."[1]

Johnson's reference to "what we have learned in this tragic century" touches on the extent to which the "lessons of the past" reinforced the commitment to Vietnam. The overriding "lesson"—drawn from the experience of the Western democracies in confronting aggression in the 1930s—was that the only means to prevent a major war against totalitarian states was to halt aggressive behavior in its initial stages, that is, "to nip aggression in the bud." Failure to stop Nazi Germany, Fascist Italy, and Imperial Japan in their first piecemeal acts of aggression, so the reasoning went, had only led to more aggression and ultimately to World War II. The containment of the Soviet Union, the sending of troops to fight in Korea in 1950, intervention against leftist movements in Latin America and the Middle East, and other aspects of American cold war policy—all were seen in the context of avoiding the mistakes of the past. In this way of looking at the world, Ho Chi Minh's movement to unify Vietnam was seen as an example of piecemeal Communist aggression. In a major address on Vietnam policy in 1965, Johnson stated, "Let no one think for a moment that retreat from Vietnam would bring an end to conflict. The battle would be renewed in one country and then another. The central lesson of our time is that the appetite of aggression is never satisfied. To withdraw from one battlefield means only to prepare for the next."[2]

U.S. leaders quickly drew parallels between Vietnam and instances where Communist pressures had been resisted. United Nations ambassador Adlai Stevenson stated publicly in 1964 that "the point is the same in Vietnam today as it was in Greece in 1947 and in Korea in 1950."[3] That same year Johnson asserted that "the challenge we face in southeast Asia today is the same challenge that we have faced with courage and that we have met with strength in Greece and Turkey, in Berlin and Korea."[4]

The commitment to Vietnam, which can be traced initially to the global containment strategy reinforced by the lessons of the 1930s, quickly took on a life of its own. U.S. options in Vietnam became limited by the "investment trap"; that is, the more the United States invested of its resources in Vietnam, the more difficult it became to withdraw or reduce its commitment. Speaking of the early U.S. troop commitment, Chester Cooper, who served in the Johnson administration, later wrote, "The 75,000 American troops in Vietnam were now a hostage. They represented too large a force to pull out without a tremendous loss of prestige, yet they were too small a combat force . . . to take over the burden of the fighting from the clearly ineffectual South Vietnamese forces."[5] At the time of those first direct military commitments, one dissident senator prophetically warned Johnson, "remember, escalation begets escalation."[6] As escalation almost inevitably followed, the result was to make Vietnam a test of American "credibility." Failure to support South Vietnam would seemingly erode the U.S. standing as a major world power. In his appeal for support from America's "silent majority," President Nixon in November 1969 warned that "this first defeat in our Nation's history would result in a collapse of confidence in American leadership, not only in Asia but throughout the world. . . . A nation cannot remain great if it betrays its allies and lets down its friends."[7]

Nixon's rhetoric touched on another element in accounting for Vietnam's importance to the United States—the long tradition of the American sense of mission. In the post–World War II period, that historic vision of promoting liberty merged with a strong anticommunist ideology. U.S. leaders repeatedly presented the rivalry with the Soviet Union as a moral struggle, thus encouraging the public to look upon international problems in absolute terms. Justifying the doctrine of containment, President Truman stated in 1947 that "it must be the policy of the United States to support free peoples who are resisting attempted subjugation by armed minorities or by outside pressures. . . . We must assist free peoples to work out their own destinies in their own way."[8] His successor, Dwight Eisenhower, in accepting the Republican nomination in 1952, stated that "you have summoned me . . . to lead a great crusade—for freedom in America and freedom in the world."[9] Freedom was seen as indivisible. As president, Eisenhower summoned support for the cause in Vietnam by warning Americans that "when the freedom of a man in Vietnam or in China is taken away from him, I think our freedom has lost a little."[10]

In Vietnam such rhetoric echoed the historic American sense of destiny in Asia. "To win the hearts and minds" of Vietnamese reflected the same mentality that had sent missionaries to gain "China for Christ" or that had talked of the "white man's burden" in the Philippines. Vietnam seemed a place where Western ideals could be realized. The sense of fostering nationhood was evident in the determined efforts to build representative institutions, in the praise of Ngo Dinh Diem as an "Asian Churchill," and in persistent effort to cast South Vietnamese leaders within an American mold. U.S. leaders presented the call to arms in Vietnam as a noble mission. "We want nothing for ourselves," Johnson told Americans in 1965, "only that the people of South Vietnam be allowed to guide their own country in their own way."[11] Four years later Nixon stated that "everything is negotiable except the right of the people of South Vietnam to determine their own future," and he called for perseverance in Vietnam because "any hope the world has for the survival of peace and freedom will be determined by whether the American people have the moral stamina and the courage to meet the challenge of free world leadership."[12] These sentiments may sound disingenuous when contrasted with certain aspects of U.S. policy in Vietnam, but the appeal to a national tradition of moral leadership nonetheless undergirded the commitments of a succession of presidential administrations.

The Americans who served in Vietnam, especially the young soldiers sent to battle, generally saw themselves as crusaders. The generation that fought in Vietnam had been especially inspired by President John Kennedy's impassioned inaugural address. John Wheeler, in his chronicle of the Vietnam generation, observes, "We believed John Kennedy. We wanted to give to our country. We only dimly realized what it meant to be sent abroad to 'pay any price, bear and burden . . . to assure the survival and the success of liberty.' "[13] Myra McPherson, who has interviewed many Vietnam veterans, adds, "Today I wonder if [Kennedy] truly knew just how much patriotism he inspired in young American boys. . . . His message carried a special message for them. . . . Over and over [the veterans] repeated it, these men in their late thirties now: 'ask not what your country can do for you. Ask what you can do for your country. . . .' Always they say it with a sense of emotion, as if it were a message meant for each alone. . . . It is, they say, the single most memorable sentence of their lives. It propelled many of them into Vietnam."[14] Experience in Vietnam often led to disillusionment, but the ideals were integral to the American effort.

That such a relatively small and obscure country would become of overriding importance to the United States can thus be seen as a result of several factors: a global strategy that looked upon the confrontation with the Communist powers as a "zero-sum game" and cast Southeast Asian nations into potential "dominoes"; the "lessons of the past" that taught the importance of halting aggression and thus perceived Vietnam as another place where the Communist powers were "testing" Western resolve; the parallel growth of U.S. commitment and "credibility" that made disengagement tantamount to surrendering America's position of world leadership; and the historic conviction of American mission that encouraged leaders, as well as civilians and military personnel in the field, to see in Vietnam an opportunity to realize Western ideals.

WHY DID THE UNITED STATES FAIL TO ACHIEVE ITS OBJECTIVES?: THE "WINNABLE" ANALYSIS

The question about the reasons for U.S. failure divides analysts of the Vietnam War between those who look upon the conflict as "winnable" and those who consider it "unwinnable." To the former, more effective use of U.S. military power could have altered the outcome, while the latter consider U.S. objectives as unattainable given the course of Vietnamese history and the risks of World War III.

The winnable school of thought, which has been advanced by Vietnam War revisionists, reflects the frustration over a conflict in which the United States, through its superior firepower and mobility, seemingly won all of the war's battles but lost the war. Books by General David Richard Palmer, General Bruce Palmer, General Phillip B. Davidson, Colonel Harry Summers, and Captain Shelby Stanton—each of whom served in Vietnam—trace failure to misguided civilian and military leadership. Each seeks to answer the problem posed by Summers: "On the battlefield itself, the Army was unbeatable. In engagement after engagement the forces of the Viet Cong and of the North Vietnamese Army were thrown back with terrible losses. Yet, in the end, it was North Vietnam, not the United States, that emerged victorious. How could we have succeeded so well, yet failed so miserably?"[15]

The classic principles of military strategy call for concentrating strength against the enemy and seizing the initiative, but American power was diffused, reactive, and applied gradually. The Johnson administration's emphasis on gradual escalation deprived the military of the opportunity to engage in a direct, immediate assault against the enemy. The air war against North Vietnam, in particular, was flawed, since the military objective of reducing support of Southern insurgency was partly subordinated to the political objective of inflicting sufficient "pain" to bring Hanoi to the bargaining table. The United States had the ability to achieve its objectives quickly and easily. In the opinion of General Davidson, U.S. strategy should have been "to strike the Viet Cong and North Vietnam as soon as possible to bring the war to a quick and satisfactory conclusion. Such an attack with overwhelming [nonnuclear] force would not only have achieved United States objectives in South Vietnam, but when compared to the protracted war we fought, it would have been a more humane conflict."[16]

The U.S. military command, in particular General William Westmoreland and his commitment to the search-and-destroy strategy, compounded the problems. This strategy squandered U.S. manpower in the essentially negative objective of winning a war of attrition. Westmoreland's plan, in Summers's words, "committed the United States Army . . . to the strategic defensive in pursuit of the negative aim of wearing the enemy down."[17] The emphasis on attrition led to counterinsurgency throughout South Vietnam, resulting in heavy American and South Vietnamese casualties without fully engaging the enemy. The American Command's delusion that the body count could bring victory underestimated North Vietnam's determination and capability. Intelligence sources correctly predicted that the North Vietnamese could indefinitely replace losses inflicted by the American search-and-destroy strategy. This misguided strategy enabled the enemy to retain the initiative, which the North Vietnamese and Viet Cong dramatically illustrated in the 1968 Tet Offensive.

Rather than pursuing the search-and-destroy strategy, the United States should have carried the war fully and directly against North Vietnam. The central mistake, according to the winnable school, was in the American concept of the Vietnam conflict as a case of Southern insurgency supported by the North, rather than as a case of Northern aggression against the South. The overriding objective should have been to prevent the North's infiltration of the South. "If the infiltration could not be brought under control," Colonel Summers argues, "South Vietnam could never solve its internal problems."[18]

The key to victory was in concentrating U.S. power against North Vietnam to prevent its infiltration of men and supplies into the South. This meant strengthening bases south of the Demilitarized Zone and establishing lines of defense into Laos. Air power should have concentrated on interdiction in the sparsely populated areas of North Vietnam and Laos and along the Demilitarized Zone. U.S. naval power should have been employed to blockade Haiphong and other Northern ports, and a large naval presence capable of amphibious landings should have been maintained in the Gulf of Tonkin to keep Hanoi guessing about American intentions. A "major mistake," according to General Bruce Palmer, was assuring North Vietnam that its territory would not be invaded. Rather, the "United States should have kept its intentions ambiguous and never taken Hanoi off the hook with respect to an invasion."[19] The United States, in Colonel Summers's words, lost "a major strategic advantage—escalation dominance—the ability to pose a threat to the enemy to raise the level of warfare beyond his ability (or willingness) to respond."[20]

Had the United States concentrated on sealing off the North, the Viet Cong, thus denied external support, would have gradually "withered on the vine." In addition, while shielding South Vietnam, the United States could have concentrated on building the South Vietnamese army into an effective counterinsurgency force. The reduced U.S. military presence throughout South Vietnam would have facilitated the development of nationhood.

Instead of concentrating on counterinsurgency, the United States' civilian and military leaders should have recognized that the war in Vietnam was a conventional, not a guerrilla, war. It was conventional in two respects: (1) it was a war of Northern aggression against the South, and (2) after large U.S. and North Vietnamese forces entered the war by 1967, most of the key fighting was in larger battles fought by conventional means. "The war was a standard contest being waged between national armies using conventional tactics," Captain Stanton contends, but "at the same time policy planners in Washington continued to misread battlefield reality. They remained mesmerized by 'counterinsurgency' which had been effectively terminated with the large-scale introduction of NVA and U.S. divisions to the battlefront."[21]

In arguing that the war's objectives were attainable, the revisionists offer an attractive argument. Their criticism of the attrition strategy and their suggestion that a less conspicuous U.S. military presence in South Vietnam would have strengthened that nation are especially telling. Whether the alternative strategy would have worked, however, is problematic. "If only" history is by definition speculative, but in this instance its value is made even more questionable by the immense problems attendant to sealing off North Vietnam. As commander, Westmoreland considered such alternatives but rejected them as impractical and costly. "Some have considered it practicable to seal the land frontiers against North Vietnamese infiltrations," Westmoreland later wrote, "yet small though [South Vietnam] is, its land frontiers extend for more than 900 miles." Its defense would have required "many millions of troops."[22] Moreover, the winnable argument tends to discount the extent of Southern opposition to the Saigon government; the Viet Cong insurgency was not a creation of North Vietnam but emerged independently before gaining the vital backing of the North. Finally, the revisionists minimize the problems attendant to nation building in South Vietnam. Even without any Northern troops in the South, the Saigon government would have still experienced the deficiencies of leadership and popular support that continually undermined its effectiveness.

THE "UNWINNABLE" ANALYSIS

Differing sharply with the winnable school are those writers who see the United States as fundamentally doomed in its political and military efforts. The United States, from this perspective, committed its resources and prestige to a cause that had virtually no chance of success. The American effort to build a noncommunist state in South Vietnam defied the principal development of post–World War II Vietnamese history. The Communist leadership in Hanoi, centered on the widely respected Ho Chi Minh, represented Vietnamese nationalist aspirations. The August Revolution and the subsequent war against the French gave the Viet Minh a legitimacy that the American-sponsored government in the South could never emulate. Accordingly, nation building in the South faced immense, fundamentally insuperable problems. Speaking of the efforts of the Diem government to rewrite history in ways that would establish its nationalist credentials, the respected scholar-journalist Bernard Fall observed, "So hoary a mythology is difficult to accept even by the peasants who comprise 90 per cent of the population. They know full well who fought the French and who did not."[23] The frustrating American record over two decades—the inability to foster a sense of nationhood, to find leaders who could rally the disparate political and religious groups, to stimulate rural reforms—was wholly predictable, given the course of post–World War II Vietnamese history. The U.S. failure can be traced, in large part, to the imbalance between the two Vietnamese governments. Put bluntly, the Americans were supporting a losing cause. "What was wrong in backing a weak, corrupt, inefficient regime against a brutally powerful, fanatically puritanical, ruthlessly efficient adversary," two scholars have written, "was that our side was likely to lose."[24]

Once the commitment to South Vietnam led to direct military involvement, the United States, despite its overwhelming capabilities, found itself engaged in a limited war in which the odds against winning were considerable. The difficulties were evident from the moment the war became Americanized. A Joint Chiefs of Staff study group stated in 1965 that "there appears to be no reason we cannot win if such is our will—and if that will is manifested in strategy and tactical operations."[25] This assurance, of course, implied unlimited options. The White House, however, never gave the military such freedom, and sound reasons dictated this restraint. However important Vietnam was to the United States in terms of its global interests, those same interests necessitated fighting a limited war. Neither Johnson nor Nixon was prepared to risk a major war over Vietnam with the Soviet Union or China or both. Recalling how China had intervened in the Korean War when U.S. forces invaded North Korea and were poised to unify Korea under a pro-Western government, U.S. leaders recognized that the major Communist powers would not tolerate North Vietnam's defeat. Thus, from the outset the United States made clear that it would not invade North Vietnam. The objective was not Hanoi's surrender, only that it abandon its warfare in the South. Likewise, the fears of extending the war led to the Johnson administration's refusal to mine Haiphong harbor or to attack North Vietnamese sanctuaries in Cambodia.

The U.S. military capability in Vietnam was also limited by domestic and global constraints. Any chance to achieve U.S. objectives would have required a considerably greater level of commitment than the Johnson administration deemed feasible. The maintenance of military obligations elsewhere in the world and the Johnson administration's determination to avoid mobilization and to sustain domestic reform programs limited the level of U.S. commitment in Vietnam. When Johnson was considering intervention in 1965, he was warned that attainment of U.S. objectives would require 700,000 to 1,000,000 men and seven years of warfare in order to force the Communists from the field and to pacify the South. Such a level of commitment was beyond what the Johnson administration ever considered. The result was a compromise that sought to find North Vietnam's "threshold of pain" through gradual escalation of U.S. military power.

U.S. analysts recognized the difficulties of this strategy; they consistently foresaw the achievement of military objectives as no more than a 50-50 proposition. The escalation of 1965–1967 was based not so much on expectations that it would be sufficient to force the North Vietnamese and Viet Cong to abandon their warfare but that it would be sufficient to deny them victory and thus force them to the bargaining table. That thinking, of course, played into the hands of Hanoi, which planned for protracted warfare.

The unwinnable school's analysis suggests that the basic problem facing the United States was that South Vietnam's survival could not be explained as vital to U.S. national security. The commitment and warfare were undertaken in the belief that preventing Communist unification of Vietnam was important in terms of global geopolitical interests, but it was not so essential that it would have justified the force levels and risks that would have enhanced the prospects of achieving objectives. Even General Bruce Palmer, a leading critic of White House restraints on the military, observes that "national security was a legitimate interest . . . but South Vietnam was not vital to the United States."[26] The inability of leaders to demonstrate that U.S. security was at stake in Vietnam contributed to declining popular support for the war and to the demoralization of soldiers sent to Vietnam. Talk of "falling dominoes" and "credibility" proved to be vague concepts on which to justify a war and to sustain an army's momentum.

Questions about how the United States could have failed in Vietnam will trouble Americans for years to come, as will the "lessons" of the war. Perhaps one might tentatively conclude, however, that the great disparity between American and North Vietnamese power was balanced by Hanoi's capacity to draw support from the Soviet Union and China, by the necessary limitations placed on U.S. warfare, and ultimately by the superior dedication of the North Vietnamese to their cause. To the North Vietnamese and Viet Cong, the war against the United States and its South Vietnamese "puppets" was everything. The dream of ending foreign interference and of achieving national unification, promised in the August Revolution, mobilized civilians and the army. To the United States, the war in Vietnam was important, but given its global commitments and the ambiguity of its interests in Vietnam, it could never become "everything." In the end, a people and army fighting to liberate their nation were able to outlast a superpower fighting to save the first "domino" and to uphold "credibility."

Notes

1. *Public Papers of the Presidents of the United States: Lyndon B. Johnson, 1967* (Washington, D.C.: U.S. Government Printing Office, 1968), 49–50.
2. *Public Papers of the Presidents of the United States: Lyndon B. Johnson, 1965* (Washington, D.C.: U.S. Government Printing Office, 1967), 394–99.
3. *Department of State Bulletin* 50, 8 June 1964, 908.
4. *Public Papers of the Presidents of the United States: Lyndon B. Johnson, 1963–64* (Washington, D.C.: U.S. Government Printing Office, 1965), 930.
5. Chester Cooper, *The Lost Crusade: America in Vietnam* (Greenwich, Conn.: Fawcett, 1972), 344.

6. Michael Mansfield cited in Herbert Schandler, *The Unmaking of a President: Lyndon Johnson and Vietnam* (Princeton, N.J.: Princeton University Press, 1977), 30.

7. *Public Papers of the Presidents of the United States: Richard Nixon, 1969* (Washington, D.C.: U.S. Government Printing Office, 1971), 901–9.

8. *Department of State Bulletin* 16, 23 March 1947, 536–37.

9. Eisenhower quoted in Cooper, *Lost Crusade*, 30.

10. *The Pentagon Papers: The Defense Department History of United States Decisionmaking on Vietnam* [Sen. Gravel edition] (Boston: Beacon, 1971), 1:606.

11. *Public Papers of Lyndon B. Johnson, 1965*, 394–99.

12. *Public Papers of Richard Nixon 1969*, 901–9.

13. John Wheeler, *Touched with Fire: The Future of the Vietnam Generation* (New York: Avon, 1984), 6.

14. Myra MacPherson, *Long Time Passing: Vietnam and the Haunted Generation* (New York: Doubleday, 1984), 47.

15. Summers, *On Strategy*, 21–22.

16. Davidson, *Vietnam at War*, 798.

17. Summers, *On Strategy*, 118.

18. Ibid., 170.

19. Bruce Palmer Jr., *The 25-Year War: America's Military Role in Vietnam* (Lexington: University Press of Kentucky, 1984), 29–30, 177.

20. Summers, *On Strategy*, 76–80.

21. Stanton, *The Rise and Fall of an American Army*, 347.

22. William C. Westmoreland, *A Soldier Reports* (New York: Doubleday, 1976), 147.

23. Bernard Fall, *Viet-Nam Witness, 1953–66* (New York: Praeger, 1966), 218.

24. David Fromkin and James Chace, "What Are the Lessons of Vietnam?" *Foreign Affairs* 63 (1985): 722–46.

25. *Pentagon Papers*, 4:291.

26. B. Palmer, *25-Year War*, 28.

CHRONOLOGY

111 B.C.	China conquers peoples of Red River Delta area of northern Vietnam.
A.D. 39	Trung sisters lead rebellion against Chinese.
939	Vietnamese forces defeat Chinese, marking the end of one thousand years of Chinese rule.
1802	Vietnam unified under Emperor Gia Long, founder of Nguyen dynasty.
1847	French naval bombardment of Da Nang.
1857	French assault on Da Nang marks the beginning of its military conquest of of Indochina.
1883	French establish control over Annam and Tonkin, rule Cochin China as a colony.
1887	France establishes the Indochinese Union, composed of Cochin China, Annam, Tonkin, Cambodia, and Laos.
1890	Ho Chi Minh born.
1898	Spanish-American War results in U.S. annexation of the Philippines.
1899–1902	U.S. troops suppress the Philippine insurrection.

1906   Phan Boi Chau founds the Modernization Society.

1914–1918   World War I.

1919   Ho Chi Minh, known as Nguyen Ai Quoc, petitions the Paris Peace Conference for recognition of Vietnamese self-determination.

1920   Ho Chi Minh joins the French Communist party.

1923   Ho Chi Minh goes to Moscow and later to China, where he organizes Vietnamese opposition to French.

1925   Phan Boi Chau, on trial in Hanoi, is sentenced to confinement for life.

1927   Vietnam Nationalist party (VNQDD) established.

1930   VNQDD rebellion fails, French suppress the movement. Ho Chi Minh and others form the Indochinese Communist party. Communist rebellion fails; cadres take refuge in China.

1932   Bao Dai returns to Vietnam from schooling in France to ascend to the throne under French tutelage.

1939   Outbreak of World War II in Europe.

1940   France falls to Germany. Japanese occupy the northern part of Indochina.

1941   Japanese forces complete their occupation of Indochina; the French administration remains intact. Ho Chi Minh and his followers organize the Viet Minh. Japan attacks U.S. bases at Pearl Harbor.

1942   Vo Nguyen Giap begins the organization of Viet Minh guerrilla groups for anti-Japanese activities in northern Vietnam.

1945   March: Japanese overthrow the French administration in Indochina, establish direct control, and proclaim nominal Vietnamese "independence."

               April: Death of Franklin Roosevelt; Harry S. Truman becomes president.

               August: United States drops atomic bombs on Hiroshima and Nagasaki; Japan surrenders. The August Revolution brings the Viet Minh to power throughout Vietnam; Bao Dai abdicates in favor of the Viet Minh.

September: Ho Chi Minh proclaims independence in the name of the Democratic Republic of Vietnam. British and Chinese forces begin occupying Vietnam to receive Japanese surrender and pave way for the return of French authority.

October: Viet Minh and Americans in northern Vietnam organize the Vietnam-American Friendship Association.

1946   March: Ho-Sainteny Agreement provides for French recognition of Vietnam as a "free state" within the French Union, stationing of French troops in the North, and a referendum on Vietnamese unification.

June: French, in violation of the March agreement, proclaim a separate government for Cochin China.

July: United States grants independence to the Philippines.

September: Ho Chi Minh, after futile negotiations in Paris to implement the March agreement, leaves after signing a modus vivendi calling for an end to French-Vietnamese clashes.

November: Shooting between French and Vietnamese soldiers at Haiphong leads to French naval bombardment.

December: Viet Minh forces attack French garrisons in Hanoi, marking the beginning of the French–Viet Minh War.

1947   August: Britain grants independence to India and Pakistan.

1948   January: Britain grants independence to Burma.

1949   March: Elysée Agreement makes Vietnam an "associated state" within the French Union and provides for the return of former emperor Bao Dai as "head of state."

October: People's Republic of China proclaimed by Mao Tse-tung, marking the completion of Communist victory in the Chinese civil war.

December: Netherlands grants independence to Indonesia.

1950   January: People's Republic of China and the Soviet Union
            recognize the Democratic Republic of Vietnam.

            February: United States and Britain recognize the Bao Dai
            government.

            May: United States begins military assistance to the French
            war effort in Indochina.

            June: Outbreak of war in Korea.

            September–October: French suffer severe defeats in northern
            Vietnam.

1951   January–March: French halt Viet Minh advance in the North.

1953   May: General Navarre becomes commander of French forces,
            puts forth his plan to win the war.

            July: Armistice ends the Korean War.

            November: French forces occupy Dien Bien Phu to forestall
            the Viet Minh assault on Laos and to establish a base for an
            offensive against the Viet Minh.

1954   January: United States, Britain, France, and the Soviet
            Union agree to hold a conference on Korea and Indochina at
            Geneva that spring.

            March: Battle of Dien Bien Phu begins.

            April: President Eisenhower sets forth the "domino theory" as
            his administration considers military intervention at Dien
            Bien Phu.

            May: French defeated at Dien Bien Phu. Indochina phase of
            the Geneva Conference begins.

            June: Ngo Dinh Diem named prime minister of State of
            Vietnam. Pierre Mendes-France becomes prime minister of
            France and promises to reach an agreement in Vietnam
            within a month.

            July: Geneva Armistice and Final Declaration provide for the
            temporary division of Vietnam pending 1956 nationwide
            elections.

September: Southeast Asia Treaty Organization established with the United States, Britain, France, Australia, New Zealand, Pakistan, Thailand, and the Philippines as members.

1955   January: United States begins direct assistance to the South Vietnamese government.

February: U.S. advisers replace the French in training the South Vietnamese army.

April–May: South Vietnamese army defeats Binh Xuyen forces.

June: South Vietnamese army attacks Hoa Hao forces.

July: People's Republic of China and the Soviet Union conclude aid agreements with North Vietnam.

August: Diem refuses negotiations with North Vietnam on reunification elections.

October: Diem defeats Bao Dai in referendum, proclaims the Republic of Vietnam with himself as president.

1956   March: Constituent National Assembly elected in South Vietnam.

July: Month when unification elections should have been held as provided in Geneva Agreements passes without incident.

December: North Vietnamese tell followers in South to persist in "political struggle" and to prepare for "self-defense."

1957   May: Diem visits the United States, addresses Congress, and gains Eisenhower's reaffirmation of U.S. support.

November: In Laos, the royal government and the Pathet Lao agree to a coalition government and integration of forces; Souvanna Phuoma selected as head of the neutral coalition government.

1958   July–August: In Laos, a U.S.-backed anticommunist group forces Souvanna Phuoma to resign and establishes a new government from which the Pathet Lao are purged.

1959   May: North Vietnamese approve a limited armed struggle in the South and the infiltration of men and supplies to the South.

1960   January: Viet Cong uprising in Ben Tre province in the Mekong Delta.

            March: Southern dissidents issue "Declaration of Former Resistance Fighters."

            August: In Laos, a neutralist coup puts Souvanna Phuoma back in power; a rightist counterattack leads to civil war.

            September: North Vietnamese adopt the objectives of a socialist state in the North and a struggle for reunification in the South.

            November: John F. Kennedy defeats Richard Nixon in the U.S. presidential election.

            December: National Liberation Front established. Crisis in Laos as U.S.-supported rightists overthrow neutralist government. U.S. military advisers in South Vietnam: about 900.

1961   May: Vice President Lyndon Johnson visits South Vietnam, urges more U.S. aid. Laos cease-fire and Geneva Conference on Laos begins; results in a coalition neutral government under Souvanna Phuoma.

            October: Walt Rostow and General Maxwell Taylor visit South Vietnam and urge increased U.S. assistance.

            December: U.S. military advisers in South Vietnam: 3,200.

1962   February: U.S. Military Assistance Command-Vietnam (MACV) established.

            December: U.S. military advisers in South Vietnam: nearly 12,000.

1963   January: Viet Cong defeats South Vietnamese at Ap Bac.

            May: South Vietnamese troops fire on Buddhist protesters at Hué.

            June: Buddhist monk commits suicide by self-immolation.

August: South Vietnamese forces attack Buddhist temples. Henry Cabot Lodge replaces Frederick Nolting as U.S. ambassador in South Vietnam.

October: United States, through CIA, assures General Duong Van Minh and others of its support in the planned coup against Diem.

November: Duong Van Minh and other generals overthrow Diem; Diem and his brother are murdered. John Kennedy assassinated; Lyndon Johnson becomes president.

December: North Vietnam decides to intensify struggle in the South. U.S. military advisers in South Vietnam: 16,000.

1964   January: General Nguyen Khanh seizes power in Saigon.

April: General William Westmoreland named MACV commander.

July: South Vietnamese naval forces carry out raids along the North Vietnamese coast.

August: Gulf of Tonkin crisis: a North Vietnamese patrol boat attacks a U.S. destroyer, and two days later a murky second "incident" occurs. U.S. air attacks on North Vietnam. Congress passes Gulf of Tonkin resolution giving the president wide authority to uphold U.S. interests in Southeast Asia.

November: Viet Cong attack Bien Hoa air base. Lyndon Johnson defeats Barry Goldwater in the U.S. presidential election. Demonstrations in Saigon against Khanh's government.

December: Viet Cong bombs Brinks hotel in Saigon. U.S. military advisers in South Vietnam: 23,200.

1965   February: Viet Cong attacks U.S. base at Pleiku; Johnson orders retaliatory air raids against North Vietnam. General Khanh's government overthrown.

March: First U.S. combat troops arrive in Vietnam. Operation Rolling Thunder begins.

April: Johnson, in speech at Johns Hopkins University, offers North Vietnam participation in a regional economic development program if it agrees to end the war; North Vietnamese reject offer. Johnson approves Westmoreland's request for a ground combat force of 40,000 troops.

June: Air Marshall Nguyen Cao Ky becomes South Vietnam's prime minister in the newly established military government, the ninth change in government since November 1963.

July: Johnson approves General Westmoreland's request for additional forces.

November: U.S.–North Vietnamese clash at Ia Drang valley, the first large, open battle of the war.

December: Johnson suspends bombing on Christmas in an attempt to induce the North Vietnamese to negotiate. U.S. troop strength: nearly 200,000.

1966   January: Johnson resumes bombing at the end of the month.

February: Johnson meets with South Vietnamese leaders in Honolulu.

March: Demonstrations led by Buddhists in Hué, Da Nang, and Saigon against South Vietnamese government; South Vietnamese troops quell protests.

October: Operation Attleboro attacks Communist bases near Cambodian border.

December: U.S. troop strength: nearly 400,000.

1967   January: North Vietnam states that the United States must halt its bombing of the North as a condition for peace negotiations. Operation Cedar Falls attacks Communist bases in the Iron Triangle.

February: Operation Junction City Attacks Communist bases near Cambodian border.

March: Johnson meets with Premier Ky and General Nguyen Van Thieu in Guam.

September: South Vietnamese elect Thieu as president and Ky as vice president. North Vietnamese and Viet Cong begin major actions. U.S. begins fortification of Khe Sanh. Johnson, in a speech at San Antonio, offers to stop the bombing in exchange for productive discussions.

November: Westmoreland, during a visit to the United States, speaks confidently of a successful outcome of the war.

December: North Vietnamese reaffirm that they will negotiate when the United States stops its bombing. U.S. troop strength: nearly 500,000.

1968   January: North Vietnamese attack on Khe Sanh begins. North Vietnamese and Viet Cong launch the Tet Offensive.

February: United States and South Vietnamese regain control of Southern cities; Hué recaptured after 25 days of fighting. Westmoreland requests 206,000 additional troops.

March: General Creighton Abrams replaces Westmoreland as MACV commander. Johnson announces he will not seek another term as president, suspends the bombing of the North except near the Demilitarized Zone, and calls for peace talks. Request for additional troops is rejected.

May: United States and North Vietnam agree to preliminary negotiations in Paris.

October: Johnson orders an end to all bombing of North Vietnam.

November: Richard Nixon defeats Hubert Humphrey in the U.S. presidential election.

December: U.S. troop strength: 535,000.

1969   January: Paris negotiations are expanded to include South Vietnamese government and National Liberation Front representatives.

March: United States begins secret bombing of Cambodia.

May: National Liberation Front peace plan demands unconditional U.S. troop withdrawal and a coalition government in the South excluding Thieu.

June: Nixon, with the announcement of the withdrawal of 25,000 U.S. forces, begins the gradual reduction of the U.S. military presence.

September: Ho Chi Minh dies in Hanoi at age 79.

November: Nixon appeals to the "silent majority" for support of his Vietnam policy. My Lai massacre (a year earlier) is revealed.

December: U.S. troop strength: 475,000.

1970   February: Henry Kissinger and Le Duc Tho begin secret talks in Paris.

March: Prince Sihanouk is overthrown in Cambodia; Lon Nol heads the new government.

April: U.S.–South Vietnamese forces attack North Vietnamese sanctuaries in Cambodia.

May: Protests against the Cambodian invasion throughout the United States; at Kent State University, national guardsmen kill four students.

June: U.S. ground troops withdrawn from Cambodia.

December: U.S. troop strength: 334,000.

1971   February: Operation Lam Son 719: South Vietnamese forces attack North Vietnamese supply lines in Laos.

March: Lieutenant William Calley is convicted of the murder of South Vietnamese civilians at My Lai.

June: *New York Times* begins publication of the Pentagon Papers, a secret study of U.S. involvement in Vietnam.

October: Thieu, running unopposed, is elected to another term as president.

December: U.S. troop strength: 140,000.

1972   February: Nixon visits China.

March: Easter 1972 Offensive: North Vietnamese assault on northern provinces of South Vietnam.

April: Nixon orders the bombing of the area near Hanoi and Haiphong.

May: North Vietnamese troops occupy Quang Tri City. Kissinger, in a private meeting with Le Duc Tho, states that the United States is prepared to drop its insistence on the withdrawal of Northern troops from the South. Nixon orders the mining of Haiphong harbor; intensified bombing of North Vietnam. Nixon visits Soviet Union.

June–September: South Vietnamese, with U.S. air support, recapture Quang Tri City.

October: Kissinger and Le Duc Tho reach the basis of a settlement to end the war; Thieu opposes the agreement.

November: Nixon defeats George McGovern in the U.S. presidential election.

December: Nixon orders the bombing of the Hanoi-Haiphong area.

1973   January: Nixon letter assures Thieu of "continued assistance in postsettlement period." Cease-fire agreement signed in Paris.

March: Last U.S. troops leave Vietnam. North Vietnam releases the last of U.S. prisoners of war.

August: United States ends the bombing of Cambodia in accordance with a congressional prohibition.

1974   February: South Vietnamese offensive against areas long under Communist control; retaliation leads to heavy fighting.

August: Nixon resigns the presidency and is replaced by Gerald Ford.

December: North Vietnamese leadership adopts a plan to defeat the Thieu government within two years.

1975   January: In Cambodia, the Khmer Rouge lay siege to Phnom Penh. North Vietnamese capture Phuoc Long province, north of Saigon.

March: North Vietnamese capture Ban Me Thuout. Thieu orders abandonment of northern provinces. Fall of Hué and Da Nang.

April: Khmer Rouge take control in Cambodia and establish Democratic Kampuchea. Thieu resigns; authority is transferred to General Duong Van Minh. U.S. evacuation of American and allied personnel from Saigon. Fall of Saigon.

1976   November: Jimmy Carter defeats Ford in the U.S. presidential election.

1977   January: Carter pardons most of the Vietnam-era draft evaders.

October: Vietnam is admitted to the United Nations.

1978   June: Vietnam joins COMECON, a Soviet Union–sponsored economic group.

November: Vietnam signs the Treaty of Friendship with the Soviet Union.

December: Vietnam invades Cambodia and replaces the Khmer Rouge with the People's Republic of Kampuchea, headed by Heng Samrin.

1979   February: Chinese forces attack Vietnam but are repulsed after heavy fighting.

1980   November: Ronald Reagan defeats Carter in the U.S. presidential election.

1982   November: Vietnam veterans memorial unveiled in Washington, D.C.

1986   December: Vietnam Communist party elects Nguyen Van Linh as general secretary; Premier Pham Van Dong and other "old guard" leaders are eased from office.

1987   August: Mission to Vietnam headed by General John Vessey results in an accelerated program of identifying MIAs.

1988   October: United Nations General Assembly passes a resolution declaring that Cambodia, after Vietnamese withdrawal, must not return to the "universally condemned policies and practices of the past."

1989   April: Vietnam promises that its forces will be withdrawn from Cambodia by September.

September: Vietnam completes troop withdrawal from Cambodia.

1992   November: Bill Clinton defeats George Bush in presidential election.

1993   October: United Nations–supervised elections in Cambodia establish coalition government.

1994   February: President Clinton lifts Vietnam embargo.

1995   July: President Clinton extends diplomatic recognition to Vietnam.

BIBLIOGRAPHIC ESSAY

This essay is intended to offer suggestions for further reading on the major topics covered in the text. Literature on the U.S.-Vietnamese relationship is already extensive and rapidly expanding—a reflection of the continuing popular and scholarly interest in the Vietnam War.

On the U.S. political-military involvement in Vietnam, George C. Herring, *America's Longest War: The United States and Vietnam, 1950–1975*, 3d ed. (New York: McGraw-Hill, 1996), William J. Duiker, *U.S. Containment Policy and the Conflict in Indochina* (Stanford, Calif.: Stanford University Press, 1994), and Robert D. Schulzinger, *A Time for War: The United States and Vietnam, 1941–1975* (New York: Oxford University Press, 1997) provide comprehensive overviews of U.S. policy making and military operations. William Conrad Gibbons, *The U.S. Government and the Vietnam War: Executive and Legislative Roles and Relationships*, 4 vols. (Washington D.C.: U.S. Government Printing Office, 1984–1995) is an especially rich source for the full dimensions of American policy making. William S. Turley's *The Second Indochina War: A Short Political and Military History* (Boulder, Colo.: Westview, 1986) traces the war from both sides. James Harrison's *The Endless War: Fifty Years of War in Vietnam* (New York: Free Press, 1982) sets the war within the context of the history and ideology of the Vietnamese Communist movement. Paul Kattenberg's *The Vietnam Trauma in American Policy, 1945–1975* (New Brunswick, N.J.: Transaction, 1980) is a balanced study written by a former official who was involved in America's policymaking in Vietnam. Stanley Karnow, a journalist with vast experience in Southeast Asia, has written *Vietnam: A History* (New York: Viking, 1983), a balanced interpretation that captures the events and personalities of the French and American wars in Indochina. Michael Maclear's *The Ten Thousand Day War* (New York: St. Martin's, 1981), written to accompany the Canadian Broadcasting Corporation's television series, also has much valuable information. Widely praised when it was published in 1972, Frances FitzGerald's *Fire in the Lake: The Vietnamese and the Americans in Vietnam* (Boston: Little, Brown & Co., 1972) traces America's failure to its ignorance of Vietnamese history and culture. Gabriel Kolko's *Anatomy of a War: Vietnam, the United States, and the Modern Historical Experience* (New York: Pantheon, 1985) attributes the war's outcome to the underlying political and social structures of the United States, the Vietnamese Communist movement, and the South Vietnamese government. More recent studies that thoughtfully stress the cultural gap are Marilyn B. Young's *The Vietnam Wars, 1945–1990* (New York: Harper Collins, 1990) and Michael H. Hunt's *Lyndon Johnson's War: America's Cold War Crusade in Vietnam, 1945–1968* (New York: Hill and Wang, 1996). James William Gilbert's *The Perfect War: The War We Couldn't Lose and How We Did* (Boston: Atlantic Monthly Press, 1986) traces U.S. frustration to a technocratic mentality and system that ignored the realities of Vietnam. Another valuable interpretation is Neil Sheehan's *A Bright Shining Lie: John Paul Vann and America in Vietnam* (New York: Random House, 1988), which relates the career of the controversial Vann to the ultimate U.S. futility in Vietnam. Other useful overviews of U.S. involvement include: James Stuart Olson, *Where the Domino Fell: America and Vietnam, 1945 to 1990*, 2d ed. (New York: St. Martin's 1996), George Moss, *Vietnam: An American Ordeal*, 2d ed. (Englewood Cliffs, N.J.: Prentice Hall, 1994), and Patrick J. Hearden, *The Tragedy of Vietnam* (New York: Harper Collins, 1991).

There are several valuable edited collections of documents and/or essays, including: David L. Anderson, ed., *Shadow on the White House: Presidents and the Vietnam War* (Lawrence: University Press of Kansas, 1993), which presents essays by historians on how six presidents beginning with Truman and ending with Ford confronted the intractable problems of Vietnam; Robert J. McMahon, ed., *Major Problems in the History of the Vietnam War*, 2d ed. (Lexington, Mass.: D. C. Heath, 1995) draws on scholarly essays and documents to address the basic issues of the war; William A. Williams, Thomas McCormick, Lloyd Gardner, and Walter LaFeber, eds., *America in Vietnam: A Documentary History* (Garden City, N.Y.: Doubleday, 1985) relies on documents and brief essays by the editors to study pertinent questions; Jeffrey P. Kimball, ed., *To Reason Why: The Debate about the Causes of U.S. Involvement in the Vietnam War* (New York: McGraw Hill, 1990) draws on a wide range of sources to examine the various dimensions of American involvement; and Gareth Porter, ed., *Vietnam: A History in Documents* (New York: Meridian, 1981) provides a rich collection of American and Vietnamese documents from 1941 to 1975.

On the rise of Vietnamese nationalism and the ascendancy of the Communist movement, the works of William Duiker, Huynh Kim Khanh, David Marr, John T. McAlister, Paul Mus, and Ken Post are all instructive. Duiker's *The Rise of Nationalism in Vietnam, 1900–1941* (Ithaca, N.Y.: Cornell University Press, 1976) analyzes the various expressions of nationalism, and

Marr's *Vietnamese Anti-Colonialism 1885–1925* (Berkeley: University of California Press, 1971) and *Vietnamese Tradition on Trial, 1920–1945* (Berkeley: University of California Press, 1981) focus on the social and intellectual forces that shaped nationalism. McAlister collaborated with the noted French scholar Paul Mus to write *The Vietnamese and Their Revolution* (New York: Harper and Row, 1970), which analyzes the social context of Vietnamese nationalism through 1945; their study reflects Mus's earlier writing, especially his classic *Viet-Nam: sociologie d'une guerre* (Paris: Editions de Seuil, 1952). McAlister's *Vietnam: The Origins of Revolution* (Princeton, N.J.: Center for International Studies, Princeton University, 1969) traces the August Revolution and the origins of the French–Viet Minh War. Khanh's *Vietnamese Communism, 1925–1945* (Ithaca, N.Y.: Cornell University Press, 1982) underscores the Communist success in appealing to traditional patriotism. The most comprehensive study of the Vietnamese Communist movement is the ongoing multivolume work of Ken Post, *Revolution, Socialism, and Nationalism in Viet Nam*, 4 vols. (Belmont, Calif.: Wadsworth, 1989–1990). Further insights into the Communist movement are offered by Jean Lacouture's *Ho Chi Minh: A Political Bibliography* (New York: Random House, 1968), which is the best biography of the Vietnamese leader, and by the writings of Douglas Pike, especially his *History of Vietnamese Communism* (Stanford, Calif.: Stanford University Press, 1978).

The fullest accounts of the mounting U.S. involvement and commitment during the 1945–1965 period are provided by Anthony Short, *The Origins of the Vietnam War* (London: Longman, 1989) and George McT. Kahin, *Intervention: How America Became Involved in Vietnam* (New York: Knopf, 1986). On the early U.S. response to Vietnamese nationalism and the French–Viet Minh conflict, see: Stein Tonnesson, *The Vietnamese Revolution of 1945: Roosevelt, Ho Chi Minh, and de Gaulle in a World at War* (London: Peace Research Institute, 1991); Gary R. Hess, *The United States' Emergence as a Southeast Asian Power, 1940–1950* (New York: Columbia University Press, 1987); Archimedes L. A. Patti, *Why Viet Nam? Prelude to America's Albatross* (Berkeley: University of California Press, 1980); Ronald H. Spector, *Advice and Consent: The Early Years of the U.S. Army in Vietnam, 1941–1960* (New York: Free Press, 1983); Lloyd C. Gardner, *Approaching Vietnam: From World War II through Dienbienphu* (New York: Norton, 1988); Ronald E. Irving *The First Indochina War: French and American Policy, 1943–1954* (London: Croom Helm, 1975); Robert M. Blum, *Drawing the Line: The Origins of the American Containment Policy in East Asia* (New York: Norton, 1982), Andrew J. Rotter, *The Path to Vietnam: Origins of the American Commitment to Southeast Asia* (Ithaca, N.Y.: Cornell University Press, 1987); and Michael Schaller, *The American Occupation of Japan: Origins of the Cold War in Asia* (New York: Oxford University Press, 1985).

The U.S. involvement in the 1954 crisis and the Geneva settlement has been studied in considerable depth. Among the most useful works are Denise

Artaud and Lawrence Kaplan, eds., *Dienbienphu: The Atlantic Alliance and the Defense of Southeast Asia* (Wilmington, Del.: Scholarly Resources, 1989), which includes essays by French, British, and American scholars; Melanie Billings-Yun, *Decision against War: Eisenhower and Dien Bien Phu, 1954* (New York: Columbia University Press, 1986); John F. Burke and Fred I. Greenstein, *How Presidents Test Reality: Decisions on Vietnam, 1954 and 1965* (New York: Russell Sage Foundation, 1989); John F. Prados, *"The Sky Would Fall": Operation Vulture, the U.S. Bombing Mission, Indochina, 1954* (New York: Dial, 1983); Melvin Gurtov, *The First Vietnam Crisis: Chinese Communist Strategy and United States Involvement, 1953–1954* (New York: Columbia University Press, 1967); and Robert F. Randle, *Geneva 1954: The Settlement of the Indochinese War* (Princeton, N.J.: Princeton University Press, 1969).

The growing U.S. involvement during the Eisenhower administration is thoughtfully covered by David Anderson in *Trapped by Success: The Eisenhower Administration and Vietnam, 1953–1961* (New York: Columbia University Press, 1991). On the Kennedy administration, William J. Rust, *Kennedy and Vietnam: American Foreign Policy, 1960–63* (New York, 1985) and John M. Newman, *JFK and Vietnam: Deception, Intrigue, and the Struggle for Power* (New York: Warner, 1992) both see Kennedy as planning to disengage from Vietnam; the latter work argues that this led to a military-inspired conspiracy against Kennedy. Roger Hilsman, *To Move a Nation* (Garden City, N.Y.: Doubleday, 1967) is the memoir-history of a key State Department official involved in Vietnam policymaking during the Kennedy years. For an understanding of South Vietnam under Ngo Dinh Diem, the best sources are Dennis Warner, *The Last Confucian* (New York: Penguin, 1963) and Robert Scigliano, *South Vietnam: Nation under Stress* (Boston: Houghton Mifflin, 1965). Ellen J. Hammer, *A Death in November: America in Vietnam, 1963* (New York: E. P. Dutton, 1987), sharply criticizes U.S. complicity in the overthrow of Diem. Among her targets is the Saigon press corps, whose Vietnam experience and influence have been analyzed by William Prochnau in *Once upon a Distant War* (New York: Vintage, 1995).

The scholarly writing on the U.S. escalation of the 1960s has been facilitated by the gradual opening of documentary sources. The pivotal Gulf of Tonkin incident has been meticulously analyzed by Edwin E. Moise in *Tonkin Gulf and the Escalation of the Vietnam War* (Chapel Hill: University of North Carolina Press, 1996). The best accounts of Johnson's movement toward Americanization of the war are: Larry Berman, *Planning a Tragedy: The Americanization of the War in Vietnam* (New York: Norton, 1982), which focuses on Johnson's political and military miscalculations; Leslie Gelb and Richard Betts, *The Irony of Vietnam: The System Worked* (Washington, D.C.: Brookings Institution, 1978), which documents the extent to which leaders were consistently informed of the difficulties facing the United States but went ahead to avoid the political consequences of losing Vietnam; Yuen

Foong Khong, *Analogies at War—Korea, Munich, Dien Bien Phu—The Vietnam Decisions of 1965* (Princeton, N.J.: Princeton University Press, 1992), which stresses how policymakers were guided by the "lessons of history"; the previously mentioned Burke and Greenstein study, *How Presidents Test Reality*, which unfavorably compares Johnson's relatively closed advisory system with the open decision making of Eisenhower; and Brian Van DeMark, *Into the Quagmire: Lyndon Johnson and the Escalation of the Vietnam War* (New York: Oxford University Press, 1991), which sees Johnson as a reluctant warrior caught in events that were largely beyond his control. The sharpest critic of Johnson and McNamara is H. R. McMaster whose *Dereliction of Duty: Lyndon Johnson, Robert McNamara, the Joint Chiefs of Staff, and the Lies That Led to Vietnam* (New York: Harper Collins, 1997) indicts them for manipulating the public and the Joint Chiefs as they deceptively took the country to war.

Johnson as commander in chief and the impact of the war on him personally and on his administration have been effectively chronicled in several works, including: Doris Kearns, *Lyndon Johnson and the American Dream* (New York: Harper & Row, 1976), which is a sympathetic portrait based in part on Johnson's personal reflections; Kathleen J. Turner, *Lyndon Johnson's Dual War: Vietnam and the Press* (Chicago: University of Chicago Press, 1983), which chronicles Johnson's effort to sustain popular support for his war policy; Larry Berman, *Lyndon Johnson's War* (New York: Norton, 1989), which sees Johnson as an ineffective leader, unable to coordinate ends with means; David Barrett, *Uncertain Warriors: Lyndon Johnson and His Vietnam Advisers* (Lawrence: University Press of Kansas, 1993), which argues that contrary to most accounts, Johnson employed an open advisory system; Warren I. Cohen and Nancy Bernkopf Tucker, eds., *Lyndon Johnson Confronts the World: American Foreign Policy, 1963–1968* (New York: Cambridge University Press, 1994), which includes thoughtful essays on Johnson's Vietnam policy and others that underline the war's impact on U.S. foreign policy generally; George C. Herring, *LBJ and Vietnam: A Different Kind of War* (Austin: University of Texas Press, 1994), which carefully examines the shortcomings of Johnson's efforts at military coordination, pacification, public relations, and negotiations; and Lloyd C. Gardner, *Pay Any Price: Lyndon Johnson and the Wars for Vietnam* (Chicago: Ivan Dee, 1996), which traces the inner workings of the Johnson White House and sees Johnson futilely linking U.S. objectives in Vietnam with his aspirations for reform at home. Frank Vandiver, *Shadows of Vietnam: Lyndon Johnson's Wars* (College Station: Texas A& M University Press, 1997) offers a sympathetic portrait.

Memoirs of key officials are also useful, including: Lyndon B. Johnson, *The Vantage Point: Perspectives of the Presidency* (New York: Holt, Rinehart, & Winston, 1971); Dean Rusk with Richard Rusk, *As I Saw It* (New York: Norton, 1990); Henry Cabot Lodge, *The Storm Has Many Eyes* (New York: Norton, 1973); Walt W. Rostow, *The Diffusion of Power: An Introduction to Recent History* (New York: Macmillan, 1972); and Robert S. McNamara with

Brian DeMark, *In Retrospect: The Tragedy and Lessons of Vietnam* (New York: Random House, 1995). Important biographies include: Deborah Shapley, *Promise and Power: The Life and Times of Robert McNamara* (Boston: Little, Brown & Co., 1993); Thomas Schoenbaum, *Waging Peace and War: Dean Rusk in the Truman, Kennedy, and Johnson Years* (New York: Simon & Schuster, 1988); Warren Cohen, *Dean Rusk* (Totowa, N.J.: Cooper Square, 1980); David D. Leo, *George Ball, Vietnam, and the Rethinking of Containment* (Chapter Hill: University of North Carolina Press, 1991); James A. Bill, *George Ball: Behind the Scenes in U.S. Foreign Policy* (New Haven: Yale University Press, 1997); Anne Blair, *Lodge in Vietnam: A Patriot Abroad* (New Haven: Yale University Press, 1995); and Douglas Kinnard, *The Certain Trumpet: Maxwell Taylor and the American Experience in Vietnam* (Washington, D.C.: Brassey's, 1991).

The domestic reaction to the war has been studied in various works. The popular response is fully examined by John Mueller in *War, Presidents, and Public Opinion* (New York: John Wiley & Co., 1973), and the clash between "doves" and "hawks" is thoroughly analyzed by David W. Levy in *The Debate over Vietnam* (Baltimore, Md.: Johns Hopkins University Press, 1991). Joseph G. Morgan's *The Vietnam Lobby: The American Friends of Vietnam* (Chapel Hill: University of North Carolina Press, 1997) traces the activities and influence of the principal pro-Saigon group in America. On the other side, the origins, extent, and impact of the antiwar protest are examined in two works: Charles DeBenedetti assisted by Charles Chatfield, *An American Ordeal: The Antiwar Movement of the Vietnam Era* (Syracuse, N.Y.: Syracuse University Press, 1990) and Melvin Small, *Johnson, Nixon, and the Doves* (New Brunswick, N.J.: Rutgers University Press, 1988). The career and influence of Senator J. William Fulbright, the foremost Establishment critic of the war, has been the subject of much writing, the most insightful being William Berman's *William Fulbright and the Vietnam War: The Dissent of a Political Realist* (Kent, Ohio: Kent State University Press, 1988) and Randall B. Wood's comprehensive *Fulbright: A Biography* (New York: Cambridge University Press, 1995). Television coverage has been frequently charged with presenting a biased antiwar perspective, a view sustained in Peter Braestup's account of the Tet Offensive, *Big Story*, 2 vols. (Boulder, Colo.: Westview, 1977). Balanced appraisals that stress the relative objectivity of the media are provided by Daniel Hallin, *The "Uncensored" War* (New York: Oxford University Press, 1986) and Martin F. Herz, *The Prestige Press and the Christmas Bombing, 1972: Images and Reality in Vietnam* (Washington, D.C.: Ethics and Public Policy Center, 1980). Along the same lines, Melvin Small's *Covering Dissent: The Media and the Anti-Vietnam War Movement* (New Brunswick, N.J.: Rutgers University Press, 1994) demonstrates that the media typically presented war protesters unfavorably.

Since the end of the war, "revisionist" studies have defended U.S. involvement as morally and politically justifiable and have argued that the war was winnable. Guenter Lewy, *America in Vietnam* (New York: Oxford University Press, 1978), the first major revisionist work, is especially notable for its defense of U.S. military actions on grounds of international law. The fullest argument on behalf of the U.S. commitment is offered by Norman Podhoretz in *Why We Were in Vietnam* (New York: Simon & Schuster, 1982). Timothy J. Lomperis's *The War Everyone Lost—and Won* (Baton Rouge: Louisiana State University Press, 1984) sees the United States as actually having won the counterinsurgency campaign but then losing the war because it failed to resist the North Vietnamese conventional campaign of 1975. Lomperis has extended this argument in *From People's War to People's Rule: Insurgency, Intervention, and the Lessons of Vietnam* (Chapel Hill: University of North Carolina Press, 1996), which compares the Western response to various leftist insurgencies.

The wave of revisionism has been enhanced by the writing of several military officers who have underscored the success of most U.S. operations and have contended that civilian restraints denied the possibility of a conventional victory. William Westmoreland's memoir, *A Soldier Reports* (Garden City, N.Y.: Doubleday, 1976), set the tone for much of this writing by blaming inept civilian leaders for his frustrations as U.S. commander. Similar sentiments are found in Dave Richard Palmer, *Summons of the Trumpet: A History of the Vietnam War from a Military Man's Viewpoint* (Novato, Calif.: Presidio, 1978); Shelby Stanton, *The Rise and Fall of an American Army: U.S. Ground Forces in Vietnam, 1965–1973* (New York: Dell, 1985); and Phillip B. Davidson, *Vietnam at War: The History, 1946–1975* (Novato, Calif.: Presidio, 1988). Douglas Kinnard's valuable study *The War Managers* (Hanover, N.H.: University Press of New England, 1977), which is based on a survey of generals who served in Vietnam, underscores not only the prevalence of blaming civilian leadership but also the diversity of military opinion on how the war could have been more effectively waged. Palmer, Stanton, Davidson, and most of the generals in the Kinnard study question the appropriateness of the search-and-destroy strategy, a point that two other military officers—Harry G. Summers and Bruce Palmer Jr.—have examined more fully. The most influential critique of U.S. strategy is offered by Summers in *On Strategy: A Critical Analysis of the Vietnam War* (Novato, Calif.: Presidio, 1982), which contrasts U.S. strategy with established military doctrines. In his more comprehensive study, *The 25-Year War: America's Military Role in Vietnam* (Lexington: University Press of Kentucky, 1984), Palmer also questions Westmoreland's strategy and a wide range of U.S. military practices. Challenging the revisionist contention that the military leadership could have brought victory had the civilian leadership allowed them, Robert Buzzanco, in *Masters of War: Military Dissent and Politics in the Vietnam War* (New York: Cambridge University Press, 1996), contends that military leaders wanted to avoid involvement in Vietnam but shrewdly shifted responsibility for failure.

There are several valuable studies of U.S. military operations. These include: Allan R. Millett, ed., *A Short History of the Vietnam War* (Bloomington: Indiana University Press, 1978); Thomas C. Thayer, *War without Fronts: The American Experience in Vietnam* (Boulder, Colo.: Westview, 1985); and Thomas D. Boettcher, *The Valor and the Sorrow* (Boston: Little, Brown & Co., 1985). The air war has been the subject of much interest. Drew Middleton's *Air War: Vietnam* (New York: Bobbs-Merrill, 1978) and especially James Clay Thompson's *Rolling Thunder: Understanding Policy and Program Failure* (Chapel Hill: University of North Carolina Press, 1980) underscore the limited effectiveness of the bombing campaign. A useful comparative perspective is provided by William W. Momyer's *Air Power in Three Wars (WWII, Korean, Vietnam)* (Washington, D.C.: U.S. Government Printing Office, 1978). How the theory and practice of earlier bombing campaigns influenced that in Vietnam is central to the argument of Mark Clodfelter's comprehensive *The Limits of Air Power: The American Bombing of North Vietnam* (New York: Free Press, 1989).

The ground war has been most effectively recounted by the men who fought. There are numerous such studies; among the best are Al Santoli, *Everything We Had: An Oral History of the Vietnam War by Thirty-Three American Soldiers Who Fought It* (New York: Ballantine, 1981); Peter Goldman and Tony Fuller, *Charlie Company: What Vietnam Did to Us* (New York: Ballantine, 1983); Mark Baker, *Nam: The Vietnam War in the Words of the Soldiers Who Fought There* (New York: William Morrow, 1981); Joe Klein, *Payback: Five Marines and Vietnam* (New York: Ballantine, 1984); Tom Mangold and John Penycate, *The Tunnels of Cu Chi* (New York: Random House, 1985); and Robert Goff and Robert Sander, *Brothers: Black Soldiers in Nam* (Novato, Calif.: Presidio, 1982). Also especially noteworthy are two widely praised works: Michael Herr, *Dispatches* (New York: Avon, 1978), a collection of essays by a war correspondent, and Philip Caputo, *A Rumor of War* (New York: Rinehart & Winston, 1977), a compelling story written by one of the first U.S. Marines to serve in Vietnam. For an understanding of how the United States recruited men to fight in Vietnam, see Christian G. Appy, *Working-Class War: American Combat Soldiers in Vietnam* (Chapel Hill: University of North Carolina Press, 1993).

There are a number of studies of specific battles and campaigns. The "lessons" derived from the earliest U.S.–North Vietnamese ground confrontation is discussed in Harold G. Moore and Joseph L. Galloway's *We Were Soldiers Once . . . and Young: Ia Drang—The Battle That Changed the War in Vietnam* (New York: Random House, 1972). On the large search-and-destroy operations, Bernard W. Rogers, *Cedar Falls–Junction City: A Turning Point* (Washington, D.C.: U.S. Army Center of Military History, 1974) provides a good summary. For a critical appraisal of Operation Cedar Falls, the journalist Jonathon Schell's classic account of the elimination of the village of Ben Suc is reprinted, along with some other of his essays, in *The Real War* (New York: Pantheon, 1987). The background to the Tet Offensive and its military and strategic impact are explored by James J. Wirtz in *The Tet Offensive:*

Intelligence Failure in War (Ithaca, N.Y.: Cornell University Press, 1991) and by Don Oberdorfer in *Tet!* (Garden City, N.Y.: Doubleday, 1971). Ronald Spector in *After Tet: The Bloodiest Year In Vietnam* (New York: Vintage, 1993) discusses the often-ignored intense post-Tet warfare. On the battle of Khe Sanh, Robert Pisor's *The End of the Line: The Siege of Khe Sanh* (New York: Ballantine, 1982) recounts fully U.S. and North Vietnamese operations. Other valuable accounts of the important campaigns include: Ngo Quong Truong, *The Easter Offensive of 1972* (Washington, D.C.: U.S. Army Center of Military History, 1980) and Nguyen Duy Hinh, *Lan Son 719* (Washington, D.C.: U.S. Army Center of Military History, 1979).

The scholarship on America's enemy is relatively sparse but instructive. The most authoritative overview of the war from North Vietnam's perspective and analysis of the reasons for its success is William Duiker's *Sacred War: Nationalism and Revolution in a Divided Vietnam* (New York: McGraw-Hill, 1995). North Vietnam's response to an air war and its military plans are explained in Jon M. Van Dyke's *North Vietnam's Strategy for Survival* (Palo Alto, Calif.: Pacific Press, 1972). Two works explore the role of the North Vietnamese army: Douglas Pike, *PAVN: The People's Army of Vietnam* (Novato, Calif.: Presidio, 1986) and Greg Lockhart, *Nation in Arms: The Origins of the People's Army of Vietnam* (Wellington, Australia: Allen & Unwin, 1991). Two additional books draw on documents and interviews to see the war from the perspective of North Vietnamese–Viet Cong combatants: David Chanoff and Doan Van Toai, *Portrait of the Enemy* (New York: Random House, 1986) and Michael Lee Lanning and Dan Cragg, *Inside the VC and NVA: The Real Story of North Vietnam's Armed Forces* (New York: Fawcett, 1991).

For the wartime South, FitzGerald's previously cited *Fire in the Lake* provides a thorough statement of the problems of the U.S. relationship with its ally. The journalist Robert Shaplen's insightful essays, many focusing on the problems in the South, have been published in *The Road from War: Vietnam, 1965–1970* (New York: Harper & Row, 1970). The memoir of Nguyen Cao Ky, *Twenty Years and Twenty Days* (New York: Stein & Day, 1976), recounts, from the vantage point of the former president and later vice president of the Saigon government, the mounting disappointment with the United States. Another high official, Tran Van Do, has published a comparable memoir, *Our Endless War: Inside South Vietnam* (Novato, Calif.: Presidio, 1978). A balanced appraisal of the South Vietnamese political structure is provided in Allen E. Goodman's *Politics of War: The Basis of Political Community in South Vietnam* (Cambridge, Mass.: MIT Press, 1973). Nigel Thrift and Dean Forbes's *The Price of War: Urbanization in Vietnam, 1954–1985* (London: Allen & Unwin, 1985) analyzes the long-term implications of warfare.

What was happening in the rural areas of the South was critical to the outcome of the war, and several efforts have been made to study specific locales. These include: James W. Trullinger, *Village at War: An Account of Revolution in Vietnam* (New York: Longman, 1980); Jeffrey Race, *War Comes to Long An: Revolutionary Conflict in a Vietnamese Province* (Berkeley: University of California Press, 1972); and William Andrews, *The Village War: Vietnamese Communist Revolutionary Activity in Dinh Truong Province, 1960–1964* (Columbia: University of Missouri Press, 1973). The program and tactics of the Viet Cong are described by Douglas Pike in *Viet Cong: National Liberation Front of South Vietnam*, rev. ed. (Cambridge, Mass.: MIT Press, 1972).

The international dimensions of the war are most fully studied by R. B. Smith in *An International History of the Vietnam War*, 2 vols. (New York: St. Martin's, 1983–1985). Daniel S. Papp's *Vietnam: The View from Moscow, Peking, Washington* (Salisbury, N.C.: McFarland, 1981) focuses on the 1965–1972 period. North Vietnam's relationship with the major communist powers has been analyzed in several studies, including: Donald Zagoria, *Vietnam Triangle: Moscow, Peking, Hanoi* (New York: Pegasus, 1967); W. R. Smyser, *The Independent Vietnamese: Vietnamese Communism between Russia and China, 1955–1969* (Athens: Ohio University Press, 1980); Lesek Buszinski, *Soviet Foreign Policy and Southeast Asia* (New York: St. Martin's, 1986); King Chen, *Vietnam and China, 1938–1954* (Princeton, N.J.: Princeton University Press, 1969); and Ilya V. Gaiduk, *The Soviet Union and the Vietnam War* (Chicago, Ivan Dee, 1996).

Several works focus on the ending of the war. The most comprehensive and balanced study of developments from the 1973 peace settlement to the 1975 Communist victories in Vietnam and Cambodia is Arnold R. Isaacs, *Without Honor: Defeat in Vietnam and Cambodia* (Baltimore, Md.: Johns Hopkins University Press, 1983). On the peace negotiations, Gareth Porter's *A Peace Denied: The United States, Vietnam, and the Paris Agreements* (Bloomington: Indiana University Press, 1975) is a thorough account, particularly in explaining the North Vietnamese position. Allan E. Goodman's *The Lost Peace: America's Search for a Negotiated Settlement of the Vietnam War* (Stanford, Calif.: Stanford University Press, 1975) examines the U.S. negotiating efforts. Developments in Vietnam are traced in William E. LeGro's *Vietnam from Cease-Fire to Capitulation* (Washington, D.C.: U.S. Army Center of Military History, 1981). The collapse of the South has been recounted in several works, including Alan Dawson, *55 Days: The Fall of South Vietnam* (Englewood Cliffs, N.J.: Prentice-Hall, 1977) and David Butler, *The Fall of Saigon* (New York: Simon & Schuster, 1985).

The tragedy of Cambodia beginning in 1970 has been recounted in two works by William Shawcross. In *Sideshow: Kissinger, Nixon, and the Destruction of Cambodia* (New York: Pocket Books, 1979), Shawcross sharply criticizes U.S. intervention in 1970, and in *The Quality of Mercy: Cambodia, Holocaust, and Modern Conscience* (New York: Simon & Schuster, 1984), he deplores the lack of international concern for Cambodia's plight during the rule of the Khmer Rouge. The latter issue is fully explored also by Jamie Frederic Metzl in *Western Responses to Human Rights Abuses in Cambodia, 1975–80* (New York:

St. Martin's, 1996). Two books by Ben Kiernan, *How Pol Pot Came to Power: A History of Communism in Kampuchea, 1930–1975* (London: Verso, 1985) and *The Pol Pot Regime: Race, Power, and Genocide in Cambodia under the Khmer Rouge, 1975–1979* (New Haven, Conn.: Yale University Press, 1996) recount fully the origins, implementation, and overthrow of the Khmer Rouge government. Also valuable are the works of Craig Etcherson, *The Rise and Demise of Democratic Kampuchea* (Boulder, Colo.: Westview, 1984); Michael Vickery, *Cambodia 1975–1982* (Boston: South End Press, 1984); and Elizabeth Becker, *When the War Was Over: The Voices of Cambodia's Revolution and Its People* (New York: Simon & Schuster, 1986). The *New York Times* correspondent Syndey H. Schanberg's *The Death and Life of Dith Pran* (New York: Viking, 1985) tells the story of his search for his Cambodian colleague, which inspired the critically acclaimed motion picture *The Killing Fields*.

On developments in Vietnam since 1975, both William Duiker's *Vietnam since the Fall of Saigon* (Athens: Ohio University Center for International Studies, 1985) and Melanie Berseford's *Vietnam: Politics, Economies, and Society* (London: Pinter, 1988) provide useful information. The tensions with China are underscored in Robert S. Ross's *The Indochina Tangle: China's Vietnam Policy, 1975–1979* (New York: Columbia University Press, 1988), King C. Chen's *China's War with Vietnam, 1979: Issues, Decisions, and Implications* (Stanford, Calif.: Hoover Institute Press, 1987), and William J. Duiker, *China and Vietnam: The Roots of Conflict* (Berkeley: University of California Institute of East Asian Studies, 1987).

The issues in U.S.-Vietnamese relation since 1975 are set forth by Frederick Z. Brown in *Second Chance: The United States and Indochina in the 1990s* (New York: Council on Foreign Relations, 1989). H. Bruce Franklin, *M.I.A. or Mythmaking in America* (New Brunswick, N.J.: Rutgers University Press, 1993) studies the development of the MIA issue in American culture and politics.

INDEX

Abrams, Creighton W., 108, 114
Agent Orange. *See* herbicides, use of
Aguinaldo, Emilio, 25, 26
Anderson, Terry, 152
Annam, 7, 9, 13, 104. *See also* France, empire
Ap Bac, 73
ARVN (Army of the Republic of Vietnam). *See* South Vietnam, army of
ASEAN (Association of Southeast Asian Nations), 141, 149, 150, 151
Attleboro, Operation, 95
August Revolution, 19–20, 30, 33, 35, 38, 55, 102, 154, 165
Australia, 46, 49

Bao Dai, 20, 38–39, 41, 49, 52; and appointment of Ngo Dinh Diem, 54, 55; and disposition of, 58, 60
"Bao Dai Solution," 38, 40, 55
Bien Hoa, 84, 136
Binh Xuyen, 56, 57, 59, 65
"boat people," 145, 149, 158
Brezizinski, Zbigniew, 145
Brogan, Denis, 71
Buck, Pearl, 28

Buddhism. *See* South Vietnam, Buddhist political activity
Bui Quang Chieu, 12
Bui Tin, 136, 137
Bundy, McGeorge, 71, 85
Burma, 18, 24, 33, 40, 159
Bush, George, 153
Buttinger, Joseph, 16

Calley, William, 101
Cambodia, 3, 4, 7, 36, 48–50, 71, 77, 141, 145; economy and society, 143, 146–47, 148, 150, 153; and Laos, 71; political development, 38, 53, 118–19, 142–43, 145–46, 148–50, 152–54; and U.S.-North Vietnam war, 97, 102, 116–20, 121, 127, 142–43
Cao Dai, 56, 65, 66, 77
Caputo, Philip, 85–86, 87
Carter, Jimmy, 144–45, 147
Cedar Falls, Operation, 95
China, 4, 5, 15, 22–23, 24; communist revolution, 33, 39–40; cultural influence on Vietnam, 1–2, 4; occupation of Vietnam (1945–1946), 34–35

THE AUTHOR

Gary R. Hess is professor of history at Bowling Green State University. His principal interests are in U.S.-Asian relations, and his books include *America Encounters India, 1941–1947, Sam Higginbottom of Allahabad: Pioneer of Point Four to India,* and *The United States' Emergence as a Southeast Asian Power, 1940–1950.* He is also the author of *The United States at War, 1941–1945* and the editor of *America and Russia: Cold War Confrontation to Coexistence.* His articles have appeared in *Journal of American History, Diplomatic History, Pacific Historical Review, Political Science Quarterly,* and other journals, and he is on the board of editors of *Diplomatic History.* He has been a Fulbright scholar/lecturer in India four times and is a past president of the Society for Historians of American Foreign Relations.

THE EDITOR

Akira Iriye is Charles Warren Professor of American History at Harvard University and visiting professor of history at the International University of Japan. His most recent publications include *China and Japan in the Global Setting* (1992), *The Globalizing of America: United States Foreign Relations, 1913–1945* (1993), and *Cultural Internationalism and World Order* (1997).